365 Ultimate Pancake Recipes

(365 Ultimate Pancake Recipes - Volume 1)

Nancy Maye

Copyright: Published in the United States by Nancy Maye/ © NANCY MAYE

Published on October, 12 2020

All rights reserved. No part of this publication may be reproduced, stored in retrieval system, copied in any form or by any means, electronic, mechanical, photocopying, recording or otherwise transmitted without written permission from the publisher. Please do not participate in or encourage piracy of this material in any way. You must not circulate this book in any format. NANCY MAYE does not control or direct users' actions and is not responsible for the information or content shared, harm and/or actions of the book readers.

In accordance with the U.S. Copyright Act of 1976, the scanning, uploading and electronic sharing of any part of this book without the permission of the publisher constitute unlawful piracy and theft of the author's intellectual property. If you would like to use material from the book (other than just simply for reviewing the book), prior permission must be obtained by contacting the author at author@bisquerecipes.com

Thank you for your support of the author's rights.

Content

365 AWESOME PANCAKE RECIPES 9

1. 12 Grain Buttermilk Pancakes Recipe 9
2. ALOHA PINA COLADA FLAPJACKS Recipe 9
3. African Dish Sweet Potato Onion And Thyme Pancakes Recipe 10
4. Almond Flour Blueberry Pancakes Recipe 10
5. Amaretto Almond Pancakes Recipe 10
6. Amaretto Pancakes Recipe 11
7. Ambrosia Pancakes With Orange Syrup Recipe 11
8. Angelgirls Griddle Cakes Recipe 12
9. Apple Blueberry Pancakes Recipe 12
10. Apple Pancackes Recipe 12
11. Apple Pancake Recipe 13
12. Apple Pancakes From Mrs Bray Recipe 13
13. Apple Pancakes Mountain Style Recipe 13
14. Apple Pie Pancakes Recipe 14
15. Apple Raisin Oven Pancake Recipe 14
16. Applesauce Oatmeal Pancakes Recipe 15
17. Applesauce Pancakes Recipe 15
18. Arabic Almond Pancakes Recipe 15
19. Aunt Jemimas Pancake Mix Recipe 16
20. Awesome Almond Buckwheat Pancakes Recipe 16
21. BAKED BLUEBERRY PANCAKE Recipe 17
22. BANANA SPLIT PANCAKES Recipe ... 17
23. BEST BUTTERMILK PANCAKES Recipe 17
24. Baby Blackberry Pancakes Recipe 18
25. Bacon Pancakes Recipe 18
26. Bacon Sausage Pancakes Recipe 18
27. Bacon And Banana Pancakes Recipe 19
28. Bacon And Coriander Pancakes Recipe 19
29. Baked Apple Pancake Recipe 20
30. Baked Gingerbread Pancake Recipe 20
31. Baked Marmalade Pancake Recipe 21
32. Baked Norweigan Pancake Recipe 21
33. Baked Peach Pancake Recipe 21
34. Baked Peach Pancakes With Honey Raisin Syrup Recipe 22
35. Baked Pear Cheese Pancakes Recipe 22
36. Baked Pear Pecan Pancake Surprise Recipe 22
37. Baked Upside Down Banana Pancake Recipe 23
38. Banana And Blueberry Pancakes With Cinnamon Vanilla Butter Recipe 23
39. Banana Blueberry Pancakes Recipe 24
40. Banana Bread Pancakes Recipe 24
41. Banana Buttermilk Buckwheat Pancakes Recipe 25
42. Banana Buttermilk Pancakes Recipe 25
43. Banana Buttermilk Pancakes With Berry Sauce Recipe 25
44. Banana Foster Pancakes Recipe 26
45. Banana Nutella Pancakes Recipe 26
46. Banana Oat Pancakes Recipe 27
47. Banana Pancake Snowmen 27
48. Banana Pancakes Recipe 28
49. Banana Pancakes With Coconut Syrup Recipe 28
50. Bavarian Apple Pancake Recipe 29
51. Bears Gingerbread Pancakes Recipe 29
52. Beer Pancakes Recipe 30
53. Beestings Pancakes For Beltaine Recipe ... 30
54. Best Buttermilk Bilberry Pancakes Recipe 30
55. Best Buttermilk Pancakes On The Planet Recipe 31
56. Bilberry Cinnamon Pancakes Recipe 31
57. Birdys Awesome Pancakes Recipe 31
58. Bisquick Blueberry Pancakes Recipe 32
59. Blackberry Cheese Pancakes Recipe 32
60. Blackberry Cinnamon Pancakes Recipe 33
61. Blackberry Cornmeal Pancakes With Orange Butter Recipe 33
62. Blackberry Filled Dutch Pancake Recipe .. 33
63. Blackberry Pancakes Recipe 34
64. Blackberry Puffed Pancakes Recipe 34
65. Blender Orange Pancakes Recipe 35
66. Blender Pancakes Recipe 35
67. Blue Cornmeal Pancakes Recipe 35
68. Blue Moon Oatmeal Brown Sugar Pancakes Recipe 36
69. Blue Puff Ramekin Pancakes Recipe 36
70. Blueberry Bran Pancakes Weight Watchers Recipe 36
71. Blueberry Buckwheat With Flaxseed Pancakes Recipe 37

72. Blueberry Buttermilk Pancakes Recipe 37
73. Blueberry Cheese Pancakes Recipe 38
74. Blueberry Cornmeal Pancakes Recipe 38
75. Blueberry Cornmeal Pancakes With Orange Butter Recipe 39
76. Blueberry Cottage Cheese Pancakes Recipe 39
77. Blueberry Flax Pancakes Recipe 40
78. Blueberry Hazelnut Pancakes Recipe 40
79. Blueberry Oatmeal Pancakes Recipe 40
80. Blueberry Pancakes With Blueberry Sauce Recipe 41
81. Blueberry Ricotta Pancakes Recipe 41
82. Bread Crumb Griddle Cakes Recipe 42
83. Bread Crumb Pancakes Recipe 42
84. Broke Man Pancakes Recipe 43
85. Buckwheat Banana Panners Recipe 43
86. Buckwheat Blueberry Pecan Pancakes Recipe 43
87. Buckwheat Pancakes Recipe 44
88. Buckwheat And Yogurt Pancakes Recipe . 44
89. Buffalo Berry Corn Cakes With Maple Syrup Recipe 44
90. Buttermilk Cranberry Pancakes Recipe 45
91. Buttermilk Pancakes With Bing Cherry Syrup Recipe 45
92. Buttermilk Pancakes With Oatmeal Recipe 46
93. Buttermilk Peach Pancakes Recipe 46
94. Canadian Pancakes Recipe 47
95. Caramel Apple Baked Pancake Recipe 47
96. Carries Vanilla Amaretto Pancakes Recipe 48
97. Cave Dweller Potato Pancakes Recipe 48
98. Cheaters Buckwheat Buttermilk Pancakes Recipe 48
99. Cheesecake Pancakes Recipe 48
100. Chestnut Pancakes With Bacon And Creme Fraiche Regular And Gluten Free Recipe 49
101. Chocolate Banana Cream Pancakes Recipe 49
102. Chocolate Chip Pancakes With Cinnamon Cream Recipe 50
103. Chocolate Chip Pancakes With Cinnamon Sauce Recipe 51
104. Chocolate Pancakes Recipe 51
105. Chocolate Apple Pancakes Recipe 52

106. Chunky Monkey Pancakes Recipe 52
107. Cilantro Corn Pancakes Recipe 53
108. Cinnamon And Nutmeg Pancakes Recipe 53
109. Cinnamon Apple Puffy Pancake Recipe ... 53
110. Cinnamon Oat Pancakes Recipe 54
111. Cinnamon Roll Pancakes Recipe 54
112. Cinnamon Swirl Pancakes Recipe 55
113. Cinnamon Apple Pancakes Recipe 56
114. Cinnapple Pancakes Recipe 56
115. Classic Potato Pancakes Recipe 56
116. Cloud Pancakes Recipe 57
117. Coconut Pancake With Coconut Cream And Tropical Fruit Recipe 58
118. Coconut Pancakes Recipe 58
119. Copycat Ihop Harvest Grain And Nut Pancakes Recipe 59
120. Corn Meal Griddle Cakes Recipe 59
121. Cornmeal Griddle Cakes Recipe 59
122. Cornmeal Pancakes With Applesauce Recipe... 60
123. Cottage Cheese Healthy Pancakes Recipe. 60
124. Cranberry Apple Puff Pancake Recipe 60
125. Cranberry Pancakes Recipe......................... 61
126. Cranberry Wow Pancakes Recipe 61
127. Cream Cheese Pancakes Recipe 62
128. Creamy Pancakes With Peaches Recipe 62
129. Crepes With Strawberry Filling Recipe 63
130. D Bomb Buttermilk Pancakes Recipe 63
131. Daddys Baked Pancake Recipe 64
132. Delicious Chocolate Chip Pancakes Recipe 64
133. Duncan Estate Acadian Plogues Ployes Dated 1954 Recipe.. 65
134. Dutch Apple Pancake Recipe 65
135. Dutch Baby Casserole Recipe 65
136. Dutch Baby Pancake Recipe....................... 66
137. Dutch Baby Recipe...................................... 66
138. Dutch Pancake Recipe................................. 66
139. Dutch Puff Pancakes Recipe 67
140. Easy Cinnamon Vanilla Pancakes Recipe . 67
141. Easy Coconut Flour Banana Pancakes Recipe.. 68
142. Easy Elegant Buckwheat Pancakes Recipe 68
143. Easy Simple Basic Vegan Pancakes Recipe 68
144. Eggless Banana Pancakes Recipe................ 69
145. Eierkuchen Puffy German Egg Cakes

Recipe 69
146. Enhanced Pancake Mixes Recipe 70
147. Extra Special Oatmeal Pancakes Recipe ... 70
148. Fabulous Buttermilk Pancakes Recipe 70
149. Fat Free Low Sugar Pumpkin Pancakes Recipe 71
150. Favorite Homemade Pancakes Recipe 71
151. Finnish Pancake Recipe 71
152. Fireside Pancakes Recipe 72
153. Fluffy Cottage Cheese Pancakes Recipe ... 72
154. Fluffy Free Pancakes Recipe 72
155. Fluffy Pancakes Recipe 73
156. Fluffy Pecan Pancakes Recipe 73
157. Fluffy Eggless Pancakes Recipe 74
158. French Ports Baked Pancakes Recipe 74
159. Fresh Corn Cakes Recipe 74
160. Friendly Monster Portrait Recipe 75
161. Fruit Glazed Oatmeal Mini Cakes Recipe 75
162. Fruit Yogurt Pancake Recipes Recipe 76
163. German Apple Pancake 76
164. German Apple Pancake Recipe 77
165. German Pancake Recipe 77
166. German Pancake With Sweet Apple Filling Recipe 77
167. German Pancakes Recipe 78
168. German Pancakes With Buttermilk Syrup Recipe 78
169. German Puff Pancakes With Spiced Apples Recipe 79
170. Ginger Pancakes Recipe 79
171. Gingerbread Man Pancakes Recipe 80
172. Gingerbread Pancakes Recipe 80
173. Gingerbread Pancakes Topped With Apples And Whipped Cream Recipe 81
174. Gluten Free Gingerbread Pancakes Recipe 81
175. Gluten Free Dairy Free German Apple Pancakes Recipe 81
176. Gluten Free Dutch Babies Recipe 82
177. Gluten Free Pumpkin Pancakes Recipe 82
178. Good Morning Pumpkin Pancakes Recipe 83
179. Grandmas Pancakes Recipe 83
180. Grizzly Bears Pancake Recipe 83
181. Guilt Free Oatmeal Pancakes Recipe 84
182. Healthy Flax Pancake Mix Recipe 84
183. Hearty Poppy Seed Pancakes Recipe 85

184. Herbed Potato Pancakes Recipe 85
185. Highland Mountain Dutch Apple Pancakes Recipe 86
186. Holiday Pancakes Recipe 86
187. Homemade Buttermilk Pancake Mix Recipe 86
188. Homemade Pancakes Recipe 87
189. Hotel Pancakes Recipe 87
190. Individual Baked Pear Pancakes Recipe 87
191. Irish Pancakes Recipe 88
192. Irish Potato Pancakes Boxty Recipe 88
193. Jumbo Pancake Roll Recipe 89
194. Latkes Minus The Potato Recipe 89
195. Latkes My Way Recipe 89
196. Lazy Day Pancakes Recipe 90
197. Lemon Pancakes With Fresh Berries Recipe 90
198. Lemon Poppyseed Pancakes Recipe 91
199. Lemon Souffle Pancakes Recipe 91
200. Lemon Ricotta Pancakes Recipe 92
201. Light And Fluffy Pancakes Recipe 92
202. Make Ahead Pancake And Waffle Batter Recipe 92
203. Mango Pancakes Recipe 93
204. Maple Wholewheat Pancakes Recipe 93
205. Marlboro Three Grain Pancakes Recipe ... 94
206. Marshmallow Milk Pancakes Recipe 94
207. Matzah Brei Light And Airy Pancakes Recipe 95
208. Metabolism Boosting Healthy Pancakes Recipe 95
209. Milk Egg Wheat Gluten Corn Free Buckwheat Pancakes Recipe 96
210. Miniature Dutch Apple Pancakes Recipe .. 97
211. Mixed Flour Dosa Recipe 97
212. Mixed Berry Pancakes Recipe 97
213. Momma Jans Buttermilk Pancakes Recipe 98
214. Moms Rhubarb Pancakes Recipe 98
215. Multigrain Hot Cakes Recipe 99
216. Multigrain Pancakes Recipe 99
217. Natural Cereal Pancakes Recipe 100
218. No Oil Banana Pancakes Recipe 100
219. Not Your Mammas Blueberry Ricotta Pancakes Recipe 100
220. Nutella Pancakes Recipe 101
221. Nutty Breakfast Rolls Recipe 101
222. Nutty Breakfast Rolls For Kids Recipe .. 102

223. Oatmeal Buttermilk Pancakes Recipe 102
224. Oatmeal Cottage Cheese Pancakes Recipe 102
225. Oatmeal Pancake Mix Recipe 103
226. Oatmeal Pancakes Recipe 103
227. Oatmeal Pancakes From Pancake Recipes On The Net Recipe 103
228. Oatmeal Pancakes With Butter Milk Syrup Recipe 104
229. Oatmeal Spice Pancakes W/ Peach Compote Recipe 104
230. Oatpancakes Recipe 105
231. Old World Recipe Squash Latkes Recipe 105
232. Orange Cloud Pancakes Recipe 106
233. Orange Pancakes Recipe 106
234. Orange Ricotta Pancakes Recipe 106
235. Oven Apple Pancakes With Cider Sauce Recipe 107
236. Oven Baked Pancakes Recipe 107
237. Oven Pancake Recipe 108
238. Oven Pancakes Swedish American Recipe 108
239. P M S Pancakes Recipe 109
240. Pancake Breakfast Muffin Recipe............ 109
241. Pancake Breakfast For A King Recipe 109
242. Pancake Snowmen Recipe 110
243. Pancakes From Scratch Recipe 110
244. Pancakes Recipe 110
245. Pancakes Never Fail I Promise Recipe.... 111
246. Pancakes With Caramel Bananas And Pecan Nuts Recipe 111
247. Peach Pancakes With Peachy Berry Sauce Recipe 112
248. Peach Puff Pancake With Cherry Almond Sauce Recipe 112
249. Peach And Strawberry Pancakes Recipe . 113
250. Peachy Strawberry Oven Pancakes Recipe 113
251. Peanut Butter Chocolate Chunk Pancake Muffins Recipe 113
252. Peanut Butter Pancakes Recipe 114
253. Peanut Butter Pancakes With Strawberry Syrup Recipe 114
254. Pear Ginger Almond Pancakes Recipe.... 115
255. Pecan Pancakes Recipe 115
256. Perfect Buttermilk Pancakes Recipe 116
257. Perfect Pancake Recipe 116

258. Pineapple Coconut Pancakes Recipe 116
259. Plump Pumpkin Pancakes Recipe 117
260. Poffertjes Dutch Tiny Pancakes Recipe . 117
261. Polynesian Banana Pancakes Recipe 118
262. Poppy Oat Pancakes Recipe 118
263. Potato Pancakes German Style Recipe ... 118
264. Protein Pancakes Recipe 119
265. Puff Pancake Ala Orange Recipe............. 119
266. Puff Pancakes With Maple Baked Fruit Recipe 120
267. Puffed Oven Pancake With Summer Fruit Recipe 120
268. Puffed Pancake Recipe 121
269. Puffed Pancake With Blackberry Syrup Recipe 121
270. Puffy Eggnog Pancake Recipe 122
271. Pumpkin Flax Pancakes Recipe 122
272. Pumpkin Pancakes Recipe 122
273. Pumpkin Pancakes With Cran Pom Maple Syrup Recipe 123
274. Pumpkin Pancakes Or Waffles Recipe ... 123
275. Rage Of The Town Raspberry Pancaes Recipe 124
276. Raspberry Filled Dutch Pancake Recipe 124
277. Really The Best Pancakes Ever Recipe ... 125
278. Red Velvet Chocolate Chips Pancakes Recipe 125
279. Revised Chocolate Chip Pancakes Low Calorie Recipe 126
280. Rhode Island Johnny Cakes Recipe 126
281. Rice Bran Buttermilk Pancakes Recipe... 126
282. Ricotta And Mozarella Corncakes Recipe 126
283. Ricotta Cheese And Buttermilk Pancakes Recipe 127
284. Ricotta Cheese Pancakes Recipe.............. 127
285. Ricotta Cinnamon Pancakes With Sauteed Apples Recipe 128
286. Ricotta Hotcakes With Honeycomb Butter Recipe 128
287. Ricotta Pancakes With Brown Sugar Cherry Sauce Recipe 129
288. Ricotta Pancakes With Blueberry Compote Recipe 130
289. Ricotta Lemon Pancakes Recipe.............. 130
290. Romantic Black Forest Pancakes Recipe 131
291. Russian Blinys Pancakes Recipe.............. 131

292. Scandinavian Puff Pancakes Recipe 132
293. Scottish Pancakes Recipe 132
294. Shawn Boys Johnny Cakes Recipe 133
295. Simple Master Mix For Baking Recipe 133
296. Simple Anyberry Syrup Recipe 134
297. Simply Awesome Buttermilk Pancakes Recipe 134
298. Smoky Corn Pancakes With Salsa Butter Recipe 135
299. Soft N Fluffy Pancakes Recipe 135
300. Sour Cream Blueberry Pancakes Recipe . 135
301. Sour Cream Pancakes Recipe 136
302. Sour Milk Griddle Cakes Dated 1928 Recipe 136
303. Sourdough Pancakes With Fruit Sauce Recipe 137
304. Soy Dessert Pancakes Recipe 137
305. Soynog Pancakes Recipe 137
306. Spamcakes Recipe 138
307. Special Pecan Pancakes Recipe 138
308. Spice Pancakes Recipe 138
309. Spice Pancakes With Lemon Sauce Recipe 139
310. Spiced 2 Grain Pancakes Recipe 139
311. Spiced Puffed Pancake With Fresh Fruit And Lemon Yogurt Sauce Recipe 140
312. Spiced Pumpkin Pancakes Recipe 140
313. Steamed Semolina Savoury Cake Recipe. 141
314. Strawberry Pancake With Almonds Recipe 141
315. Strawberry Pancakes Recipe 142
316. Sunday Morning Buttermilk Pancakes Recipe 142
317. Superb Sourdough Pancakes Recipe 142
318. Supper Pancakes Recipe 143
319. Swedish Oven Pancakes Recipe 143
320. Swedish Pancakes Recipe 143
321. Sweet Chestnut Pancakes Regular And Gluten Free Recipe 144
322. Sweet Potato And Banana Pancakes Recipe 144
323. Sweet Potato Pancakes Recipe 144
324. Sweetcakes Pancake Mix Recipe 145
325. Sweetstacks Pancakes Recipe 145
326. Swirl Springroll Recipe 145
327. Tagine Estate Blueberry Sour Cream Pancakes Tried And True Recipe 146

328. Thanksgiving Latkes Recipe 146
329. The Best Pancake Recipe 146
330. The Spirit Of Apple Prune Pancake Recipe 147
331. Thin New Hampshire Maple Syrup Pancakes Recipe 147
332. Top Of The World Pancakes Recipe 148
333. Topsy Turvy Pancakes Recipe 148
334. Triple Coconut Pancakes Recipe 148
335. Tropical Cakes With Golden Mango Sauce Recipe 149
336. Vanentines Day Carrotcake Pancakes Recipe 149
337. Vanilla Buttermilk Pancakes With Blood Orange Marsala Syrup Recipe 150
338. Vegan Cinnamon Pancakes Recipe 151
339. Vegan Pancakes Recipe 151
340. Wheat Free Milk Free Corn Cakes Recipe 151
341. Wheat Germ Pancakes Recipe 152
342. Wheat Germ Pancakes With Yogurt And Berry Sauce Recipe 152
343. Wheat Pancakes My Kids Will Eat Recipe 152
344. Wheat Free PancakesWaffles Recipe 153
345. Wheat N Ter Pancakes Recipe 153
346. Whole Grain Pancakes Recipe 153
347. Whole Wheat Applesauce Pancakes Recipe 154
348. Whole Wheat Buttermilk Blueberry Pancakes Recipe 154
349. Whole Wheat Nutty Pancakes Recipe 155
350. Whole Wheat Ricotta Pancakes With Citrus Buttered Honey Syrup Recipe 155
351. Wholesome Cornmeal Pancakes Recipe 156
352. Wild Blackberry Pancakes Recipe 156
353. Wildcat Cafe Blueberry Pancakes Recipe 157
354. Wisconsin Buttermilk Pancakes With Strawberry Sauce Recipe 157
355. Zucchini Pancakes Dated 1964 Recipe... 158
356. Zucchini Pancakes Recipe 158
357. Zuider Zee Pancake Recipe 158
358. Banana Pancakes Recipe 159
359. Chocolate Chip Pancakes Recipe............. 159
360. Cornmeal Pancakes Recipe 159
361. Fiber Full Bran Pancakes Recipe 160
362. German Potatoe Pancake Lippischer Pickert

Recipe 160
363. Homemade Pancakes Recipe 160
364. Mixed Berry Pancakes Recipe 161
365. Peanut Butter Banana Pancakes Recipe ..161

INDEX 162

CONCLUSION 165

365 Awesome Pancake Recipes

***

1. 12 Grain Buttermilk Pancakes Recipe

Serving: 15 | Prep: | Cook: 10mins | Ready in:

Ingredients

- Dry Mix (Makes 5 cups)
- 2 cups 12-grain flour
- 1 cup whole wheat pastry flour
- 1 cup all purpose flour
- ½ tsp cinnamon
- ½ tsp nutmeg
- 2 tbsp sugar
- 4 (1-g) packets stevia
- 2 ¼ tbsp baking powder
- 1 tsp baking soda
- ½ tbsp salt
- 1 tbsp maca powder (use gelatinized or roasted for optimum absorption)
- 2 tbsp dried whole egg powder
- ¼ cup buttermilk powder
- For one (4-child serving) batch of pancakes:
- 1 egg
- 1 tbsp oil or melted butter
- 1 cup low fat milk (or buttermilk!)
- 1 1/3 cups 12-Grain buttermilk pancake mix

Direction

- Dry Mix
- Whisk all the ingredients together. Store in an airtight container in the pantry or fridge.
- To make one (4-child serving) batch of pancakes:
- In a medium bowl, whisk together egg, oil or butter, milk and pancake mix.
- Stir with a whisk until moistened but still lumpy.
- Cook on a hot, greased griddle until cooked through.

2. ALOHA PINA COLADA FLAPJACKS Recipe

Serving: 16 | Prep: | Cook: 4mins | Ready in:

Ingredients

- 2 cups all-purpose flour
- 2 tbsp baking powder
- 1/3 cup sugar
- 1/2 tsp salt
- 1 (14oz) can crushed pineapple
- water
- 2 eggs
- 1 cop milk
- 1/4 cup butter;melted
- pancake syrup
- 1 cup toasted coconut

Direction

- In a large bowl, combine flour, baking powder, sugar & salt.
- Drain pineapple & reserve juice.
- Set pineapple aside.
- Add water to juice to equal 1 cup liquid.
- In a medium bowl, beat eggs well.
- Stir in juice/water mixture, milk and butter.
- Add to flour mixture; stir only until combined. (Batter will be lumpy)
- Using 1/4 cup of batter for each pancake, pour onto pre-heated greased fry pan.
- Sprinkle each pancake with 1 tbsp. of drained pineapple.
- Cook 2 minutes; or until underside is golden.
- Flip & cook until brown.

- Pour syrup and sprinkle toasted coconut on each pancake.

3. African Dish Sweet Potato Onion And Thyme Pancakes Recipe

Serving: 16 | Prep: | Cook: 4mins | Ready in:

Ingredients

- 3- eggs, slightly beaten
- 1/2- cup milk
- 2- tablespoon olive oil
- 1-1/4 cups flour
- 12 - ounces sweet potatoes, peeled and coarsley grated
- 2- onions, thinly sliced
- 2-teaspoon dried thyme
- sunflower or peanut oil for frying
- salt and freshly ground pepper

Direction

- Combine the eggs, milk and olive oil in a small bowl
- Place the flour in a large bowl and slowly stir in the egg mixture until a smooth batter is formed..............
- Add the sweet potatoes, onions, and thyme, season and mix well.....
- Pour a little oil into the frying pan and heat until hot but not smoking...
- Place a small ladle of the pancake mixture in the frying pan and press into shape, then repeat with more of the mixture until the base of the pan is full.
- Fry for about 2 minutes on each side until the pancakes are golden brown
- Remove and drain on a paper towel before serving ....enjoy

4. Almond Flour Blueberry Pancakes Recipe

Serving: 4 | Prep: | Cook: 10mins | Ready in:

Ingredients

- 1 1/2 cups almond flour/Meal
- 1/4 cup milk
- 4 eggs
- 1/4 cup coconut oil
- 1/2 tbls vanilla
- 1/2 teas baking soda
- 1/2 teas baking powder
- pinch salt
- 2 tbls frozen blueberries

Direction

- Combine almond flour, milk, eggs, oil, vanilla, baking soda, salt and blueberries
- Ladle pancake batter onto griddle.
- When bubbles start to pop on surface of pancake, flip them.
- Serve with butter and pure maple syrup.

5. Amaretto Almond Pancakes Recipe

Serving: 8 | Prep: | Cook: 5mins | Ready in:

Ingredients

- 1 C - All purpose bleached flour (softer than unbleached flour)
- 2 t – sugar
- ½ t – salt
- ½ t – baking powder
- ¾ c – buttermilk
- ¼ c – milk
- 1 – Large egg
- 2 T – unsalted butter melted
- 1 t – vanilla extract
- ¾ C – sliced almonds
- 1 T - Amaretto

- Topping:
- ¼ t – almond extract
- ½ C – Vermont medium amber grade A maple syrup
- ¼ C - sliced almonds

Direction

- Heat a large non-stick skillet or griddle to 375 degrees.
- Mix flour, sugar, salt, baking powder, sliced almonds and baking soda in a medium bowl. Microwave buttermilk and milk in a bowl to get to room temperature. Whisk in egg, butter and vanilla.
- Add wet ingredients to dry ingredients until just barely mixed to the point of no lumps.
- Pour batter ¼ cup at a time. Work in batches to avoid overcrowding. When pancake bottoms are golden brown and the tops start to bubble (2-3 minutes) flip the pancake and cook until golden brown on the remaining side.
- Combine Almond Extract and syrup and microwave for 45 seconds. Serve hot. Garnish pancakes with sliced almonds.

6. Amaretto Pancakes Recipe

Serving: 4 | Prep: | Cook: 20mins | Ready in:

Ingredients

- 2 cups all purpose baking mix
- 2 eggs
- 1 cup milk
- 1/4 cup Amaretto
- 1/2 cup almonds sliced
- Amaretto butter:
- 2 tablespoons Amaretto
- 1/2 cup butter softened
- Amaretto syrup:
- 1/4 cup Amaretto
- 1 cup maple syrup

Direction

- Beat pancakes ingredients together until smooth then cook on butter lined griddle until done.
- Combine butter and syrup and spread over warm pancakes.
- Combine amaretto and syrup then heat to boiling and cool slightly then pour over pancakes.

7. Ambrosia Pancakes With Orange Syrup Recipe

Serving: 4 | Prep: | Cook: 10mins | Ready in:

Ingredients

- 1 egg
- 1 cup all purpose flour
- 1/2 cup flaked coconut
- 3/4 cup milk
- 1 teaspoon grated orange rind
- 1 tablespoon brown sugar
- 2 tablespoons vegetable oil
- 1 tablespoon baking powder
- 1/4 teaspoon salt
- shortening as needed
- orange Syrup:
- 1 cup orange sections coarsely chopped
- 1 cup maple flavored syrup

Direction

- Beat egg until fluffy then add remaining ingredients except shortening and beat just until smooth.
- For thinner pancakes stir in additional 2 tablespoons milk.
- Heat griddle or skillet over medium heat or to 375 and grease griddle with shortening if necessary.
- For each pancake pour scant 1/4 cup batter onto hot griddle.
- Cook pancakes until puffed and dry around edges then turn and cook other side until golden brown.

- For syrup combine ingredients in a small saucepan then cook until thoroughly heated.

8. Angelgirls Griddle Cakes Recipe

Serving: 12 | Prep: | Cook: 7mins | Ready in:

Ingredients

- 1 1/2 cup self rising flour
- 2 tablespoons sugar
- 1 1/2 cup milk
- 2 large eggs
- 3 tablespoons butter
- 1 tablespoon oil
- 2 teaspoons vanilla extract
- 1/2 teaspoon cinnamon-or to taste

Direction

- Preheat a griddle or a large non-stick skillet. When drops of water sizzle and bounce around on it, it is ready.
- In a medium mixing bowl, combine flour, sugar, and cinnamon. Set aside.
- In a large mixing bowl, beat eggs and milk together with an electric mixer until mixture turns light yellow.
- Add butter, oil, and vanilla. Beat until combined.
- Add flour mixture. Beat on low until just combined and smooth. Do not overbeat.
- Brush preheated griddle or skillet with additional butter or oil.
- Pour batter onto griddle in 1/4 cup increments, leaving space between each cake.
- Flip griddle cakes when edges look dry and tops are covered with bubbles. This should take approx. 2 minutes.
- Cook on other side for approx. 1 1/2 to 2 minutes.
- Repeat with remainder of batter.
- Serve griddle cakes hot with lots of warm melted butter and syrup.
- Note:

- If you don't have self-rising flour, simply add 1 teaspoon baking powder, 1 teaspoon baking soda, and 1/2 teaspoon salt to all-purpose flour. Prepare as directed.
- Suggestion:
- Add bananas, blueberries, strawberries, or chocolate chips to pancake batter.

9. Apple Blueberry Pancakes Recipe

Serving: 10 | Prep: | Cook: 15mins | Ready in:

Ingredients

- Bisquick prepared according to box
- Handful of blueberries
- 1 eating apple

Direction

- Prepare Bisquick according to box.
- Wash and core apple, but leave skin on.
- Chop apple in hand blander.
- Add to Bisquick mix and stir.
- Wash blueberries and fold into Bisquick/apple mixture.
- Grill in hot pan until golden brown.
- Enjoy with maple or blueberry syrup!

10. Apple Pancackes Recipe

Serving: 4 | Prep: | Cook: 30mins | Ready in:

Ingredients

- 40 oz Lucky Leaf apple pie filling, No sugar Added
- 2 Tbsp light butter
- 1 tsp ground cinnamon
- 3/4 cup egg Beaters egg Beaters
- 1/2 cup fat-free skim milk

- 1/2 cup all-purpose flour
- 1 Tbsp light sour cream
- 1 tsp lemon zest
- 1/4 tsp table salt
- 1/4 cup powdered sugar

Direction

- Preheat oven to 350 degrees F.
- In a 10-inch cast iron skillet, warm the apple pie filling, butter, cinnamon. In a bowl, beat the egg beaters until frothy. Add the milk, flour, sour cream, lemon zest, and salt. Beat just until batter is smooth. Pour over the hot apple mixture in the skillet, and immediately put the pan in the oven. Bake for 20 to 25 minutes, or until the pancake is puffed up and golden brown. Using a small, fine sieve, lightly dust the top of the pancake with confectioners' sugar. Serve warm.

11. Apple Pancake Recipe

Serving: 2 | Prep: | Cook: 25mins | Ready in:

Ingredients

- 2 eggs
- 1/2 cup milk
- 1/2 teaspoon vanilla
- 1/3 cup flour
- 2 tablespoons brown sugar, divided
- 1/8 teaspoon salt
- 1/2 teaspoon cinnamon
- 1/4 teaspoon nutmeg
- 2 teaspoons butter, melted
- 1 apple, peeled, cored and sliced

Direction

- Preheat oven to 400 degrees.
- In large bowl, whisk together eggs, milk and vanilla. Add flour, 1 tablespoon of the brown sugar, salt, cinnamon and nutmeg; mix until well blended. Set aside.
- Pour melted butter into bottom of a glass pie plate. Arrange apple slices around bottom and then pour batter over the top. Sprinkle with remaining tablespoon of brown sugar.
- Bake 25-30 minutes, or until lightly browned and puffed.

12. Apple Pancakes From Mrs Bray Recipe

Serving: 4 | Prep: | Cook: 10mins | Ready in:

Ingredients

- 1 1/3 cups of pancake mix
- 2/3 cup of evaporated milk
- 2/3 cup of water
- (I substitute 1 cup of whole milk, I like a thicker batter)
- 1 cup of finely chopped peeled apples
- 2 tbsp of melted butter
- 1/2 teaspoon of cinnamon
- 1/4 teaspoon of lemon juice
- 1 teaspoon of sugar

Direction

- Mix pancake mix and milk mixture, slowly.
- Fold in the apples.
- Stir in butter, cinnamon, lemon juice and sugar.
- Bake on a slightly greased griddle.
- Don't beat the batter until smooth, makes it tough.
- When drops of water dance on the griddle it is o.k.

13. Apple Pancakes Mountain Style Recipe

Serving: 4 | Prep: | Cook: 15mins | Ready in:

Ingredients

- 2 large eggs
- 1/2 cup milk
- 1 tablespoon sugar
- 1/3 cup flour
- 1/4 teaspoon salt
- 3 tablespoons butter
- 1 medium Red Delicious, peeled, cored, sliced in rings
- 2 Tablespoons sugar
- 1/4 teaspoon cinnamon
- 3-4 Tablespoons cognac

Direction

- Beat eggs until light and foamy, beat in milk and 1 tablespoon sugar, blend in flour and salt. Preheat oven 450°. Melt butter in 10" ovenproof skillet. Arrange apples in single layer and cook until sizzling.
- Pour batter over and shake to distribute evenly. Cover and cook to brown underside approximately 3-4 minutes. Uncover, place in oven until puffs and bubbles, approximately 5 minutes.
- Sprinkle with cinnamon and sugar. Warm cognac and ignite on pancake. Serve immediately.

14. Apple Pie Pancakes Recipe

Serving: 4 | Prep: | Cook: 5mins | Ready in:

Ingredients

- 1 1/2 cups flour
- 2 tbsp sugar
- 1 tbsp baking powder
- 1/2 tsp apple pie spice or cinnamon
- 1/4 tsp salt
- 2 eggs
- 1 cup apple juice
- 3 tsp butter, melted or use oil
- 2 tsp vanilla
- 1/4 cup snipped dried apple or 1/2 cup fresh apples
- cooking spray

Direction

- In bowl, stir together flour, sugar, powder spice and salt. Make a well in the center, set aside.
- In a small bowl, use a fork to mix together eggs, juice butter and vanilla. Add this mixture to flour mixture. Stir just until moistened. batter will be lumpy. Stir in apple.
- Use 1/4 cup measuring cup full of mixture, pour onto a hot, lightly greased griddle or skillet.
- Serve warm.

15. Apple Raisin Oven Pancake Recipe

Serving: 4 | Prep: | Cook: 30mins | Ready in:

Ingredients

- 1 large baking apple cored and thinly sliced
- 1/3 cup golden raisins
- 2 tablespoons packed brown sugar
- ½ teaspoon ground cinnamon
- 4 eggs
- 2/3 cup milk
- 2/3 cup all purpose flour
- 2 tablespoons margarine or butter, melted
- powdered sugar
- berries

Direction

- Preheat oven to 350 degrees. Spray 9 inch pie plate with no stick cooking spray.
- Combine apples, raisins, brown sugar and cinnamon in medium bowl. Transfer to pie plate. Bake uncovered 10-15 minutes or until apple begins to soften. Remove from oven.
- Increase oven temperature to 450 degrees.

- Meanwhile, whisk eggs, milk, flour and butter until blended. Pour over apples. Bake 15 minutes or until pancake is golden brown.
- Sprinkle with powdered sugar and garnish with your favorite berries.

16. Applesauce Oatmeal Pancakes Recipe

Serving: 5 | Prep: | Cook: | Ready in:

Ingredients

- 1 cup quick-cooking oats
- 1/2 cup whole wheat flour
- 1/4 cup all-purpose flour
- 1 tablespoon baking powder
- 1 cup skim milk
- 2 tablespoons sugarless applesauce
- 4 egg whites

Direction

- In a bowl, combine the oats, flour and baking powder, in another bowl, combine milk, applesauce and egg whites; add to dry ingredients and mix well.
- Pour batter by 1/4 cupfuls onto a heated griddle coated with non-stick cooking spray.
- Cook until bubbles appear on the top; turn and cook until lightly browned.
- Yield 5 servings (two pancakes each).

17. Applesauce Pancakes Recipe

Serving: 10 | Prep: | Cook: 10mins | Ready in:

Ingredients

- 1 cup all purpose flour
- 1 tsp. baking soda
- 1/8 tsp salt
- 2 Tbl. toasted wheat germ
- 1 cup nonfat buttermilk
- 1/4 cup applesauce
- 2 tsp. vegetable oil
- 1 egg, lightly beaten
- vegetable cooking spray
- Reduced calorie maple syrup (optional)
- fresh fruit slices (optional)

Direction

- Combine first 4 ingredients in a medium bowl; make a well in center of mixture.
- Combine buttermilk and next 3 ingredients.
- Add buttermilk mixture to dry ingredients, stirring just until dry ingredients are moistened.
- Coat a non-stick griddle or non-stick skillet with cooking spray, and preheat to 350 degrees. For each pancake. Pour 1/4 cup batter onto hot griddle, spreading to a 5-inch circle. Cook pancakes until tops are covered with bubbles and edges look cooked, turn pancakes, and cook other side.
- If desired serve with maple syrup and fresh fruit slices.

18. Arabic Almond Pancakes Recipe

Serving: 1012 | Prep: | Cook: 15mins | Ready in:

Ingredients

- 4 cups flour
- 1/2 teaspoon yeast
- 1 cup milk
- water
- 2 eggs
- 1 cup confectioner's sugar
- 3 tablespoons corn oil
- 1 tablespoon ground cardamom
- 1 teaspoon baking powder
- 2 cups almonds, roasted and ground

Direction

- Put the flour in a bowl, add the milk, eggs, baking powder, yeast and water; mix together to form a batter; set aside to rise.
- Grease a frying pan with a little oil, pour into the pan half a ladle of batter.
- Spread the batter quickly into a thin pancake and fry over medium heat until the top bubbles, then turn over and brown the other side. Repeat using all batter.
- Mix the sugar, cardamom and almonds together.
- Stuff each pancake with the mixture; roll into finger shapes, and arrange on a serving dish; sprinkle with some ground almonds. Serves 10-12 persons.

19. Aunt Jemimas Pancake Mix Recipe

Serving: 35 | Prep: | Cook: | Ready in:

Ingredients

- 2 cups Self-rising flour
- 2 cups Bisquick
- 1/2 cup sugar
- 1/2 cup Non-dairy creamer powder

Direction

- THE MIX: In an 8-cup container, stir together flour, Bisquick, sugar and creamer. Cover tightly. Refrigerate mix to use within 3 months.
- Makes 7 cups of mix.
- TO USE THE MIX:
- 1 Egg
- 8 ounces 7-up
- 1 3/4 cups prepared pancake mix
- TO USE: Into blender, put egg, 7-up and prepared pancake mix. Blend at high speed until smooth, 1 minute. Allow 1/3 cup batter for each 6" pancake.

20. Awesome Almond Buckwheat Pancakes Recipe

Serving: 2 | Prep: | Cook: 10mins | Ready in:

Ingredients

- Combine:
- 1/3 c buckwheat flour
- 1/3 c whole wheat (or whole spelt) flour
- 3/4 tsp baking powder
- 1/4 tsp salt
- 2 tsp sugar (optional)
- *****
- Combine separately:
- 1/3 c yogurt
- 1/2 c milk (or substitute)
- 1 egg
- 1 Tbsp melted butter
- *****
- slivered almonds

Direction

- Mix wet and dry ingredients until just incorporated - batter can be a bit lumpy.
- Heat a frying pan over medium heat with about a teaspoon of butter. You can spray your pan with oil (grape seed works well) instead if you like.
- Pour in 1/4 of the batter and generously sprinkle with slivered almonds.
- When bubbles start to appear in your pancake, flip it and cook until slightly browned on bottom.
- Repeat with the rest of the batter adding a bit more butter to the pan each time.
- Serve warm with maple syrup.
- Enjoy

21. BAKED BLUEBERRY PANCAKE Recipe

Serving: 2 | Prep: | Cook: 25mins | Ready in:

Ingredients

- 2 Tbsp butter (do not substitute)
- 1/2 to 3/4 cup blueberries (I have made it with both fresh and frozen)
- 1 cup Bisquick
- 1 egg
- 1/2 cup milk

Direction

- Set oven to 350 degrees.
- Melt butter in pie plate.
- Spread blueberries in butter.
- Mix Bisquick, egg and milk together.
- Pour the batter over the blueberries.
- Bake at 350 degrees for 25 minutes.
- Serve with melted butter and syrup of your choice.

22. BANANA SPLIT PANCAKES Recipe

Serving: 10 | Prep: | Cook: 10mins | Ready in:

Ingredients

- 1 large egg
- 1 cup buttermilk
- 2 Tbsp butter; melted
- 1/2 cup mashed banana
- 1 tbsp sugar
- 1 cup flour
- 1 tsp baking powder
- 1/2 tsp baking soda
- 1/2 tsp salt
- 1/8 tsp nutmeg
- oil for pan
- 1 large banana; sliced
- 6-8 strawberries; sliced
- 1/2 cup melted nutella
- 1 cup syrup

Direction

- In a medium bowl, whisk together the egg, buttermilk, butter, banana, and sugar.
- In a separate bowl, sift together the flour, baking powder, baking soda, salt, and nutmeg.
- Pour the liquid ingredients over the dry ingredients and stir together with a fork or small whisk just to combine (over stirring makes the pancakes tough).
- It is okay if the batter is a little bit lumpy.
- Heat a non-stick griddle or skillet over medium-high heat.
- Brush the pan lightly with oil and drop the batter onto the heated skillet in mounded cup portions.
- Cook the pancakes until the batter starts to brown around the edges and little bubbles start to form over the surface of the batter, 1 to 2 minutes.
- Use your spatula to lift a corner of the pancake to see if it is brown and lacy and ready to turn.
- Flip the pancake and finish cooking, 1 to 2 minutes longer.
- Repeat with the remaining pancake batter, brushing the pan with more oil when needed to prevent sticking.
- Serve the warm pancakes drizzled with melted butter, sliced bananas, fresh strawberries, warmed Nutella, and/or syrup

23. BEST BUTTERMILK PANCAKES Recipe

Serving: 4 | Prep: | Cook: 2mins | Ready in:

Ingredients

- 1 1/4 cups all-purpose flour
- 1/4 cup sugar
- 1 tsp baking powder
- 1 tsp baking soda

- 1/8 tsp salt
- 4 tbsp buttermilk powder
- 1 1/4 water
- 1/4 cup vegetable oil
- 1 egg

Direction

- Mix all wet ingredients together.
- Mix all dry ingredients together.
- Mix both until just blended.
- Let sit for 5 minutes.
- Portion by 1/4 cupfuls onto hot griddle set at 350f.
- Cook until dry around edges and bubbly in middle, flip and cook until golden brown. About 1 minute each side.
- Makes 10 cakes.
- Note: substitute fresh buttermilk for water and powder if using.

24. Baby Blackberry Pancakes Recipe

Serving: 4 | Prep: | Cook: 10mins | Ready in:

Ingredients

- 3/4 cup milk
- 1/2 cup unbleached all purpose flour
- 2 large eggs
- 1-1/2 tablespoons granulated sugar
- 1/2 teaspoon pure vanilla extract
- 3 tablespoons unsalted butter
- 1 tablespoon confectioners' sugar
- 1-1/2 cup fresh blackberries

Direction

- Preheat oven to 450 with rack in center of oven.
- Have a glass pie plate or cast iron skillet ready.
- Mix milk, flour, eggs, sugar and vanilla until smooth in a blender.
- Put butter in pie plate or skillet and place in hot oven until butter is melted.
- Brush butter up sides and onto rim of pan so the entire inside surface is well coated.
- Slowly pour batter into pie plate or skillet and bake 20 minutes.
- Reduce oven to 350 and continue baking 10 minutes longer.
- Remove from oven and sift confectioners' sugar over top.
- Serve immediately with fruit spooned into center.

25. Bacon Pancakes Recipe

Serving: 8 | Prep: | Cook: 10mins | Ready in:

Ingredients

- 2 cups flour
- 1 teaspoon baking powder
- 1/2 teaspoon salt
- 3 tablespoons sugar
- 2 eggs
- 2 tablespoons butter melted
- 1-1/2 cups buttermilk
- 3/4 cup cooked drained and crumbled bacon

Direction

- Mix flour, baking powder, salt and sugar.
- In a small bowl beat eggs, milk and butter then add to flour mixture then gently stir in bacon.
- Allow to stand 5 minutes then pour by spoonfuls onto hot lightly greased griddle.
- Cook until bubbles break on top then turn and cook until underside is golden

26. Bacon Sausage Pancakes Recipe

Serving: 3 | Prep: | Cook: 20mins | Ready in:

Ingredients

- General:
- • One bowl of pancake batter, minus the shortening. Use your own favorite or see below.
- • 4 to 6 slices (to your taste) of smoked bacon, chopped pretty fine. You can also use any kind of sausage here, kielbasa, Portuguese, summer, etc.; all finally chopped.
- • 1 egg, cooked to your liking, per serving.
- The batter:
- • 1 cup all purpose flour
- • 1 cup buttermilk
- • 1 tsp baking powder
- • ½ tsp baking soda
- • 1 Tbs sugar
- • ½ tsp salt
- • 1 egg
- • 1 tsp vanilla extract (optional)
- • 2 Tsp shortening. You need to adjust this for the fat content of the meat you use. If you use 6 strips of fatty bacon you won't need any additional shortening. The fat from the meat and what shortening you add should equal 2 Tbs.

Direction

- 1. Cook the meat of your choice (until done but not crisp) with enough shortening to total 2 Tbs. I often do this in the microwave.
- 2. While the meat is cooking mix up your batter, no shortening yet.
- 3. When the meat is cooked allow to cool a little and add to the batter. If you think you have more than 2 Tbsp. of grease in the meat poor some off.
- 4. Beat the meat/batter mixture thoroughly to make sure the shortening is well mixed in.
- 5. I'm sure you know how to cook pancakes and these are no different than standard pancakes in that regard . The pancakes need to be well done and not doughy in the middle.
- 6. Top each serving with an egg cooked to taste and serve.
- Yes, I have used this meat/batter combo to make waffles and they come out great.

27. Bacon And Banana Pancakes Recipe

Serving: 4 | Prep: | Cook: 17mins | Ready in:

Ingredients

- 4 slices-bacon
- 1T-butter
- 1& 1/2-bananas
- 1/2 C-brown sugar
- pancake mix (your choice of out of the box or homade)

Direction

- Cut bacon into 1/4 inch strips.
- Add to pan with butter.
- Render out fat slowly.
- Extract bacon and keep fat in pan.
- Heat to medium high.
- Add bananas and brown sugar.
- This should make a nice syrup.
- Add all ingredients, bacon, bananas, and syrup to batter and make par usual.
- I can usually get 8 pancakes out of this amount, and just to forewarn you don't need any additional syrup.

28. Bacon And Coriander Pancakes Recipc

Serving: 6 | Prep: | Cook: 20mins | Ready in:

Ingredients

- 12 slices bacon
- 1 cup flour
- 2 eggs beaten

- 8 ounces milk
- 2 tablespoons finely chopped coriander leaves

Direction

- Dice bacon finely and set it aside.
- Sift flour into a bowl and make a well in the middle.
- Stir in eggs and half the milk and beat until batter is smooth.
- Gradually beat in remaining milk then stir in the chopped coriander.
- Fry a heaped tablespoon of bacon in a small pan until it is crisp.
- Pour enough batter for one pancake over the bacon and fry until the underside is light brown.
- Turn it over and fry the other side.
- Turn the pancake out onto a clean tea towel and fold the towel over it to keep it warm.
- Repeat until all the pancakes are cooked.

29. Baked Apple Pancake Recipe

Serving: 9 | Prep: | Cook: 25mins | Ready in:

Ingredients

- 4 tablespoons butter
- 4 cups diced and peeled apples
- 2 tablespoons brown sugar
- 2 tablespoons lemon or lime juice
- ½ teaspoon ground cinnamon
- 4 large eggs, lightly beaten
- 1 cup whole milk
- 1 cup all purpose flour
- 1 teaspoon vanilla
- 1/8 teaspoon salt
- Confectioners' sugar for dusting

Direction

- Preheat oven to 425 degrees F.
- Melt half the butter, add the apples and sauté until tender.
- Sprinkle with the brown sugar, lemon/lime juice, and cinnamon and stir to combine. Remove from heat.
- Preheat a 9x13 baking dish for 5 minutes then add the remaining 2 tablespoons butter to it and coat the bottom and sides.
- Spoon the sautéed apple mixture over the bottom evenly.
- By hand, whisk together eggs, milk, flour, vanilla, and salt until blended.
- Pour the batter over the hot fruit. Bake until puffed and golden brown (about 20-25 minutes).
- Remove from oven and dust with confectioners' sugar.
- Serve and enjoy!

30. Baked Gingerbread Pancake Recipe

Serving: 4 | Prep: | Cook: 15mins | Ready in:

Ingredients

- 1/2 cup milk
- 1/2 cup all purpose flour
- 2 tablespoons all purpose flour
- 1/2 cup unsweetened applesauce
- 1/2 cup egg substitute
- 1 tablespoon dark molasses
- 1 tablespoon granulated sugar
- 1/4 teaspoon ground ginger
- 1/4 teaspoon ground cinnamon
- 1/4 teaspoon table salt
- 1 cup lemon yogurt

Direction

- Preheat oven to 425 then coat oven proof skillet with cooking spray.
- Combine all ingredients together except yogurt and whisk until lump free.
- Pour batter into skillet and bake until pancake is firm about 12 minutes.

- Immediately remove pancake from oven and cut into wedges and top with yogurt.

31. Baked Marmalade Pancake Recipe

Serving: 8 | Prep: | Cook: 20mins | Ready in:

Ingredients

- 2 eggs
- 1/2 cup all purpose flour
- 1/2 cup milk
- 1/4 teaspoon almond or vanilla extract
- 1/4 pound unsalted butter
- 6 tablespoons orange marmalade
- 2 tablespoons confectioners' sugar

Direction

- Preheat oven to 400.
- In medium bowl whisk eggs, flour, milk and almond extract until blended.
- Melt butter in a large ovenproof skillet over moderate heat.
- Remove skillet from heat and pour in batter tilting to cover bottom of pan evenly.
- Immediately place in oven and bake 15 minutes.
- Transfer to a serving plate then spread with marmalade and dust with sugar and serve.

32. Baked Norweigan Pancake Recipe

Serving: 4 | Prep: | Cook: 40mins | Ready in:

Ingredients

- 1/4 cup butter
- 4 eggs
- 1-1/2 cups milk
- 6 tablespoons butter
- 1/2 cup sugar divided
- 3/4 cup regular all purpose flour
- 1/4 teaspoon salt
- 3 cups mixed berries
- sour cream
- brown sugar

Direction

- Put butter in 9" baking dish and place dish in 425 oven for 10 minutes but do not burn.
- While that is heating beat together eggs, milk, butter, 3/4 cup sugar, flour and salt until smooth.
- Remove hot pan from oven and add mixture then quickly return to hot oven for 30 minutes.
- Add remaining sugar to 3 cups berries and stir to dissolve.
- When pancake is done remove from oven then spoon berries into center and cut in wedges.
- Serve with sour cream and brown sugar.

33. Baked Peach Pancake Recipe

Serving: 4 | Prep: | Cook: 25mins | Ready in:

Ingredients

- 2 cups fresh or frozen sliced peeled peaches
- 4 tsp sugar
- 1 tsp lemon juice
- 3 eggs
- 1/2 cup all purpose flour
- 1/2 cup milk
- 1/2 tsp salt
- 2 Tbsp butter
- ground nutmeg
- sour cream, optional

Direction

- In a bowl, combine peaches with sugar and lemon juice; set aside. In a mixing bowl, beat eggs until fluffy. Add flour, milk and salt; beat until smooth. Place butter in a 10-in. skillet; bake at 400 degrees for 3-5 minutes or until melted. Immediately pour batter into hot skillet. Bake for 20-25 minutes or until pancake has risen and is puffed all over. Fill with peach slices and sprinkle with nutmeg. Serve immediately with sour cream if desired.

34. Baked Peach Pancakes With Honey Raisin Syrup Recipe

Serving: 4 | Prep: | Cook: 30mins | Ready in:

Ingredients

- 1/4 cup butter
- 1 cup all purpose baking mix
- 3/4 cup milk
- 4 eggs
- 2 medium peaches peeled and thinly sliced
- 1/4 cup sugar
- 1/4 teaspoon cinnamon
- honey raisin Syrup:
- 1/2 cup honey
- 1/4 cup raisins
- 1/4 cup margarine
- 1/4 teaspoon cinnamon

Direction

- Heat oven to 400 then place 2 tablespoons butter in two pie pans and heat in oven until melted.
- Beat baking mix, milk and eggs then arrange sliced peaches in each pie pan.
- Divide batter evenly between pie pans then mix sugar and cinnamon and sprinkle over batter.
- Bake uncovered 25 minutes then cut and serve with syrup.
- To make syrup heat all ingredients over medium heat.

35. Baked Pear Cheese Pancakes Recipe

Serving: 2 | Prep: | Cook: 20mins | Ready in:

Ingredients

- 1/4 cup butter
- 1/2 teaspoon salt
- 4 eggs
- 1 cup shredded white cheddar cheese
- 1/2 teaspoon lemon juice
- 1 cup all purpose flour
- 1 cup milk
- 2 medium pears thinly sliced
- powdered sugar

Direction

- Preheat oven to 425 then heat butter in rectangular pan in oven until hot and bubbly.
- Beat flour, milk, salt and eggs until well blended then pour into hot pan with melted butter.
- Sprinkle with cheese then bake until sides of pancakes and puffed about 18 minutes.
- Slice pears and pour lemon juice over to keep from turning brown.
- Arrange pears over pancakes as desired then microwave 1 minutes to warm pears.
- Sprinkle with powdered sugar and serve immediately.

36. Baked Pear Pecan Pancake Surprise Recipe

Serving: 4 | Prep: | Cook: 15mins | Ready in:

Ingredients

- 3/4 cup pancake mix
- 1/2 cup water
- 3 eggs
- 1/4 cup and 1 tablespoon sugar
- 1 teaspoon cinnamon

- 1/2 cup butter
- 3 cups thinly sliced peeled pears
- 5 teaspoons brown sugar
- 1/4 cup chopped pecans
- 1/2 cup raisins
- Raspberry syrup
- vanilla yogurt

Direction

- In bowl combine pancake mix, water, eggs and 1 tablespoon sugar then mix well and set aside.
- In small bowl combine 1/4 cup sugar and 1 teaspoon cinnamon and set aside.
- Melt butter in a skillet over medium heat and sauté pears until tender.
- Place 1 teaspoon of butter and 1 teaspoon of brown sugar in each ramekin then place in oven.
- When butter and brown sugar have melted spoon in sautéed pears.
- Top with pecans and raisins then pour 3-1/2 tablespoons batter over pears.
- Sprinkle sugar cinnamon mix over batter and bake at 450 for 12 minutes.
- Top with raspberry syrup and vanilla yogurt.

37. Baked Upside Down Banana Pancake Recipe

Serving: 4 | Prep: | Cook: 30mins | Ready in:

Ingredients

- 1 stick butter
- 1 Cup real maple syrup (not pancake syrup)
- 3-4 ripe bananas
- 1 cup chopped pecans or walnuts
- 1 tsp. vanilla
- 1 recipe pancake mix (such as Bisquick)

Direction

- Preheat oven to 350 degrees.
- Move top rack of oven to high middle section.
- Melt butter in heavy 10-11 inch skillet in oven. (I use my cast iron skillet!)
- Brush sides of pan with melted butter.
- Add maple syrup and let cool a couple of minutes.
- Slice bananas evenly over the syrup and cover entire bottom of pan with bananas.
- Do not slice bananas too thin because they will shrink some during baking.
- Sprinkle pecans or walnuts over bananas.
- Mix pancake mix and add vanilla.
- Pour batter gently over bananas and spread evenly.
- Bake in oven about 30 minutes until top browns.
- Remove from oven and let cool 5 minutes.
- Invert onto a large platter. To do this, place a large platter on top of frying pan and with one quick motion turn upside down.
- Dust with powdered sugar, slice and serve.

38. Banana And Blueberry Pancakes With Cinnamon Vanilla Butter Recipe

Serving: 4 | Prep: | Cook: 10mins | Ready in:

Ingredients

- 1-1/2 cups all-purpose flour
- 2 tablespoons sugar
- 2 teaspoons baking powder
- 1/2 teaspoon salt
- 1 egg, lightly beaten
- 1-1/4 cups fat-free milk
- 3 medium ripe bananas, mashed
- 1 teaspoon vanilla extract
- 1-1/2 cups fresh or frozen blueberries (If using frozen blueberries, do not thaw)
- maple syrup, optional
- powdered sugar, optional
- cinnamon-Vanilla butter
- 1/4 cup unsalted butter, softened

- 1/2 teaspoon cinnamon
- 1/4 teaspoon vanilla extract

Direction

- For cinnamon-vanilla butter: Combine softened unsalted butter, cinnamon and vanilla extract in a bowl. Mix until well combined. Set aside.
- For pancakes: In a large bowl, combine the flour, sugar, baking powder and salt. In another bowl, combine the egg, milk, bananas and vanilla; stir into dry ingredients just until moistened. Gently stir in blueberries.
- Coat a large flat pan with cooking spray. Turn pan to low heat. Pour pancake batter by 1/4 cupfuls onto the pan. Turn when bubbles form on top; cook until second side is golden brown.
- Serve with maple syrup, sifted powdered sugar and/or cinnamon-vanilla butter, if desired.
- Enjoy!

39. Banana Blueberry Pancakes Recipe

Serving: 4 | Prep: | Cook: 20mins | Ready in:

Ingredients

- 2 cups sifted all purpose flour
- 1/4 cup granulated sugar
- 4 teaspoons baking powder
- 1 teaspoon salt
- 2 eggs well beaten
- 1-1/2 cups milk
- 1/4 cup butter melted
- 2/3 cup mashed banana
- 1 teaspoon vanilla extract
- 2 cups fresh blueberries

Direction

- Mix flour, sugar, baking powder and salt. Add eggs, milk, butter, bananas and vanilla. Stir until well blended and smooth then gently fold in blueberries. Spoon about 1/4 cup of batter for each pancake on preheated greased griddle. Turn only once.

40. Banana Bread Pancakes Recipe

Serving: 8 | Prep: | Cook: 15mins | Ready in:

Ingredients

- Pancake Ingredients:
- 1½ cups all-purpose flour
- 1 teaspoon salt
- 3 tablespoons sugar
- 1¾ teaspoons baking powder
- 2 eggs-separated
- 3 tablespoons butter-melted
- 1¼ cups milk
- 1 teaspoon cinnamon
- 1/2 teaspoon nutmeg
- 1 teaspoon vanilla
- 1/2 teaspoon ground ginger
- 2 bananas-sliced
- 1/2 cup walnuts-chopped
- banana Ingredients:
- 3 tablespoon butter
- 3 bananas-sliced on a slight horizontal
- 1/8 cup brown sugar
- 1/8 cup white sugar
- 1/2 teaspoon nutmeg

Direction

- Directions:
- Lightly spoon flour into dry measuring cups, and level with a knife. Combine flour in bowl with salt, spices, sugar and baking powder. Combine egg yolks, butter, vanilla, and milk. Quickly mix ingredients together-batter will be lumpy. Whip egg whites and gently fold into mixture. Gently fold in bananas, walnuts (reserve 1 tablespoon of nuts for garnish).

Ladle onto griddle pan on low-medium heat. Cook until bottom is golden brown. Flip, repeat. Top with nuts and caramelized bananas. For a special treat, try serving with warmed applesauce.
- Caramelized Bananas:
- Melt butter in non-stick saucepan over medium heat. Add sugars and heat until they dissolve. Add bananas and sauté until mixture thickens and bananas start to brown. Optional — add 2 tablespoons coffee-flavored liqueur and cook 3-5 minutes until thick.

41. Banana Buttermilk Buckwheat Pancakes Recipe

Serving: 4 | Prep: | Cook: 20mins | Ready in:

Ingredients

- 1 cup all purpose flour
- 1/3 cup whole wheat flour
- 1/2 cup buckwheat flour
- 2 tablespoons granulated sugar
- 1 teaspoon baking soda
- 4 teaspoons baking powder
- 2 eggs slightly beaten
- 1-1/2 cups buttermilk
- 1/2 cup milk
- 2 ripe bananas mashed
- 1/4 cup butter melted

Direction

- Stir together flours, sugar, salt, baking soda and baking powder.
- Beat eggs in separate bowl then stir in buttermilk, milk, bananas and butter.
- Add liquid mixture to dry ingredients stirring just until blended well.
- Heat greased griddle or skillet over medium heat.
- For each pancake pour scant 1/4 cup batter onto hot griddle.

- Cook pancakes until puffed bubbly and dry around edges.
- Turn and cook other sides until golden brown.

42. Banana Buttermilk Pancakes Recipe

Serving: 6 | Prep: | Cook: 10mins | Ready in:

Ingredients

- 1 cup flour
- 1 teaspoon granulated sugar
- 3/4 teaspoon baking powder
- 1/2 teaspoon baking soda
- 1/2 teaspoon salt
- 1 egg lightly beaten
- 1 cup buttermilk
- 2 medium bananas thinly sliced

Direction

- Sift together all dry ingredients then make well in middle and add in egg and buttermilk.
- Combine with a few quick strokes but do not over mix.
- Heat griddle.
- Add bananas to batter and spoon onto griddle in desired size pancakes.
- When top of pancakes are covered with air bubbles gently check bottom with a spatula.
- Once golden brown turn pancake and cook other side.
- When cooked add to a warmed plate and stack with butter.
- Serve with your favorite syrup or sprinkled with powdered sugar and nutmeg.

43. Banana Buttermilk Pancakes With Berry Sauce Recipe

Serving: 8 | Prep: | Cook: 20mins | Ready in:

Ingredients

- 1 cup granola
- 2 cups unbleached white flour
- 2 teaspoons baking soda
- 4 teaspoons baking powder
- 3/4 teaspoon salt
- 4 ripe bananas pureed
- 1/4 cup honey
- 2 cups buttermilk
- 2 eggs separated with whites whipped to medium peaks
- 1/4 cup vegetable oil
- Berry Sauce:
- 1/3 cup orange juice
- 2 cups fresh or frozen blueberries
- 1 cup fresh or frozen blackberries
- 1 cup fresh or frozen raspberries
- 1 teaspoon orange zest
- 1 teaspoon lemon zest
- 1/2 cup honey
- 1/4 cup berry liquor
- 1 tablespoon cornstarch

Direction

- Mix all dry ingredients together.
- Mix wet ingredients except whites then combine with dry ingredients.
- Stir in egg whites and stir gently until just combined being careful not to over mix.
- Cook in a lightly greased pan or griddle until small bubbles form on surface.
- Flip and brown the other side then top with butter and berry sauce.
- Reserve 1/4 cup of each berry then add orange juice and remaining berries to saucepan.
- Cook at a simmer for 15 minutes then add zest and honey.
- Simmer while stirring until blended then remove from heat and add liquor.
- Return to heat and simmer 5 minutes.
- Add cornstarch to 2 tablespoons cold water then stir until liquefied and add to pan.
- Stir constantly until thickened approximately 2 minutes then add reserved berries.
- Stir gently until it returns to a simmer then turn off heat and cool just until warm.
- Spoon over pancakes and serve immediately.

44. Banana Foster Pancakes Recipe

Serving: 6 | Prep: | Cook: 15mins | Ready in:

Ingredients

- 1 stick butter
- 6 bananas, sliced
- 1 cup maple syrup
- ½ cup slivered pecans
- 1 tsp crème d'banana liqueur
- 1 tsp light rum
- whipped cream
- additional chopped pecans, optional
- strawberries, optional

Direction

- Melt the butter in a large skillet; add bananas and pecans. Sauté about one minute.
- Add syrup and heat. Stir in liqueur; keep warm.
- Using your favorite pancake recipe, prepare pancakes allowing three pancakes preserving.
- Arrange pancakes on individual plates and top with banana mixture.
- Garnish with a dollop of whipped cream, sprinkle with additional chopped pecans, and top with a fanned strawberry.

45. Banana Nutella Pancakes Recipe

Serving: 4 | Prep: | Cook: 10mins | Ready in:

Ingredients

- 1 cup pancake mix (I used Arrowhead Mills buttermilk Pancake & Waffle Mix)

- 1 cup + 1 tbsp milk
- 1 tbsp canola oil (vegetable oil) + more for skillet or griddle
- 1/4 cup nutella
- 1 banana (average size), sliced with 1/4 reserved to slice for garnish (waiting to slice this part keeps from browning)
- confectioners sugar, for garnish

Direction

- Lightly coat skillet or griddle with oil and heat over medium to medium-high heat.
- Combine mix with milk, oil and Nutella. Whisk until smooth. Measure about 1/2 cup of batter and slowly pour into pan, be sure to leave a couple inches between each. Turn when bubbles form on surface and edges begin to dry and cook on other side for about 3 minutes or until golden brown.
- *The batter is brown so keep a close eye so as not to overcook them.
- *This will probably need to be done in batches. I cooked about 2 at a time. I placed them on a plate tented in foil to keep warm.
- *For thicker pancakes, use less liquid. For thinner pancakes, use more liquid.
- To serve, sprinkle tops with confectioners' sugar (sifted) and slices of banana.

46. Banana Oat Pancakes Recipe

Serving: 4 | Prep: | Cook: 35mins | Ready in:

Ingredients

- 1 c. old-fashioned oats
- 1 c. nonfat milk
- 1 c. mashed ripe bananas (about 3 medium)
- 2 large eggs, beaten to blend
- 2 tbsp toasted wheat germ
- 1 tsp gound cinnamon
- 1 1/2 c. reduced-fat (light) oat bran pancake mix or other mixed grain pancake mix.
- 6 tbsp (3/4 stick) butter
- maple syrup
- berries and sliced bananas

Direction

- Combine oats and milk in large bowl. Let stand until oats are soft, about 15 minutes. Mix in mashed bananas, eggs, wheat germ and cinnamon. Gradually stir in pancake mix (batter will be very thick).
- Preheat oven to 250. Melt 2 tablespoons butter in large non-stick skillet over medium-low heat. Using generous 1/4 cup batter for each pancake, drop in 4 pancakes, spacing apart. Cook pancakes until brown on bottom and some bubbles begin to break around edges, about 3 minutes. Turn pancakes over. Cook until brown on bottom and firm to touch in center, about 3 minutes (pancakes will be thick). Transfer pancakes to baking sheet; place in oven to keep warm. Repeat with remaining butter and batter in 2 more batches. Serve pancakes with syrup and, if desired, berries and bananas.

47. Banana Pancake Snowmen

Serving: 2 | Prep: | Cook: 5mins | Ready in:

Ingredients

- 1 cup complete buttermilk pancake mix
- 3/4 cup water
- 1/3 cup mashed ripe banana
- 1 teaspoon confectioners' sugar
- Pretzel sticks, chocolate chips, dried cranberries and/or halved banana slices

Direction

- In a small bowl, stir the pancake mix, water and banana just until moistened.
- Pour a scant 1/2 cup batter onto a greased hot griddle, making three circles to form a snowman. Turn when bubbles form on top. Cook until the second side is golden brown.

Transfer to a serving plate. Repeat with remaining batter.
- Sprinkle with confectioners' sugar. Decorate snowmen with pretzels, chocolate chips, cranberries and/or banana if desired.
- Nutrition Facts
- 1 snowman (calculated without decorations): 133 calories, 1g fat (0 saturated fat), 0 cholesterol, 417mg sodium, 28g carbohydrate (7g sugars, 1g fiber), 3g protein. Diabetic Exchanges: 2 starch.

48. Banana Pancakes Recipe

Serving: 4 | Prep: | Cook: 15mins | Ready in:

Ingredients

- 1 1/2 cups all-purpose flour
- 3 1/2 teaspoons baking powder
- 1 teaspoon salt
- 1 tablespoon splenda
- 1 1/4 cups milk
- 1 egg
- 3 tablespoons butter, melted
- 2 bananas - ripened to your taste

Direction

- In a large bowl, whisk together the flour, baking powder, salt and sugar. In another bowl, mash the bananas well and add the milk, mix well, add the butter and eggs, mix well. Make a well in the center of the flour mixture and pour in the banana concoction; mix until well blended.
- Heat a lightly oiled griddle or frying pan over medium high heat. Pour or scoop the batter onto the griddle, using approximately 1/4 cup for each pancake. Brown on both sides and serve hot.

49. Banana Pancakes With Coconut Syrup Recipe

Serving: 6 | Prep: | Cook: 6mins | Ready in:

Ingredients

- 1 1/2 cups all-purpose flour
- 1 tbs sugar
- 1/2 tsp salt
- 1 tsp baking soda
- 1 tsp baking powder
- 1 large egg
- 1 cup buttermilk
- 1/4 cup whole milk
- 1 tbs melted unsalted butter
- 3 tbs melted unsalted butter
- 3 ripe bananas, cut into 1/3-inch slices
- coconut Syrup:
- 1 (14.5 oz) can unsweetened coconut milk
- 1 cup sweetened shredded coconut
- 3/4 cup packed brown sugar

Direction

- Sift together the flour, sugar, salt, baking soda, and baking powder.
- In a large bowl, whisk together the egg, buttermilk, milk and melted butter. Add the dry ingredients. Stir until the flour disappears, being careful not to overbeat the batter.
- Preheat oven to 200 degrees.
- Melt 1/2 tbsp. of the butter in a large cast-iron skillet over medium heat. Ladle about 1/4 cup of batter into the pan for each pancake. Immediately press 4 or 5 banana slices into each, so the batter oozes slightly over the fruit.
- Cook until bubbles appear and then flip and cook on the other side, about 3 minutes total. Transfer the pancakes to a platter and keep warm in the oven while you cook the remaining batches, adding butter to the pan as needed.
- Serve hot with warm coconut syrup.
- Coconut Syrup:
- Combine all the ingredients in a small heavy saucepan. Bring to a boil, reduce to a simmer

and cook 20 minutes, stirring occasionally. Transfer to a blender and puree until smooth. Serve immediately. Coconut syrup can be stored in the refrigerator 2 weeks and reheated.

50. Bavarian Apple Pancake Recipe

Serving: 4 | Prep: | Cook: 10mins | Ready in:

Ingredients

- 3 large eggs
- 1/8 teaspoon nutmeg
- 3 tablespoons flour
- 6 tablespoons milk
- 2 tablespoons butter melted
- 1/4 cup raisins
- 1/4 cup sliced almonds
- 2 large tart cooking apples
- 2 tablespoons butter
- 2 tablespoons sugar
- 1/2 teaspoon cinnamon
- 1/4 teaspoon nutmeg
- 1/8 teaspoon ground cloves

Direction

- Preheat oven to 450.
- In mixing bowl beat eggs and nutmeg with a whisk.
- Add flour in 3 additions and beat after each addition until mixture is smooth.
- Add milk in 2 additions beating slightly after each then lightly beat in butter.
- Pour mixture into a well-buttered pie plate then sprinkle top with raisins and almonds.
- Bake 8 minutes in hot oven then reduce heat to 350 baking 8 minutes more.
- While baking peel core and thinly slice apples.
- Melt 2 tablespoons butter in small skillet then add apples and sprinkle with sugar and spices.
- Cook slowly over low heat turning occasionally until glazed and tender.
- After pancake is cooked remove pie plate from oven and divide into halves.
- Top with sliced apples and serve hot.

51. Bears Gingerbread Pancakes Recipe

Serving: 9 | Prep: | Cook: 15mins | Ready in:

Ingredients

- 3 cups buttermilk pancake mix
- 3 tablespoons sugar
- 3 tablespoons ground cinnamon
- 1 1/4 teaspoons ground allspice
- 1/2 teaspoon ginger
- 1/2 teaspoon ground nutmeg
- 1/2 teaspoon ground cloves
- 2 1/2 cups water
- orange marmalade syrup
- Yields: 1 cup
- 2/3 cup pure maple syrup 1/3 cup orange marmalade Combine ingredients in a small saucepan and bring to a boil, stirring constantly.

Direction

- Combine dry ingredients in a large bowl, and make a well in center of mixture.
- Add water to dry ingredients, stirring just until moistened. May need to add some more milk-batter should not be too thick.
- Spoon about 2 tablespoons batter onto a hot, lightly greased griddle.
- Cook pancakes until tops are covered with bubbles and edges look cooked; turn and cook other side.
- Serve with Orange Marmalade Syrup

52. Beer Pancakes Recipe

Serving: 8 | Prep: | Cook: 15mins | Ready in:

Ingredients

- 2 Cups biscuit mix
- 1/2 tsp. cinnamon
- 1/2 Cup beer
- 2 Tbs. sugar
- 4 eggs, beaten
- 2 Tbs. oil
- cooking spray

Direction

- Mix all ingredients together (batter will be lumpy).
- Pour batter onto hot griddle or pan (approx. 1/4 cup batter for each pancake), be sure to spray on some cooking spray (like Pam) so pancakes won't stick.
- Cook until golden brown on both sides.
- Note: for thinner batter use more beer!

53. Beestings Pancakes For Beltaine Recipe

Serving: 4 | Prep: | Cook: 6mins | Ready in:

Ingredients

- 5 cups flour
- 1 teaspoon baking soda
- large pinch of salt, or to taste
- 1 egg yolk
- 2-3 teaspoons sugar
- 4-5 cups beestings
- butter or lard for frying

Direction

- Mix the flour, baking soda, salt, egg yolk and sugar in a large bowl.
- Beat in enough of the beestings to create a batter of the desired thickness.
- Drop tablespoonsful of the batter on a hot greased griddle and cook for 4 to 6 minutes on each side.
- Serve with rich butter, cream or syrup.

54. Best Buttermilk Bilberry Pancakes Recipe

Serving: 3 | Prep: | Cook: 4mins | Ready in:

Ingredients

- 2 1/2 cups cake flour
- 2 heaping tsp baking powder
- 2 tsp baking soda
- Pinch of salt
- 2 eggs, beaten
- 2 1/2 cups buttermilk, at room temperature
- 1/2 cup sugar
- 1/4 tsp vanilla extract
- 1/2 cup melted butter, at room temperature
- plus extra for griddle
- 1/2 cup of bilberries or blueberries

Direction

- Sift together the cake flour, baking powder, baking soda, and salt into a medium size bowl.
- Whisk together the flour mixture, beaten eggs, buttermilk, sugar, vanilla, and melted butter until they are very smooth.
- Let the batter sit for about 5 minutes.
- Preheat an electric griddle to 375 degrees or use non-stick griddle.
- Just before cooking the pancakes, coat the cooking surface with melted butter using a pastry brush.
- Pour batter onto hot griddle letting it spread by itself until it forms a 5 inch circle.
- You should be able to fit about 3 pancakes in the griddle at one time.
- Drop about 10 bilberries on top of the pancake.

- Flip the pancakes when their edges appear to be hardening a little.
- There should also be some small holes forming on the surface of the pancakes.
- This should take about 2 minutes total.
- Cook the pancakes on the other side for about 2 minutes or until the pancakes are golden brown.
- Serve with warm maple syrup.
- Recipe should make about 12 pancakes.

55. Best Buttermilk Pancakes On The Planet Recipe

Serving: 4 | Prep: | Cook: 5mins | Ready in:

Ingredients

- 2 cups flour
- 2 tbsp. granulated sugar
- 4 tsp. baking powder
- 1 tsp. baking soda
- 1 tsp. fine salt
- 2 cups buttermilk
- 4 tbsp. melted butter
- 1 tsp. vanilla extract
- 2 beaten eggs

Direction

- Mix the flour, sugar, baking powder, baking soda, and salt into a large bowl and whisk, set aside.
- In a smaller bowl, whisk the buttermilk, butter, vanilla, and eggs.
- Mix the wet ingredients into the dry ones, and mix gently, just to combine. Don't overmix, or you'll have tough pancakes.
- Heat a non-stick skillet over medium heat.
- Heat oil or butter, when hot, add 1/2 cup batter for each pancake.
- Let cook on one side until top gets bubbly, and turn to cook second side, repeat until you use up the batter.
- Transfer to a plate and keep warm until ready to serve.

56. Bilberry Cinnamon Pancakes Recipe

Serving: 3 | Prep: | Cook: 25mins | Ready in:

Ingredients

- 2 cups all purpose flour
- 1 tbsp baking powder
- 1/4 cup granulated sugar
- 1 tsp salt
- 1/2 tsp ground cinnamon
- 1 1/2 cups whole milk
- 1/4 cup margarine, melted and cooled
- 2 eggs, lightly beaten
- 1 1/4 cups fresh bilberries (or blueberries)

Direction

- Mix flour, baking powder, sugar, salt and cinnamon.
- Mix milk, margarine and eggs.
- Stir into dry mixture until well blended.
- Stir in bilberries.
- Heat a greased griddle until a drop of water sizzles.
- Pour 1/4 cup of the batter onto the griddle.
- Cook about 1 1/2 - 2 minutes each side.
- Makes about 8 - 12 pancakes.

57. Birdys Awesome Pancakes Recipe

Serving: 8 | Prep: | Cook: 15mins | Ready in:

Ingredients

- 1 1/2 cups all-purpose flour
- 3 1/2 teaspoons baking powder

- 1 teaspoon salt
- 1 tablespoon white sugar
- 3 tablespoons powdered buttermilk
- 1 1/2 cups milk
- 1 egg
- 3 tablespoons butter, melted

Direction

- In a large bowl, sift together the flour, baking powder, powdered buttermilk, salt and sugar. Make a well in the center and pour in the milk, egg and melted butter; mix until smooth.
- Pre-heat a griddle or frying pan over medium high heat. Pour or ladle out the batter onto the griddle, using about 1/4 cup of batter for each pancake.
- Cook until you start seeing bubbles on the raw side, flip and finish cooking on the other side. Should be nice golden brown in color.
- Slather with butter and pour the syrup on and serve. You won't be disappointed.

58. Bisquick Blueberry Pancakes Recipe

Serving: 4 | Prep: | Cook: 20mins | Ready in:

Ingredients

- 2 cups Original Bisquick® mix
- 2 teaspoons baking powder
- 1 cup milk
- 1 tablespoon sugar
- 2 tablespoons lemon juice
- 1 teaspoon lemon zest
- 1 teaspoon vanilla extract
- 2 eggs
- 1 cup fresh or frozen (thawed and drained) blueberries
- Melted butter (optional)
- maple syrup (optional)
- powdered sugar (optional)

Direction

- Heat griddle or skillet over medium-high heat.
- Combine milk, lemon juice, lemon zest, and vanilla extract together. Let sit for 2 minutes.
- Add milk mixture to remaining ingredients. Stir until blended.
- Grease cooking surface with cooking spray, vegetable oil or butter. Use a paper towel to wipe off excess grease.
- Pour by 1/4 cupfuls onto hot griddle. Arrange blueberries on batter.
- Cook until edges are dry. Turn; cook until golden.
- Serve with melted butter, powdered sugar, and maple syrup.

59. Blackberry Cheese Pancakes Recipe

Serving: 4 | Prep: | Cook: 20mins | Ready in:

Ingredients

- 1-1/2 cups cottage cheese
- 4 eggs
- 1/2 cup flour
- 1/4 cup granulated sugar
- 2 tablespoons butter melted
- 2 teaspoons vanilla
- 1 cup blackberries
- Blackberry Syrup:
- 1 pint fresh blackberries
- 1/4 cup water
- 1/2 cup granulated sugar
- 1 tablespoon fresh lemon juice

Direction

- Combine cottage cheese, eggs, flour, sugar and butter in a bowl then mix well.
- Stir in vanilla then add blackberries.
- Cook batter on a hot greased griddle until light brown on both sides turning once.
- Serve with butter and blackberry syrup.

- To make syrup carefully wash blackberries then pour into heavy pot with water and sugar.
- Bring to boil then reduce heat and simmer 10 minutes stirring occasionally.
- Press through a fine sieve to remove seeds then add lemon and cool and serve.

60. Blackberry Cinnamon Pancakes Recipe

Serving: 4 | Prep: | Cook: 20mins | Ready in:

Ingredients

- 2 cups sifted flour
- 3 teaspoons baking powder
- 1/4 cup sugar
- 1 teaspoon salt
- 1/2 teaspoon ground cinnamon
- 1-1/2 cups milk
- 1/4 cup shortening melted
- 2 lightly beaten eggs
- 1-1/4 cup fresh blackberries

Direction

- Mix flour, baking powder, sugar, salt and cinnamon then add milk, shortening and eggs.
- Mix lightly and stir in berries then spoon batter onto lightly greased hot griddle.
- Cook on both sides turning once.

61. Blackberry Cornmeal Pancakes With Orange Butter Recipe

Serving: 4 | Prep: | Cook: 20mins | Ready in:

Ingredients

- 2 cups flour
- 1 cup cornmeal
- 1/4 cup granulated sugar
- 2 teaspoons baking powder
- 1 teaspoon baking soda
- 1 teaspoon salt
- 1/4 teaspoon ground cinnamon
- 2 eggs
- 3 cups buttermilk
- 1/3 cup butter melted
- 2 cups fresh blackberries
- orange Butter:
- 3/4 cup butter softened to room temperature
- 2 tablespoons powdered sugar
- 1 tablespoon grated orange peel
- 2 tablespoons orange liqueur
- 2 tablespoons orange juice
- 1/4 teaspoon vanilla
- 1/4 teaspoon ground nutmeg
- 1/8 teaspoon salt

Direction

- Combine flour, cornmeal, sugar, baking powder, baking soda, salt and cinnamon then set aside.
- Beat eggs then add buttermilk and 1/3 cup melted butter.
- Add egg mixture to flour mixture and stir just until moistened then fold in blackberries.
- Spoon 1/4 cup of the batter onto a greased griddle.
- Cook until both sides are light brown on the inside and crisp on the outer edges.
- Repeat with remaining butter then serve with orange butter
- To make butter combine butter, powdered sugar and grated orange peel and beat until fluffy.
- Beat in orange liqueur, orange juice, vanilla, nutmeg and salt.

62. Blackberry Filled Dutch Pancake Recipe

Serving: 4 | Prep: | Cook: 20mins | Ready in:

Ingredients

- 1 tablespoon butter
- 3 eggs
- 1/2 cup milk
- 1/3 cup all purpose flour
- 3 tablespoons sugar divided
- 1/4 teaspoon salt
- 1-1/2 cups fresh blackberries
- 1/4 teaspoon ground cinnamon
- 1/2 cup sliced bananas

Direction

- Preheat oven to 450.
- Place butter in a pie plate then melt in oven 5 minutes tilting plate to coat evenly with butter.
- Meanwhile combine eggs, milk, flour, 1 tablespoon sugar and salt until smooth.
- Pour batter into plate and bake 8 minutes then reduce heat to 375 and bake 10 minutes longer.
- Combine blackberries with remaining sugar and cinnamon.
- Remove pancake from oven and scatter bananas over pancake then spoon blueberries over top.
- Cut into wedges and serve immediately.

63. Blackberry Pancakes Recipe

Serving: 6 | Prep: | Cook: 20mins | Ready in:

Ingredients

- 1 cup blackberries
- 2 eggs
- 2 cups buttermilk
- 2 cups flour
- 1 teaspoon baking soda
- 1 teaspoon salt
- 1 tablespoon granulated sugar
- 2 teaspoons baking powder
- 1/4 cup butter melted

Direction

- Beat eggs until light and fluffy then beat in buttermilk and soda.
- Sift flour, salt, sugar and baking powder.
- Add flour mixture to egg mixture beating well to make a thin batter.
- Add blackberries and butter.
- Fry on a hot buttered griddle until puffy and golden brown turning only once.
- Serve hot.

64. Blackberry Puffed Pancakes Recipe

Serving: 4 | Prep: | Cook: 15mins | Ready in:

Ingredients

- 2 cups blackberries
- 2 T splenda
- 3 tablespoons unsalted butter
- 3/4 cup whole milk, room temperature
- 3 large eggs, room temperature
- 3/4 cup all purpose flour
- Pinch of salt
- powdered sugar for dusting

Direction

- Preheat oven to 450°F. Stir Blackberries and Splenda sugar in medium bowl. Let stand at room temperature while preparing pancake.
- Melt butter in 10-inch ovenproof skillet (I like cast iron) over medium-high heat, swirling to coat bottom and sides of skillet. Blend milk and eggs in blender until smooth. Add flour and salt; blend batter just until incorporated. Pour batter into hot skillet.
- Transfer skillet to oven and bake pancake until puffed and golden in spots, about 11 minutes.
- Immediately cut pancake into quarters. Transfer 1 wedge to each of 4 plates. Spoon blackberries on top, dust with powdered sugar and serve

65. Blender Orange Pancakes Recipe

Serving: 4 | Prep: | Cook: 10mins | Ready in:

Ingredients

- 1 c orange juice
- 1/4 c milk
- 3 Tbsp melted butter or oil...i used olive oil
- 1 lg egg
- 3 Tbsp sugar
- 3/4 tsp salt
- 1 1/2 c all purpose flour
- 2 1/2 Tbsp baking powder

Direction

- Throw all ingredients in a blender and blend on high speed for 15 seconds. Stop and stir down Blend for another few seconds.
- Pour 1/4 cup of batter into prepared pan. I use about 1 tsp. butter in my pan, melt till bubbling and cook till bubbles appear at edges of pancakes. Flip and cook till done.

66. Blender Pancakes Recipe

Serving: 46 | Prep: | Cook: 2mins | Ready in:

Ingredients

- 1 large egg
- 1 TABLESPOON oil (of your choice or melted butter)
- 1/2 cup to 3/4 skim milk (or buttermilk) depending on how thick you like your batter.
- 1/2 teaspoon salt
- 2 teaspoons baking powder
- 2 TABLESPOONS sugar (or maple syrup)
- 1 cup flour (white or whole wheat)
- oil for pan
- Optional: 1 teaspoon vanilla extract
- Optional : 2 TABLESPOONS unprocessed bran

Direction

- Pay attention to the order in which you put ingredients in the blender. The wet ingredients go in first! This is important!
- Add, egg, oil, milk, salt, baking powder, sugar, flour into the blender.
- Blend 10-20 seconds--just until all ingredients are mixed. Scrape sides. Blend 2-3 more seconds.
- Grease skillet or frying pan and place on stovetop burner set medium high.
- Pour pancakes into pan to desired size.
- When bubbles form on pancake surface, turn. Cook for 5 or 10 seconds more. Remove from pan. Enjoy!

67. Blue Cornmeal Pancakes Recipe

Serving: 4 | Prep: | Cook: 15mins | Ready in:

Ingredients

- 3/4 cup blue cornmeal
- 3/4 cup unbleached, all-purpose flour
- 2 tsp baking powder
- 1 tbsp white sugar
- 1 egg, beaten
- 1/2 cup milk
- 2 tbsp melted butter
- 1 cup boiling water
- 1 tsp salt
- 1/2 cup toasted pine nuts

Direction

- Combine the blue cornmeal, sugar, and salt in a medium sized bowl. Add in the boiling water until all of the ingredients are moist. Cover, and set aside to stand for a few minutes.

- In a measuring cup, mix together the egg, milk, and melted butter then stir into the cornmeal mixture. Combine the flour and baking powder then incorporate into the cornmeal mixture. To thin the batter, add a bit more milk until it runs off the spoon thickly, but smoothly.
- Heat a large cast iron skillet over a medium heat, and grease with a dab of butter or oil. Use about 2 tbsp. of batter for every pancake. Immediately sprinkle a few pignoli onto each pancake. After the entire surface is covered with bubbles, flip and cook the other side until golden in color. (It can be difficult to tell when blue food is thoroughly cooked--so allow them a few extra seconds if you're not sure)
- Serve at once with maple syrup of fruit preserves.

68. Blue Moon Oatmeal Brown Sugar Pancakes Recipe

Serving: 6 | Prep: | Cook: 3mins | Ready in:

Ingredients

- 1 1/2 cups all-purpose flour
- 1 tablespoon baking powder
- 2 eggs
- 2 to 3 tablespoons vanilla
- 1 1/2 cups milk
- 3 tablespoons melted butter
- 3 tablespoons brown sugar
- 1/2 c. oatmeal

Direction

- Combine all ingredients and stir until lumps are gone. Ladle onto a hot (350 degrees) griddle coated with vegetable oil or clarified butter.
- If you would like to add extra ingredients, such as chocolate chips or berries, sprinkle them on the wet side of the pancake now, while the underside cooks.
- Look for bubbles on the wet surface (a sign that the air is cooking out of the pancakes), or use a spatula to peek underneath, making sure the pancake is golden brown. Flip and cook for another 2 to 3 minutes.

69. Blue Puff Ramekin Pancakes Recipe

Serving: 3 | Prep: | Cook: 23mins | Ready in:

Ingredients

- ¼ c. melted butter
- 3 eggs
- ¾ c. flour
- ¾ c. milk
- 1 T honey
- ½ c. blueberries (OR raspberries, peaches, etc.)

Direction

- Divide the melted butter into 3 ramekins.
- Place a dozen or so blueberries into each ramekin.
- Combine the rest of the ingredients and beat until fluffy. Divide equally between 3 ramekins.
- Bake at 425 for 20-25 minutes.
- Sprinkle with icing sugar and serve immediately with genuine maple syrup.
- Serve immediately before they sag.

70. Blueberry Bran Pancakes Weight Watchers Recipe

Serving: 4 | Prep: | Cook: 4mins | Ready in:

Ingredients

- 1 cup ready-to-eat bran flakes
- 2 large egg whites

- 1-1/4 cups buttermilk
- 2 tsp. canola oil
- 1 cup all-purpose flour
- 1 TB sugar
- 1 tsp. baking powder
- 1/2 tsp. baking soda
- 1/2 cup blueberries
- 2 tsp. powdered sugar

Direction

- Coat a non-stick skillet with cooking spray; heat over medium-high heat.
- Crush cereal in a food processor or blender, or place in a zip-close plastic bag and crush with a rolling pin; set aside.
- Stir egg whites, buttermilk, oil and cereal together in a medium bowl; allow to stand 5 minutes. Beat in flour, sugar, baking powder and baking soda with a wire whisk until well blended.
- To make pancakes, place 3 tablespoons of batter onto skillet, repeat to make 4 pancakes at a time. Gently press 5 to 6 blueberries into each pancake.
- Cook until puffed, about 2 minutes; flip and cook until golden brown, about 2 minutes more. Repeat to make 12 pancakes. Serve pancakes in a short stack dusted with powdered sugar. Yields 3 pancakes per serving.

71. Blueberry Buckwheat With Flaxseed Pancakes Recipe

Serving: 4 | Prep: | Cook: 2mins | Ready in:

Ingredients

- 3/4 cup buckwheat flour
- 1/2 cup whiteflour
- 1/4 cup flaxseed flour (grind flaxseed in coffee mill)
- 1 tsp salt
- 1 3/4 tsp baking powder
- 1-2 eggs
- 3 tbsp melted butter
- 1-1/4 cups milk
- 2 tbsp molasses
- 1 cup blueberries

Direction

- Combine dry ingredients in a large bowl sifted or stirred.
- Combine liquid ingredients and slowly add to dry mixture.
- Stir until moistened. "Let this mixture sit for 1-2 hours for lighter cakes.
- Add Blueberries stir gentle.
- Pour batter about 1/4 cup for each cake, onto hot greased griddle.
- Cook until tops of pancakes are bubbly and edges appear dry, 1 to 1 1/2 minutes. Turn over to brown other side.
- Serve with maple syrup and butter, honey or molasses.

72. Blueberry Buttermilk Pancakes Recipe

Serving: 4 | Prep: | Cook: 15mins | Ready in:

Ingredients

- 1 cup all-purpose flour
- 1/2 cup yellow cornmeal, preferably stone-ground
- 1/4 cup sugar
- 1 1/4 teaspoons baking powder
- 1/4 teaspoon baking soda
- 1/4 teaspoon salt
- 1 1/4 cups buttermilk
- 4 tablespoons (1/2 a stick) butter, melted
- 2 large egg yolks
- 1 1/2 teaspoons finely grated lemon zest
- 2 large egg whites
- 1 cup fresh or frozen blueberries

Direction

- Preheat your griddle to 350 degrees.
- In a large bowl, whisk the flour, cornmeal, sugar, baking powder and soda, and salt together.
- In a smaller bowl, whisk together the buttermilk, butter, egg yolks, and lemon zest.
- Pour the wet ingredients over the dry ingredients and gently whisk them together, mixing just until combined.
- On high speed, beat the egg whites until they have formed peaks that are stiff but not dry. Fold them into the batter until just combined.
- Fold in the blueberries.
- Spoon 1/3 cup batter onto the griddle for each pancake. Cook until the top of each pancake is speckled with bubbles and some of them have popped. Flip the pancakes and cook until the underside is lightly browned. Serve immediately or keep warm in a 200 degree oven while you finish cooking the rest of the batter. Serve with maple syrup, honey, or blueberry sauce, or plain. Makes 12 pancakes.

73. Blueberry Cheese Pancakes Recipe

Serving: 4 | Prep: | Cook: 10mins | Ready in:

Ingredients

- 2 cups all-purpose flour
- 2 tsp. baking powder
- 1/4 tsp. baking soda
- 1/4 tsp salt
- 2 TBSP. sugar
- 2 TBSP. wheat germ
- 1 1/2 cups milk
- 1 cup small curd cottage cheese.
- 1 lg. egg lightly beat
- 1/4 cup vegie oil
- 1 cup fresh or frozen blueberries

Direction

- Sift flour, baking powder, baking soda and salt. Stir in sugar and wheat germ; set aside.
- Combine milk, cheese, egg, and oil.
- Pour milk mixture all at once into the flour mixture. Stir until moist. Add additional milk a little at a time if batter is too thick. (Batter should pour easily) Gently stir in berries.
- Preheat skillet over med. heat grease skillet lightly. Pour mixture into skillet to the size you prefer. Cook until tops are bubbly and appear dry and turn over finish cooking, and serve.

74. Blueberry Cornmeal Pancakes Recipe

Serving: 0 | Prep: | Cook: 4mins | Ready in:

Ingredients

- 1/2 cup flour
- 1/2 cup yellow cornmeal
- 2 tablespoons sugar
- 1 teaspoon baking powder
- 1/2 teaspoon baking soda
- 1/2 teaspoon ground cinnamon
- 1 cup nonfat yogurt
- 3 tablespoons skim milk
- 1 tablespoon vegetable oil
- 1 egg -- lightly beaten
- 1 cup blueberries

Direction

- Combine first 6 ingredients in a large bowl; stir well. Combine yogurt and next three ingredients; add to dry ingredients, stirring until smooth. Gently stir in blueberries.
- Spoon about 1/3 cup batter onto a hot non-stick griddle or non-stick skillet. Turn pancakes when tops are covered with bubbles and edges look cooked.

75. Blueberry Cornmeal Pancakes With Orange Butter Recipe

Serving: 4 | Prep: | Cook: 15mins | Ready in:

Ingredients

- 2 cups flour
- 1 cup cornmeal
- 1/4 cup granulated sugar
- 2 teaspoons baking powder
- 1 teaspoon baking soda
- 1 teaspoon salt
- 1/4 teaspoon ground cinnamon
- 2 eggs
- 3 cups buttermilk
- 1/3 cup butter melted
- 2 cups fresh blueberries
- orange Butter:
- 3/4 cup butter softened to room temperature
- 2 tablespoons powdered sugar
- 1 tablespoon grated orange peel
- 2 tablespoons orange liqueur
- 2 tablespoons orange juice
- 1/4 teaspoon vanilla
- 1/4 teaspoon ground nutmeg
- 1/8 teaspoon salt

Direction

- Combine flour, cornmeal, sugar, baking powder, baking soda, salt and cinnamon then set aside.
- Beat eggs then add buttermilk and 1/3 cup melted butter.
- Add egg mixture to flour mixture and stir just until moistened then fold in blueberries.
- Spoon 1/4 cup of the batter onto a greased griddle.
- Cook until both sides are light brown on the inside and crisp on the outer edges.
- Repeat with remaining butter then serve with orange butter.
- To make butter combine butter, powdered sugar and grated orange peel and beat until fluffy.
- Beat in orange liqueur, orange juice, vanilla, nutmeg and salt.

76. Blueberry Cottage Cheese Pancakes Recipe

Serving: 68 | Prep: | Cook: 8mins | Ready in:

Ingredients

- Makes 18 pancakes (4")
- 1 1/4 cups all-purpose flour
- 1/3 cup sugar
- 1 tsp. baking soda
- 1/2 tsp. salt
- 1 cup sour cream
- 1 cup cottage cheese
- 2 eggs
- 1 tsp. vanilla
- 2 cups blueberries
- butter for griddle or Pam spray

Direction

- Whisk together flour, sugar, baking soda, and salt in medium bowl.
- Stir together sour cream, cottage cheese, eggs, and vanilla in large bowl.
- Add flour mixture, stir until just combined.
- Gently stir in blueberries.
- Heat oven to 200.
- Heat a griddle over medium heat. Butter griddle lightly.
- Spoon level 1/4 cup batter onto griddle for each pancake.
- Cook until lightly brown and bubbles begin to form 3-4 minutes.
- Turn and cook other side.
- Keep in warm oven on baking sheet until ready to serve.
- Garnish with berries and citrus wedges.

77. Blueberry Flax Pancakes Recipe

Serving: 4 | Prep: | Cook: 5mins | Ready in:

Ingredients

- 1 1/2 cups dry pancake mix
- 1 cup blueberries, fresh or frozen (thawed)
- 1/2 cup flax seed meal
- 2 eggs
- 1 cup skim milk

Direction

- Over medium heat, warm a non-stick skillet.
- Combine the pancake mix and flax seed meal in a medium sized bowl. Now, in another bowl (or measuring cup), stir together the eggs and milk. Mix the liquid mixture into the dry and stir until the batter is just moistened.
- Place 1/4 cup of the batter onto the hot skillet. Top with as many blueberries as you prefer and cook until bubbles form on the surface, then flip and cook until nicely browned on the opposite side.

78. Blueberry Hazelnut Pancakes Recipe

Serving: 4 | Prep: | Cook: 30mins | Ready in:

Ingredients

- • 1/2 cup (125 mL) blueberries
- • 1 1/2 cups (375 mL) self-rising flour
- • 1 tsp (5 mL) salt
- • 1 tbsp (15 mL) brown sugar
- • 2 tbsp (30 mL) sugar
- • 3 eggs
- • 2 tbsp (30 mL) hazelnut butter
- • 1 cup (250 mL) milk
- • 1/3 cup (75 mL) unsalted butter, melted and cooled
- • 2 tbsp (30 mL) canola oil

Direction

- 1. Mix all the dry ingredients in a medium-sized bowl.
- 2. In another bowl, beat eggs with hazelnut butter, adding milk and melted butter. Add mixture to dry ingredients and mix well, taking care not to over mix (a few lumps are fine).
- 3. Pour canola oil in a small bowl. Using paper towel, gently brush some oil on a non-stick pan.
- 4. Heat pan to medium heat, then lower slightly. Pour about 3 tablespoons of the mix per pancake into the pan. Drop in 1 teaspoon of blueberries per pancake. Wait till the mixture starts to form bubbles on top, then flip and continue cooking for a minute.
- 5. Remove from the pan and wipe the pan with oil again before making more pancakes.
- 6. Serve with maple syrup.

79. Blueberry Oatmeal Pancakes Recipe

Serving: 4 | Prep: | Cook: 20mins | Ready in:

Ingredients

- 1 1/2 cups quick-cook oats
- 1 tsp sugar
- 2 cups buttermilk
- 2 eggs
- 1/4 tsp salt
- 2 tsp white sugar
- 1 1/2 tsp baking soda
- 1/2 cup flour
- 1 tsp baking powder
- 1/2 tsp cinnamon
- 1/4 tsp nutmeg
- zest of 1 lemon
- 1 cup frozen blueberries, unthawed (see note if using fresh instead)

Direction

- In a mixing bowl stir together your oats and buttermilk. Let that sit for about 10 minutes to allow the oatmeal to soften up a bit.
- In a different larger mixing bowl, mix together flour, salt, sugar, baking soda, cinnamon, nutmeg, baking powder, sugar, and lemon zest.
- Heat up a large pan or griddle to medium heat and pour 1/4 cup of mix per pancake. Add your fresh blueberries to the cakes at this point (if you do it earlier the berries will get smushed and just turn your cakes purple).
- Let this cook for about 3 minutes then flip and give it another 2 minutes. The end result should be a golden brown cake on either side.

80. Blueberry Pancakes With Blueberry Sauce Recipe

Serving: 4 | Prep: | Cook: 30mins | Ready in:

Ingredients

- Pancakes
- 1 cup AP flour
- 1 cup whole wheat flour
- 3 1/2 baking powder
- 1 tsp baking soda
- 3/4 salt
- 1 tbsp sugar
- 1 1/3 cups milk, more by the tbsp if needed
- 1 egg, beaten
- 3 tbsp butter, melted & cooled
- 1 tsp vanilla extract
- 1 cup blueberries
- Blueberry Sauce
- 2 pints fresh blueberries, washed and picked over
- 1 tbsp + 1 tsp lemon juice
- 1/4 granulated sugar, or to taste
- 1/2 tbsp water
- 2 tsp vanilla extract
- whipped dessert topping, if desired

Direction

- Pancakes
- Preheat oven to 200F. Line a baking sheet with parchment paper.
- Sift together flours, baking powder & soda, salt and sugar in a large mixing bowl.
- Make a well in the center and pour in milk, egg, butter, and vanilla. Mix until smooth. Gently fold in blueberries.
- Heat a lightly or buttered griddle or frying pan over medium heat. Scoop batter, using approximately 1/3 cup for each pancake, onto the griddle or pan.
- Turn when bubbles form on surface and edges begin to dry and cook on other side for about 3 minutes or until golden brown. Transfer to lined baking sheet and place in oven to keep warm while cooking remaining pancakes.
- Blueberry Sauce
- Combine berries, lemon juice, sugar, and water in a medium non-reactive saucepan.
- Cook over medium heat, stirring frequently, until blueberries begin to break down and juices boil and thicken, about 5 minutes.
- Remove from heat, stir in vanilla, and cover to keep warm.
- To serve, divide pancakes - 2 on each plate. Divide sauce between plates. Top with whipped dessert topping if desired.

81. Blueberry Ricotta Pancakes Recipe

Serving: 4 | Prep: | Cook: 20mins | Ready in:

Ingredients

- 1/2 cup whole-wheat pastry flour
- 1/4 cup plus 2 tablespoons all-purpose flour
- 1 teaspoon sugar
- 1 teaspoon baking powder
- 1/4 teaspoon baking soda
- 1/2 teaspoon freshly grated nutmeg

- 3/4 cup part-skim ricotta cheese
- 1 large egg
- 1 large egg white
- 1/2 cup nonfat buttermilk (see Tip)
- 1 teaspoon freshly grated lemon zest
- 1 tablespoon lemon juice
- 2 teaspoons canola oil, divided
- 3/4 cup fresh or frozen (not thawed) blueberries

Direction

- 1. Whisk whole-wheat flour, all-purpose flour, sugar, baking powder, baking soda and nutmeg in a small bowl. Whisk ricotta, egg, egg white, buttermilk, lemon zest and juice in a large bowl until smooth. Stir the dry ingredients into the wet ingredients until just combined.
- 2. Brush a large non-stick skillet with 1/2 teaspoon oil and place over medium heat until hot. Using a generous 1/4 cup of batter for each pancake, pour the batter for 2 pancakes into the pan, sprinkle blueberries on each pancake and cook until the edges are dry and bubbles begin to form, about 2 minutes. Flip the pancakes and cook until golden brown, about 2 minutes more. Repeat with the remaining oil, batter and berries, adjusting the heat as necessary to prevent burning.
- NUTRITION INFORMATION: Per serving: 238 calories; 8 g fat (3 g sat, 3 g mono); 68 mg cholesterol; 30 g carbohydrate; 12 g protein; 3 g fiber; 334 mg sodium; 128 mg potassium.
- Nutrition bonus: Selenium (24% daily value), Calcium (16% dv).
- Tip: No buttermilk? Mix 1 tablespoon lemon juice into 1 cup milk.

82. Bread Crumb Griddle Cakes Recipe

Serving: 12 | Prep: | Cook: 10mins | Ready in:

Ingredients

- * 1 cup flour
- * 1 cup bread crumbs(Plain or with spices, your choice)
- * 1½ cups milk, scalded
- * 2 eggs, beaten
- * 4 teaspoons baking powder
- * 2 tablespoons shortening, melted
- * Pinch of salt

Direction

- Mix the melted shortening and the scalded milk together.
- Pour over the bread crumbs and let stand until bread crumbs are soft.
- Add the beaten eggs, flour, salt and baking powder.
- Mix and beat well.
- Cook on slightly greased hot griddle on both sides.
- Serve with Syrup, Fruit or Jam.

83. Bread Crumb Pancakes Recipe

Serving: 6 | Prep: | Cook: 20mins | Ready in:

Ingredients

- 2 C bread Crumbs
- 2 eggs
- 1 1/2 C Scalded whole milk
- 2 Tbls unsalted butter
- 1/2 C A/P flour
- 1/2 tsp Salt
- 3 tsp baking powder
- 1 Tbls sugar

Direction

- Melt the butter in your scalded milk. Next soak the bread crumbs in the milk/butter. Add the YOLKS of the 2 eggs. Mix well. Sift the flour, baking powder, salt and sugar into the bread crumb mixture.

- Beat the egg WHITES into stiff peaks. Now gently fold egg whites into bread crumb mixture.
- Drop large spoonfuls onto a greased hot griddle. Cook until golden brown on both sides. Serve with butter and syrup, a fried egg, or whatever your little heart desires.
- (I put the milk and butter in a microwave safe bowl. Heat in the microwave 1 minute at a time until I can see it begin to foam. This is microwave scalding. Takes me only about 2 minutes this way.)

84. Broke Man Pancakes Recipe

Serving: 4 | Prep: | Cook: 10mins | Ready in:

Ingredients

- 1 cup flour (I prefer freshly ground whole grain flour for flavor--white works just as well)
- 1 1/2 teaspoons baking powder
- 1/4-3/8 teaspoon salt
- 1 teaspoon cinnamon
- 3 Tablespoons sugar
- 1 cup water
- 2 Tablespoons cooking oil

Direction

- Blend first five ingredients
- Add water and oil and stir until well blended.
- Cook over medium heat in a skillet until the bubbles go flat and edges of the tops look dull, then flip and cook until they stop steaming.
- If you don't have syrup, you can increase the sugar, and if you don't have cinnamon, you can omit it.

85. Buckwheat Bananna Panners Recipe

Serving: 3 | Prep: | Cook: 3mins | Ready in:

Ingredients

- 2 eggs
- 2 TBSP coconut oil or butter, Melted
- 2 TBSP coconut milk, (or whole milk)
- 1 Ripe Bananna, Mashed
- 1 TBSP agave nectar, (or 1-2 tsp sugar)
- 1/8 tsp salt
- 3-4 Heaping TBSP buckwheat flour
- 1/4 baking powder

Direction

- Mix everything up with a wire whisk.
- Let sit for about 5 minutes.
- Grease skillet with coconut or olive oil.
- Spoon batter onto a heated (cast iron) skillet.
- Batter will be thick but will flatten when cooking.
- Top paneers with coconut oil or butter and agave nectar or maple syrup. You don't need much because they are already sweet. Enjoy this yummy healthy breakfast treat!! (I have thought about adding some cocoa to these but haven't tried it yet.)

86. Buckwheat Blueberry Pecan Pancakes Recipe

Serving: 8 | Prep: | Cook: 15mins | Ready in:

Ingredients

- 2 cups buckwheat pancake mix
- 2 egg whites
- 1-2 cups skim milk (depending how thin or thick you like your cakes)
- 1 single serving tub (like what you would put in a lunchbox) of blueberry applesauce, no sugar added

- 1/2 cup toasted, chopped pecans
- 1 cup fresh blueberries
- non-stick spray, butter flavor
- sugar-free butter pecan syrup

Direction

- Mix 1st 5 ingredients and let sit for 5 minutes.
- Heat up non-stick skillet to medium heat.
- Add pecans and blueberries to batter.
- Spray skillet and pour batter, you know the rest. Its pancakes!!

87. Buckwheat Pancakes Recipe

Serving: 2 | Prep: | Cook: 10mins | Ready in:

Ingredients

- 6 tbsp buckwheat flour
- 6 tbsp all-purpose flour
- 1 tsp white sugar
- 1 tsp baking soda
- 1 cup buttermilk
- 3 tbsp butter
- 3 tbsp melted butter
- 1 egg
- 1/2 tsp salt

Direction

- Combine the buttermilk, melted butter and egg in a medium sized bowl.
- In a separate bowl, combine the buckwheat and white flour, sugar, soda and salt. Add the dry ingredients into the egg-mixture and stir until the two have just combined.
- Heat your griddle (or large frying pan) to medium-hot, and add 1 tablespoon of margarine, butter, or oil. Let the butter melt prior to adding the batter to the frying pan, then create 4 inch pancakes out of the batter. After bubbles have formed on top, flip and cook on the other side for about 3 minutes.

Continue this process until all of you batter has been used.

88. Buckwheat And Yogurt Pancakes Recipe

Serving: 4 | Prep: | Cook: 10mins | Ready in:

Ingredients

- 2 cups buckwheat flour
- 1/4 teaspoon salt
- 1 teaspoon baking soda
- 1-1/2 cups buttermilk
- 1/2 cup plain yogurt
- 2 eggs
- 1 teaspoon maple flavoring
- 1 tablespoon canola oil
- nonstick cooking spray

Direction

- Combine flour, salt and baking soda then add remaining ingredients.
- Pour by 1/8 cup onto hot lightly sprayed griddle and cook until brown turning once.

89. Buffalo Berry Corn Cakes With Maple Syrup Recipe

Serving: 4 | Prep: | Cook: 10mins | Ready in:

Ingredients

- 2/3 cup all-purpose flour
- 2/3 cup fine stone-ground cornmeal
- 2 tablespoons sugar
- 1 1/2 teaspoons baking powder
- 1 1/2 teaspoons baking soda
- 1/2 teaspoon salt
- 1 cup buttermilk
- 1 pcs large egg, separated

- 1 cup buffalo berries or (huckleberries or blueberries)
- 2 tablespoons vegetable oil
- softened unsalted butter and warm pure maple syrup, for serving

Direction

- TOTAL TIME: 25 MIN
- In a medium bowl, whisk together the flour, cornmeal, sugar, baking powder, baking soda and salt. In a small bowl, whisk the buttermilk with the egg yolk. In a medium bowl, beat the egg white until firm peaks form. Add the buttermilk mixture to the dry ingredients and stir gently with a wooden spoon until evenly moistened; there will still be some lumps. Fold in the beaten egg white and then the Buffalo Berries (you can use huckleberries or blueberries).
- Heat a large cast-iron skillet. Add 1 tablespoon of the oil, and when it is hot, spoon 1/4 cup of the batter into the skillet for each pancake.
- Cook over moderate heat until browned on the bottom and bubbles appear on the surface, about 3 minutes. Flip and cook until browned on the second side, about 2 minutes longer. Keep the pancakes warm in a low oven while you continue with the remaining oil and batter.
- Serve the pancakes with butter and maple syrup.

90. Buttermilk Cranberry Pancakes Recipe

Serving: 6 | Prep: | Cook: 10mins | Ready in:

Ingredients

- 1 cup flour
- 1 teaspoon granulated sugar
- 3/4 teaspoon baking powder
- 1/2 teaspoon baking soda
- 1/2 teaspoon salt
- 1 egg lightly beaten
- 1 cup buttermilk
- 1/2 cup chopped dried cranberries

Direction

- Sift together all dry ingredients then make well in middle and add in egg and buttermilk.
- Combine with a few quick strokes but do not over mix.
- Heat griddle.
- Add cranberries to batter and spoon onto griddle in desired size pancakes.
- When top of pancakes are covered with air bubbles gently check bottom with a spatula.
- Once golden brown turn pancake and cook other side.
- When cooked add to a warmed plate and stack with butter.
- Serve with your favorite syrup or sprinkled with powdered sugar and nutmeg.

91. Buttermilk Pancakes With Bing Cherry Syrup Recipe

Serving: 8 | Prep: | Cook: 10mins | Ready in:

Ingredients

- 1/2 cup brown sugar firmly packed
- 1/2 cup sugar
- 1 cup warm water
- 1-1/2 cups stemmed pitted large ripe bing cherries
- 1 teaspoon almond extract
- 2 large eggs
- 2 cups all-purpose flour
- 2 tablespoons sugar
- 2 teaspoons baking powder
- 1 teaspoon baking soda
- 1 teaspoon salt
- 2 cups buttermilk
- 4 tablespoons unsalted butter melted
- 1/2 teaspoon almond extract

- 2 tablespoons vegetable oil

Direction

- In a saucepan over high heat combine the brown sugar, granulated sugar and water and stir until the sugars dissolve.
- Bring to a boil and cook uncovered for 5 minutes.
- Add cherries then reduce heat to low and simmer 10 minutes.
- Stir in the almond extract and simmer for 2 minutes more to blend the flavors.
- Remove from the heat and let cool.
- In a small bowl using an electric mixer beat the eggs until frothy.
- Add flour, sugar, baking powder, baking soda, salt, buttermilk, melted butter and almond extract.
- Continue to beat just until the mixture is smooth.
- Do not overbeat.
- Heat a griddle or a large heavy fry pan over high heat.
- Lightly grease the pan with the vegetable oil or non-stick cooking spray.
- Pour about 1/3 cup of the batter onto the griddle.
- Cook until the surface is covered with tiny bubbles about 2 minutes.
- Flip the pancake over and continue to cook 2 minutes more.
- Keep warm until all the pancakes are cooked.
- Repeat with the remaining batter adding more oil to the pan as needed.
- Serve the pancakes hot topped with a spoonful of the cherry syrup.
- Pass the remaining syrup at the table.

92. Buttermilk Pancakes With Oatmeal Recipe

Serving: 6 | Prep: | Cook: 20mins | Ready in:

Ingredients

- 2 cups quick oats, uncooked
- 1 tsp cinnamon
- 1/2 teaspoon baking soda
- 2 1/2 cups buttermilk
- 1 cup sifted all-purpose flour
- 2 teaspoons baking powder
- 1 teaspoon salt
- 2 tablespoons splenda
- 1/4 oil
- 2 eggs, beaten

Direction

- Mix oats, soda, cinnamon and buttermilk. Let stand 5 minutes.
- Sift together flour, baking powder, salt and sugar.
- Add sifted dry ingredients, oil and eggs to oats mixture.
- Stir until combined.
- For each pancake, pour about 1/4 cup batter onto hot, lightly greased griddle.
- Bake to a golden brown, turning only once.
- Serve hot with butter and syrup.

93. Buttermilk Peach Pancakes Recipe

Serving: 6 | Prep: | Cook: 10mins | Ready in:

Ingredients

- 1 cup flour
- 1 teaspoon granulated sugar
- 3/4 teaspoon baking powder
- 1/2 teaspoon baking soda
- 1/2 teaspoon salt
- 1 egg lightly beaten
- 1 cup buttermilk
- 1/2 cup fresh peaches thinly sliced and lightly sweetened

Direction

- Sift together all dry ingredients then make well in middle and add in egg and buttermilk.
- Combine with a few quick strokes but do not over mix.
- Heat griddle.
- Add peaches to batter and spoon onto griddle in desired size pancakes.
- When top of pancakes are covered with air bubbles gently check bottom with a spatula.
- Once golden brown turn pancake and cook other side.
- When cooked add to a warmed plate and stack with butter.
- Serve with your favorite syrup or sprinkled with powdered sugar and nutmeg.

94. Canadian Pancakes Recipe

Serving: 6 | Prep: | Cook: 10mins | Ready in:

Ingredients

- 2 cups all purpose flour
- 1/8 teaspoon sea salt
- 1-1/2 cups apple juice
- 2 tablespoons vegetable oil
- 2 large eggs
- 1/2 cup honey
- 2 teaspoons baking powder
- 1 granny smith apple peeled and grated
- 2 teaspoons vegetable oil

Direction

- In large bowl combine flour, salt, apple juice, oil, eggs, honey and baking powder.
- Mix on medium speed with hand mixer until smooth then fold in grated apple by hand.
- In heavy skillet add oil and heat until sizzling.
- Drop batter by spoonful into pan and cook until bubbles appear then flip.
- Serve immediately with honey or maple syrup.

95. Caramel Apple Baked Pancake Recipe

Serving: 4 | Prep: | Cook: 25mins | Ready in:

Ingredients

- 5 Tbsp. butter
- 6 Tbsp. brown sugar
- 1/4 tsp. cinnamon
- 1 cup baking apples; thinly sliced (1-2 apples)
- 1 cup flour
- 1 Tbsp. sugar
- 1 tsp. baking powder
- 1/2 tsp. baking soda
- dash salt
- 1 cup buttermilk
- 1 egg
- 3 Tbsp. melted butter

Direction

- Preheat oven to 400F. Spray 9-inch pie pan or baking dish with non-stick spray.
- In small sauté pan, melt butter and add brown sugar. Cook on medium high until sugar melts, about 4 minutes, stir in cinnamon. Pour caramel into a prepared pan. Slice apples with apple slicer and quarter, now arrange apple slices evenly on top of the caramel. Set aside.
- In medium bowl measure flour and add sugar, baking powder, baking soda and salt. Sift together. Add buttermilk and egg and whisk until blended.
- Stir in melted butter. Pour onto caramel and apples in the pan covering evenly.
- Bake for 25 minutes or until golden brown on edge. Remove from oven and let sit for 10 minutes. Invert onto a serving dish. Serves 4.

96. Carries Vanilla Amaretto Pancakes Recipe

Serving: 4 | Prep: | Cook: 10mins | Ready in:

Ingredients

- Boxed pancake mix
- 2 tsp. vanilla
- 1 shot Amaretto de Saronno
- 3/4- 1 C. Carnation Amaretto flavored liquid coffee creamer
- shortening or cooking spray
- maple syrup

Direction

- Preheat skillet and rub down with shortening on a paper towel.
- Prepare pancake mix as shown on box, except substituting the milk for the creamer.
- Add the vanilla and Amaretto.
- Stir until right consistency.
- (If mixture is too runny, add more pancake mix)
- Cook in skillet and serve with warm butter or syrup.

97. Cave Dweller Potato Pancakes Recipe

Serving: 46 | Prep: | Cook: 16mins | Ready in:

Ingredients

- 1 26 oz. bag frozen shredded potatoes, thawed overnight
- 2 tbl flour
- 2 tea salt, or to taste
- 1 teaspoon coarsely ground pepper
- ½ teaspoon thyme
- 1 carton egg Beaters
- 4 tbl corn oil
- 3 green onions, finely chopped

Direction

- Thoroughly mix all ingredients in a large bowl.
- Spoon mixture onto hot griddle and spread into ¼ inch pancakes.
- Cook about 8 minutes each side or until pancakes are browned and crispy.
- Serve with applesauce and sour cream on the side to help cover the pepper and onion taste.

98. Cheaters Buckwheat Buttermilk Pancakes Recipe

Serving: 1 | Prep: | Cook: 20mins | Ready in:

Ingredients

- 1/3 cup buttermilk pancake mix (the add milk / egg kind)
- 1/4 cup buckwheat flour
- 1/4 tsp baking powder
- 1/3 - 1/2 cup 1% milk
- 1 egg white, beaten until frothy

Direction

- Whisk together the pancake mix, flour, and baking powder.
- Combine milk and egg white, then beat into the flour mixture until just combined but still lumpy.
- Let sit 5-10 minutes while preheating a fry-pan over medium-high heat.
- Fry in batches in a small spritz of PAM until batter is finished.
- Serve with maple syrup or fresh blueberries for a great treat.

99. Cheesecake Pancakes Recipe

Serving: 5 | Prep: | Cook: 7mins | Ready in:

Ingredients

- 1 package (8 oz) cream cheese
- 2 cups Original Bisquick® mix
- 1/2 cup graham cracker crumbs
- 1/4 cup sugar
- 1 cup milk
- 2 eggs
- strawberry syrup
- 1 cup sliced fresh strawberries
- 1/2 cup strawberry syrup for pancakes

Direction

- Prep time does not include freezing of the cream cheese
- . Slice cream cheese lengthwise into four pieces.
- Place on ungreased cookie sheet; cover and freeze 8 hours or overnight.
- .
- Brush griddle or skillet with vegetable oil, or spray with cooking spray; heat griddle to 375°F or heat skillet over medium heat.
- .
- Cut cream cheese into bite-size pieces; set aside.
- In large bowl, stir Bisquick mix, graham cracker crumbs, sugar, milk and eggs with whisk or fork until blended.
- Stir in cream cheese.
- .
- For each pancake, pour slightly less than 1/3 cup batter onto hot griddle.
- Cook until edges are dry.
- Turn; cook other sides until golden brown.
- .
- In small bowl, mix strawberries and syrup; top pancakes with strawberry mixture.
- 3 pancakes a piece, for 5 servings

100. Chestnut Pancakes With Bacon And Creme Fraiche Regular And Gluten Free Recipe

Serving: 24 | Prep: | Cook: 15mins | Ready in:

Ingredients

- 6 slices thick-cut bacon, chopped
- • 3/4 cup milk
- • 2 large eggs
- • 2 teaspoons baking powder
- • 1/2 teaspoon salt
- • 1 1/2 cups coarsely chopped jarred steamed chestnuts (7 to 8 ounces), divided
- • Créme fraîche or sour cream
- • Chopped chives or maple syrup

Direction

- Cook bacon in large skillet over medium heat until brown and crisp. Using slotted spoon, transfer bacon to paper towels to drain. Transfer 2 tablespoons bacon drippings to blender; add milk and next 3 ingredients, then 1 cup chestnuts.
- Blend until batter is smooth. Pour batter into bowl; stir in remaining 1/2 cup chestnuts.
- Pour remaining drippings into small bowl. Brush same skillet with some drippings; heat over medium heat.
- Drop in batter by rounded tablespoonfuls. Cook pancakes until brown and cooked through, about 3 minutes per side.
- Transfer to plates.
- Top with crème fraiche and bacon, then chives or maple syrup.

101. Chocolate Banana Cream Pancakes Recipe

Serving: 2 | Prep: | Cook: 5mins | Ready in:

Ingredients

- 2 cups vanilla pudding
- 2 cups cream cheese
- pancake mix, eggs, & oil accordint to directions
- 2 soup spoons of chocolate chips
- 1 banana sliced into 1/2" thick slices
- chocolate sauce
- 1 tbsp. powdered sugar
- whipped topping

Direction

- VANILLA CREAM CHEEESE MIXTURE
- Combine vanilla pudding and room temperature cream cheese.
- Mix until well blended and creamy (no lumps).
- Refrigerate immediately.
- (Covered vanilla cream cheese may be stored in the refrigerator for up to five days).
- PANCAKES
- Mix batter for 2 large pancakes according to package directions or recipe.
- Pour batter for two pancakes on a 350°F pan or griddle.
- Evenly distribute chocolate chips and four banana slices per pancake immediately after pouring batter.
- Grill the pancakes until they bubble and each pancake is dry on edges.
- Flip pancakes over.
- Grill until golden brown on both sides.
- PUTTING IT TOGETHER
- Place first pancake upside down on a plate.
- Using a tablespoon, place four spoons of vanilla cream cheese mixture on the upside down pancake.
- Then place the second pancake upside down on top of the vanilla cream cheese mixture.
- (Place the pancake upside down so the bananas and chocolate chips are visible.)
- Drizzle chocolate sauce on top of the pancakes in a '"zigzag"' pattern.
- Sprinkle pancakes with powdered sugar.
- Garnish with whipped topping.

102. Chocolate Chip Pancakes With Cinnamon Cream Recipe

Serving: 10 | Prep: | Cook: 20mins | Ready in:

Ingredients

- chocolate chip PANCAKES
- 1 1/4 cups all-purpose flour
- 3 tablespoons sugar *(I add more sugar)
- 2 teaspoons baking powder
- 1/4 teaspoon salt
- 1 cup milk
- 2 large eggs, separated
- 3 tablespoons butter, melted plus 4 tablespoons, divided
- 1/2 cup miniature semi-sweet chocolate morsels
- *This recipe does not call for vanilla extract, but I add one teaspoon as I feel that it needs it.
- cinnamon Cream; recipe follows
- cinnamon CREAM
- 1 cup heavy whipping cream
- 1/4 cup confectioner's sugar
- 1/4 teaspoon ground cinnamon

Direction

- FOR THE PANCAKES:
- Preheat griddle to 350 degrees.
- In a large bowl, combine flour, sugar, baking powder and salt
- In a small bowl, combine milk, egg yolks, and 3 tablespoons melted butter; add to flour mixture, whisking until smooth.
- In a small bowl, beat egg whites at medium-high speed with an electric mixer until stiff. Gently fold into batter. Gently fold in chocolate morsels.
- Melt 2 tablespoons butter on hot griddle. Ladle about 1/4-cup batter for each pancake onto hot griddle. Cook pancakes for 2 to 3 minutes, or until tops are covered with bubbles, and edges look cooked. Turn and cook the other side. Repeat procedure with

- remaining 2 tablespoons butter and remaining batter.
- FOR THE CINNAMON CREAM:
- In a medium bowl, beat cream at medium-high speed with an electric mixer until thickened. Gradually beat in confectioner's sugar and cinnamon, beating until stiff peaks form. Cover and chill.
- Serve pancakes with Cinnamon Cream, and Maple Syrup.

103. Chocolate Chip Pancakes With Cinnamon Sauce Recipe

Serving: 10 | Prep: | Cook: 20mins | Ready in:

Ingredients

- 1 1/4 cups all-purpose flour
- 3 tablespoons sugar
- 2 teaspoons baking powder
- 1/4 teaspoon salt
- 1 cup milk
- 2 large eggs, separated
- 3 tablespoons butter, melted plus 4 tablespoons, divided
- 1/2 cup miniature semi-sweet chocolate morsels
- cinnamon Cream, recipe follows
- maple syrup, for serving
- cinnamon Cream:
- 1 cup heavy whipping cream
- 1/4 cup confectioners' sugar
- 1/4 teaspoon ground cinnamon

Direction

- Preheat griddle to 350 degrees F.
- In a large bowl, combine flour, sugar, baking powder, and salt.
- In a small bowl, combine milk, egg yolks, and 3 tablespoons melted butter; add to flour mixture, whisking until smooth.
- In a small bowl, beat egg whites at medium-high speed with an electric mixer until stiff.

Gently fold into batter. Gently fold in chocolate morsels.
- Melt 2 tablespoons butter on hot griddle. Ladle about 1/4-cup batter for each pancake onto hot griddle. Cook pancakes for 2 to 3 minutes, or until tops are covered with bubbles and edges look cooked. Turn and cook the other side. Repeat procedure with remaining 2 tablespoons butter and remaining batter.
- For the Cinnamon Cream:
- In a medium bowl, beat cream at medium-high speed with an electric mixer until thickened. Gradually beat in confectioners' sugar and cinnamon, beating until stiff peaks form. Cover and chill.
- Serve pancakes with Cinnamon Cream and maple syrup.

104. Chocolate Pancakes Recipe

Serving: 5 | Prep: | Cook: 5mins | Ready in:

Ingredients

- 1 cup milk
- 1 egg
- 2 tbsp margarine, melted
- 1 c. all-purpose flour
- 1/3 c. cocoa powder
- 1/4 c. sugar
- 1/2 tsp. baking soda
- 1/2 tsp. salt
- powdered sugar
- Any other favorite toppings such as fruit, jam, whipped cream, etc.

Direction

- In med bowl, add milk, egg, margarine. Whisk until well blended.
- In another med bowl, combine flour, cocoa, sugar, baking soda and salt. Mix well.

- Add milk mixture to dry mixture. Whisk until ingredients moistened. The batter may be slightly lumpy.
- Heat skillet to med-low or low heat depending on your stove.
- Once hot, pour 1/4 cup of batter per pancake in pan.
- Flip once batter is set around edges. Then cook till baked through.
- Once pancakes are cooked. Sprinkle with powdered sugar. Then add your favorite toppings (optional).

105. Chocolate Apple Pancakes Recipe

Serving: 46 | Prep: | Cook: 10mins | Ready in:

Ingredients

- 1 1/2 teaspoons baking powder
- 2 cups all-purpose flour
- 1 egg
- 4 tablespoons sugar
- 1 1/4 cups milk
- 1 tablspoon butter, melted
- 1 apple
- 1/3 cup chocolate chips. (try white, dark, & pp chips different times)

Direction

- Sift flour & baking powder into a mixing bowl.
- Stir in the sugar, egg, & melted butter.
- Slowly beat in milk, keep mixing until batter is smooth.
- Peel, core, & grate the apple.
- Mix apple into the batter & chocolate chips.
- Heat up the frying pan or griddle over medium heat.
- Place a little butter or oil down.
- Place about 2 tablespoons of batter onto your cooking pan.
- Cook for a few minutes until you see bubbles around the edge, then flip over to other side, cook about 1 more minute.
- Serve with syrup of your choice.

106. Chunky Monkey Pancakes Recipe

Serving: 9 | Prep: | Cook: 30mins | Ready in:

Ingredients

- 1 cup all-purpose flour
- 2 teaspoons baking powder
- 1 teaspoon baking soda
- 1/4 teaspoon salt
- 3/4 cup skim milk
- 3 tablespoons butter, melted
- 2 eggs
- 1 tablespoon white sugar
- 1 teaspoon vanilla extract
- 1 large banana, diced
- 1/2 cup miniature semisweet chocolate chips
- 1/4 cup chopped pecans
- cooking spray

Direction

- Combine flour, baking powder, baking soda, and salt in a large bowl.
- Set bowl aside. In a separate bowl, whisk together the skim milk, melted butter, eggs, sugar, and vanilla.
- Make a well in the center of the dry ingredients and stir in the wet ingredients, being careful not to over mix the batter.
- Gently fold in the banana, chocolate chips, and nuts.
- Heat a large skillet over medium heat, and coat with cooking spray.
- Pour 1/4 cupfuls of batter onto the skillet, and cook until bubbles appear on the surface.
- Flip with a spatula, and cook until browned on the other side.
- 195 calories per serving

107. Cilantro Corn Pancakes Recipe

Serving: 8 | Prep: | Cook: 10mins | Ready in:

Ingredients

- 1/2 cup all purpose flour
- 1/3 cup cornmeal
- 1 teaspoon baking powder
- 1/2 teaspoon baking soda
- 1 teaspoon sugar
- 1/4 teaspoon salt
- 1 large egg
- 1 cup buttermilk or plain yogurt
- 2 tablespoons vegetable oil
- 1 cup frozen corn kernels rinsed under cold water to thaw and drained
- 4 ounce can chopped mild green chilies
- 1/4 cup chopped fresh cilantro leaves
- 1/3 cup chopped green onions
- vegetable oil as needed
- salsa
- sour cream

Direction

- Combine flour, cornmeal, baking powder, baking soda, sugar and salt.
- Stir in cornmeal.
- Lightly beat egg, then add buttermilk, oil, corn, chilies, cilantro and onions.
- Add to dry ingredients then stir until combined.
- Heat griddle or skillet over medium heat.
- Grease griddle with shortening then pour batter onto hot griddle.
- Cook pancakes until puffed and dry around edges.
- Turn and cook other sides until golden brown.
- Serve with salsa and sour cream spooned over warm pancakes.

108. Cinnamon And Nutmeg Pancakes Recipe

Serving: 4 | Prep: | Cook: 10mins | Ready in:

Ingredients

- 1 cup milk
- 1 egg
- 2 1/2 tsp. vegetable oil
- 1 1/4 cup flour
- 3 tsp. sugar
- 1 1/2 tsp. cinnamon
- 1/2 tsp. nutmeg
- 2 tsp. baking powder
- 1/2 tsp. salt

Direction

- In a bowl combine milk eggs and veg. oil.
- Stir in the rest of the ingredients.
- Heat a lightly oiled pan over med to med high heat (may want to turn down on second batch so you don't burn them). Pour about 1/4 of the batter for each pancake and brown on both sides. Serve with your favorite syrup and a dab of butter. These are also just as great served with just butter! Enjoy!
- * If you like thinner pancakes just add more milk to your liking.
- **For even thicker pancakes let the batter sit for about 5 minutes before cooking and it will thicken up more.
- *** This recipe makes 4 descent size pancakes...if you are big breakfast eaters definitely double the recipe for 4 people.

109. Cinnamon Apple Puffy Pancake Recipe

Serving: 4 | Prep: | Cook: 20mins | Ready in:

Ingredients

- 2 granny smith apples; peeled, cored & chopped
- 4 lrg. eggs
- 1/4t. cinnamon
- 1c. flour
- 1c. milk
- pinch of salt
- 8T. unsalted butter
- 1/4c. confectioner's sugar + more for sprinkling
- 3T. fresh lemon juice, for sprinkling

Direction

- Preheat oven to 425 degrees.
- Beat together the eggs & cinnamon in a small bowl.
- Lightly beat together the flour, milk, salt & egg mixture; it's fine to leave the batter a bit lumpy.
- Melt the butter in a 14" skillet with a heat-proof handle.
- Add the apples & sauté until tender.
- Turn the heat off under the pan and pour the batter over the apples.
- Bake 15-20 minutes until puffy and golden brown.
- Sprinkle with the 1/4c. sugar and return to the oven for a minute or two.
- Use a potholder to remove the pan from the oven. I hate to admit it, but I once grabbed the handle, like a complete fool!
- Sprinkle the pancake with lemon juice and serve immediately.
- Pass more sugar for sprinkling at the table.

110. Cinnamon Oat Pancakes Recipe

Serving: 4 | Prep: | Cook: 4mins | Ready in:

Ingredients

- 1-1/3 cups (325 mL) all-purpose flour
- 1/4 cup (50 mL) packed brown sugar
- 1 tbsp (15 mL) baking powder
- 1 tsp (5 mL) cinnamon
- 1/2 tsp (2 mL) salt
- 1 cup (250 mL) quick-cooking rolled oats (not instant)
- 1/2 cup (125 mL) raisins or dried cranberries
- 1 egg
- 1-1/2 cups (375 mL) milk
- 3 tbsp (50 mL) vegetable oil

Direction

- In bowl, whisk together flour, sugar, baking powder, cinnamon and salt. Add rolled oats and raisins; stir to combine.
- Whisk together egg, milk and 2 tbsp. (25 mL) of the oil.
- Pour egg mixture over top of dry ingredients; stir until almost smooth.
- Heat skillet over medium heat; brush with some of the remaining oil.
- Pour about 1/4 cup (50 mL) batter for each pancake into pan; cook until underside is golden brown and bubbles break on top but do not fill in, 1-1/2 to 2 minutes. Turn and cook until underside is golden brown, about 1 minute.

111. Cinnamon Roll Pancakes Recipe

Serving: 1 | Prep: | Cook: 30mins | Ready in:

Ingredients

- For the Pancakes:
- 4 cups all-purpose flour
- 8 tsps baking powder
- 2 tsp. salt
- 4 cups milk
- 4 tbsps vegetable oil
- 4 large eggs, lightly beaten
- ~
- For the cinnamon Filling
- 1 cup butter, melted

- 1 1/2 cup brown sugar, packed
- 2 tbsp ground cinnamon
- ~
- For the cream cheese glaze
- 1/2 cup butter
- 4 oz. cream cheese
- 1 1/2 cups powdered sugar
- 1 tsp. vanilla

Direction

- To make the Cinnamon Filling:
- Mix the three ingredients together. Place in a disposable piping bag and snip the end off or put in a Ziploc bag and snip the corner off.
- To make the Pancakes:
- Mix the dry ingredients in one bowl and the wet ingredients in another bowl. Stir them together until everything is moistened leaving a few lumps.
- Heat your griddle to exactly 325 degrees. You don't want these too cook too quickly, and you won't want your cinnamon to burn.
- Make desired size pancake on greased griddle and then using the piping bag and starting at the center of the pancake, create a cinnamon swirl. Wait until the pancake has lots of bubble before you try to turn it. You will find that when you turn it the cinnamon swirl will melt. The cinnamon will melt out and create the craters which the cream cheese glaze will fill.
- To make the Cream Cheese Glaze:
- In a microwave safe bowl melt the butter and cream cheese and then stir together. Whisk in the powdered sugar and vanilla. Add a little milk if needed to make it a glaze consistency.
- Place pancake on plate, then cover with cream cheese glaze.

112. Cinnamon Swirl Pancakes Recipe

Serving: 8 | Prep: | Cook: 30mins | Ready in:

Ingredients

- 1 3/4 cup milk (1 %)
- 2 eggs
- 2 tablespoons sunflower oil
- 2 tablespoons truvia
- 1/2 teaspoons salt
- 1 1/2 cups flour
- 1/2 cup whey protein isolate
- 2 teaspoons baking powder
- 2 teaspoon vanilla
- 1/8 cup maple syrup
- 1/8 cup fancy molasses
- 1 tablespoon cinnamon
- 1 teaspoon nutmeg
- 1 tablespoon coconut oil

Direction

- Heat cast iron griddle, brushing with a small amount of coconut oil, at medium low heat.
- Meanwhile beat together milk, eggs, Truvia, salt and vanilla.
- Measure flour, whey isolate and baking powder over top of the wet ingredients and then whisk together quickly.
- Pour the maple syrup and fancy molasses in to a snack size zip lock bag, and pour cinnamon and nutmeg over top.
- Close the bag and massage the syrups and spices together. The molasses allows the syrup to pour slowly enough to make a pleasing swirl. Cut 1/8 inch tip off one corner to drizzle the syrup.
- Pour 1/2 cup batter on to the heated grill. Wait a few moments to allow the batter to set slightly, then starting in the center, drizzle the syrup in an outward spiral.
- When the first side is browned lightly, flip and lightly brown the second side.
- Serve with Greek yogurt, more syrup, and pomegranate.

113. Cinnamon Apple Pancakes Recipe

Serving: 14 | Prep: | Cook: 4mins | Ready in:

Ingredients

- 1-3/4 cups whole-wheat pastry flour
- 1/4 cup wheat germ or yellow cornmeal
- 1-1/2 teaspoons ground cinnamon, plus more for dusting
- 1 teaspoon baking powder
- 2 large egg whites
- 3 tablespoons light brown sugar
- 1-1/2 to 2 cups soy milk or low-fat milk
- 1 cup (heaping) peeled, cored, finely diced apple (any all-purpose variety)
- applesauce or pure maple syrup for serving

Direction

- Preheat oven to 200°F. In large bowl, mix together flour, wheat germ, cinnamon and baking powder. Set aside.
- In medium bowl, lightly beat egg whites with fork until foamy. With rubber spatula, stir in brown sugar until dissolved, then stir in 1-1/2 cups milk until well combined.
- Make a well in center of flour mixture. Pour milk mixture into well and stir until thoroughly combined, but don't over mix or pancakes will be rubbery. Add remaining 1/2 cup milk if batter seems too thick. Stir in apple.
- Lightly coat non-stick griddle or large non-stick skillet with cooking spray then heat over medium-low heat until hot. Pour 2-1/2 tablespoons batter onto skillet and cook until golden, about 2 minutes per side. (These pancakes need to brown a bit more slowly than most to be cooked all the way through.)
- Transfer pancakes to ovenproof plate, cover loosely with foil and keep warm in oven. Repeat with remaining batter, lowering heat if pancakes brown too fast. Serve warm with applesauce or maple syrup and a dusting of cinnamon.
- How many this recipe makes depends on the size of pancake that you make.
- Nutrition information: 297 calories, 14 grams protein, 3 grams total fat, 58 grams carbohydrates, 4 milligrams cholesterol, 80 milligrams sodium, 8 grams fiber

114. Cinnapple Pancakes Recipe

Serving: 6 | Prep: | Cook: 5mins | Ready in:

Ingredients

- 1 or two cups of Bisquick™
- 2 pinches of cinnamon
- 2 pinches of sugar
- ***COOK AS DIRECTED ON BOX***
- ___topping___
- 3 tsp diced apple (per serving)
- 1 pinch of powdered sugar
- add maple syrup as desired
- ;D

Direction

- Mix sugar and cinnamon together in pan cake batter.
- Cook as directed on box.
- Sprinkle on powdered sugar and apples.
- (Optional) add a pinch of brown sugar and serve with maple syrup.

115. Classic Potato Pancakes Recipe

Serving: 6 | Prep: | Cook: 20mins | Ready in:

Ingredients

- 1 medium onion, peeled

- 4 large russet or idaho potatoes (about 3 1/2 pounds), peeled
- 2 large eggs
- 2 tablespoons all-purpose flour
- 6 tablespoons vegetable oil
- 6 tablespoons unsalted butter
- applesauce and/or sour cream, for serving

Direction

- Preheat oven to 200°F. Place 2 non-stick baking sheets in oven.
- Using box grater or food processor fitted with grating disc, coarsely grate onion and place in colander set in sink. Coarsely grate potatoes, add to colander, and set aside to drain.
- In large mixing bowl, lightly beat eggs, then whisk in flour.
- Press potatoes and onion to extract as much liquid as possible, then add to egg/flour mixture. Season with salt and freshly ground black pepper. Using wooden spoon or hands, mix well, but do not overwork.
- In heavy-bottomed, 12-inch skillet over moderately high heat, heat 1 tablespoon oil and 1 tablespoon butter until hot but not smoking. Drop 4 scant 1/4-cup portions of potato mixture into pan and flatten with spatula to form four 3-inch pancakes.
- Fry until bottoms are golden-brown, 4 to 5 minutes, then turn over and fry until golden-brown and crisp, an additional 4 to 5 minutes. Transfer to paper towels to drain; season immediately with salt and pepper. Keep warm on baking sheets in oven while making remaining pancakes.
- Using paper towels, carefully wipe out pan. Add 1 tablespoon oil and 1 tablespoon butter and fry 4 more pancakes. Repeat with remaining batter, wiping out pan and adding 1 tablespoon oil and 1 tablespoon butter before each batch.
- Serve pancakes hot with applesauce and/or sour cream.
- Makes about 24 pancakes.

116. Cloud Pancakes Recipe

Serving: 4 | Prep: | Cook: 30mins | Ready in:

Ingredients

- 1/2 cup flour
- 2 teaspoons baking powder
- 1/2 teaspoon salt
- 1 cup ricotta cheese
- 4 egg yolks
- 3 tablespoons sugar
- 1/4 cup milk
- 1-1/2 cups fresh blueberries
- 4 egg whites

Direction

- In a mixing bowl, combine flour, baking powder and salt. In another mixing bowl, beat together ricotta cheese, egg yolks and sugar until well-combined. Add to flour mixture; stir until smooth. Stir in milk. Fold in fresh blueberries.
- In a small mixing bowl, beat the egg whites with an electric mixer on high speed until stiff peaks form (tips stand straight).
- Gently fold the beaten egg whites into batter, leaving a few puffs of egg white.
- Do NOT over-beat.
- Heat a lightly greased griddle or heavy skillet over medium heat until a few drops of water sizzle on the surface.
- For each pancake, pour about 1/4 cup batter onto the hot griddle. Spread batter into a circle about 4 inches in diameter.
- Cook over medium heat until tops are covered with bubbles and edges look cooked; turn and cook other side.
- Serve immediately or keep warm in a loosely covered, ovenproof dish in a 300-degree oven.

117. Coconut Pancake With Coconut Cream And Tropical Fruit Recipe

Serving: 12 | Prep: | Cook: 15mins | Ready in:

Ingredients

- coconut Pancake:
- 1 ¾ cups all-purpose flour
- 1 tsp baking powder
- 1 tbsp sugar
- 1 cup unsweetened coconut
- 1tsp salt
- 4 eggs, separated
- 1 cup milk
- 1 cup coconut milk
- 2 tbsp unsalted butter, melted butter, for greasing the pan
- coconut cream
- Ingredients
- ½ cup cream, chilled
- 2 tbsp sugar
- 1 can coconut cream
- Mixed Tropical fruit
- Ingredients
- 1 c diced strawberries
- 1 kiwi, peeled, diced
- 1 c chopped fresh pineapple
- 1/4 cup coconut-flavored rum or liqueur
- Procedure

Direction

- Coconut Pancake
- In a bowl combine the flour, baking powder, sugar, coconut and salt. In a separate bowl whisk together the egg yolks, milk and coconut milk. Add the milk mixture and butter to the dry ingredients and mix lightly until just combined.
- Place the egg whites in a clean, dry stainless steel bowl and beat until stiff peaks form. Fold the egg whites through the batter in two batches.
- Heat a large non-stick frying pan over a medium heat and brush a small portion of butter over the base. For each pancake, drop 3 tablespoons of batter into the pan. Avoid overcrowding the pan with pancakes. Cook for 2 minutes on one side, turn and cook for another minute. Transfer to a plate and keep warm in the oven while you make the remaining pancakes.
- Serve the pancakes in stacks of three layering the coconut cream and tropical fruit between each layer.
- Coconut Cream
- Use an electric beater to whip the cream and sugar in a medium bowl until soft peaks form. Add the coconut cream and whip until firm peaks form. Cover with plastic wrap and place in the fridge.
- Mixed Tropical Fruit
- Combine first 4 ingredients in medium bowl. Let stand 5 minutes.
- From the Sur La Table Kitchen.

118. Coconut Pancakes Recipe

Serving: 6 | Prep: | Cook: 2mins | Ready in:

Ingredients

- 1 cup Tropical Traditions coconut flour
- 1 ½ cups wheat flour
- ½ cup shredded coconut
- ¼ cup ground flax seeds, (optional)
- 2 tablespoons baking powder
- ½ - 1 teaspoons salt
- 3 eggs
- 2 ¼ cups milk
- 3 tablespoons honey
- ¾ cup coconut oil, melted

Direction

- In one bowl, combine the flours, shredded coconut, flax, baking powder and salt.
- Separate the egg whites and yolks. Combine the egg yolks, milk, honey and coconut oil; stir into dry ingredients just until moistened.

- Beat the egg whites until stiff. Gently fold egg whites into batter.
- Pour batter by ¼ cupful onto a greased hot griddle. Turn when bubbles form on top of pancakes; cook until the second side is golden brown.

119. Copycat Ihop Harvest Grain And Nut Pancakes Recipe

Serving: 4 | Prep: | Cook: 10mins | Ready in:

Ingredients

- ¾ C. oats
- ¾ C. whole-wheat flour
- 2 tsp baking soda
- 1 tsp baking powder
- ½ tsp salt
- 1 ½ C. buttermilk
- ¼ C. vegetable oil
- 1 egg
- ¼ C. sugar
- 3 T. fine chopped blanched almonds
- 3 T. chopped walnuts

Direction

- Lightly oil a skillet or griddle, and preheat it to medium heat.
- Grind the oats in a blender or food processor until fine, like flour.
- Combine ground oats, whole wheat flour, baking soda, baking powder and salt in a medium bowl.
- In another bowl combine buttermilk, oil, egg and sugar with an electric mixer until smooth.
- Combine dry ingredients with wet ingredients, add nuts and mix well with mixer.
- Ladle 1/3 cup of the batter onto the hot skillet and cook the pancakes for 2 to 4 minutes per side or until brown.

120. Corn Meal Griddle Cakes Recipe

Serving: 18 | Prep: | Cook: 5mins | Ready in:

Ingredients

- 1 cup cornmeal
- 1 cup natural flour
- 1 t. salt
- 4 t. baking powder
- 1/4 cup shortening, melted
- 1 egg, well beaten
- 2 1/2 cups milk

Direction

- Mix dry ingredients, combine egg and milk and stir into dry ingredients. Stir in shortening and add more milk if necessary to make a thin batter.

121. Cornmeal Griddle Cakes Recipe

Serving: 46 | Prep: | Cook: 20mins | Ready in:

Ingredients

- 1 1/2 cup flour, sifted
- 1/2 cup yellow cornmeal
- 4 tsp baking powder
- 1 1/2 tsp salt
- 1 tbsp sugar
- 2 lg eggs, separated
- 2 cups skim milk
- 1/4 cup vegetable oil

Direction

- Sift flour and other dry ingredients together in a large bowl.
- Beat yolks then add them to the milk. Add oil, and whisk together.

- Add to the dry ingredients and stir just until moistened and smooth. DO NOT Over stir. It will be lumpy.
- Beat eggs whites until stiff and fold gently into the batter.
- Pour by 1/4 cupfuls onto hot griddle. (350 f-375 f, depending upon yours)
- Cook until edges are dry and top is bubbly, flip over until light brown.
- Hold in a warm oven until all are cooked.
- Serve with lots of butter, syrup or preserves.

122. Cornmeal Pancakes With Applesauce Recipe

Serving: 4 | Prep: | Cook: 10mins | Ready in:

Ingredients

- 1 cup all purpose flour
- 3/4 cup cornmeal
- 1 tablespoon granulated sugar
- 1-1/2 teaspoons baking powder
- 1/2 teaspoon apple pie spice
- 1/4 teaspoon salt
- 2 slightly beaten eggs
- 1 cup milk
- 1 teaspoon cooking oil
- Nonstick spray coating
- 3/4 cup unsweetened applesauce

Direction

- Stir together flour, cornmeal, sugar, baking powder, apple pie spice and salt.
- In small mixing bowl combine eggs, milk and oil.
- Add all at once to flour mixture and stir just until blended but still slightly lumpy.
- Spray a griddle with non-stick spray coating then preheat griddle over medium heat.
- For each pancake pour about 1/4 cup batter onto hot griddle then cook 2 minutes per side.
- In small saucepan heat applesauce until warm then serve with pancakes.

123. Cottage Cheese Healthy Pancakes Recipe

Serving: 4 | Prep: | Cook: 4mins | Ready in:

Ingredients

- 1 pound cottage cheese
- 2/3 cup whole wheat flour
- 1/3 cup multi grain oatmeal
- 2 egg yolks
- 3 tbs. honey
- 2 tbs. milk
- 1 tsp. vanilla extract
- 1 tsp. ground cardamom
- 6 egg whites vegetable oil

Direction

- Mix cottage cheese, flour, oatmeal, egg yolks, honey, milk, vanilla and cardamom in large bowl. Beat whites in another large bowl until stiff but not dry. Fold whites into cottage cheese mixture in 2 additions. Preheat oven to 200°. Heat large non-stick skillet over medium heat. Brush with oil. Spoon batter onto skillet by 1/3 cupfuls, forming 4-inch-diameter pancakes. Cook pancakes until bottoms are brown and bubbles form on top, about 3minutes. Turn; cook until bottoms are brown and pancakes are cooked through, about 4 minutes. Transfer to plate and place in oven to keep warm. Repeat with remaining batter. Serve immediately.

124. Cranberry Apple Puff Pancake Recipe

Serving: 4 | Prep: | Cook: 20mins | Ready in:

Ingredients

- # 1 cup milk
- # 4 Large eggs
- # 1 teaspoon vanilla
- # 2 tablespoons butter or margarine
- # 1/2 cup flour
- # 1/2 teaspoon baking powder
- # Dash salt
- # 1 tablespoon sugar
- # 1/8 teaspoon Fresh ground nutmeg
- # 1/2 cup sugar
- # 1/2 teaspoon cinnamon
- # 1/8 teaspoon Fresh ground nutmeg
- # 3 tablespoons unsalted butter
- # 1/2 cup Fresh or frozen cranberries
- # 1 apple (Granny Smith is great)

Direction

- Preheat oven to 425 degrees.
- Mix first 4 ingredients and then add next 5 ingredients and mix well.
- Let stand for about 10 or 15 minutes.
- In a separate bowl mix 1/2 cup of sugar, 1/2 teaspoon cinnamon and 1/8 teaspoon of nutmeg.
- Put off to the side.
- Peel and slice apple.
- In oven proof skillet or cast iron, melt 3 tablespoons of unsalted butter sprinkle 1/2 of sugar mixture over butter.
- Spread evenly sliced apples and cranberries cook for 5-10 minutes.
- Add batter to skillet and place in oven for 15 min. then *reduce heat to 375 degrees* and cook for 10 minutes.
- Pancake is done when it gets really puffy.
- Serve with Maple Syrup or as a real treat, a scoop of ice cream. Oh so very Yummy... Enjoy!

125. Cranberry Pancakes Recipe

Serving: 4 | Prep: | Cook: 3mins | Ready in:

Ingredients

- 1 c cranberries
- 3 tb sugar (or Splenda)
- 1 c flour
- 1/2 c yellow cornmeal
- 1 1/2 ts baking powder
- 1/2 ts salt
- 1 1/2 c milk
- 1 Large egg
- 3 tb butter, melted
- 2 tb Pancake syrup

Direction

- Chop cranberries and sugar in food processor.
- Remove from processor.
- Add dry ingredients to processor and mix well.
- Add milk, egg, butter and syrup and process a few times just to blend all.
- Don't overmix.
- Return cranberries to processor and pulse one or twice to
- Mix.
- Heat griddle or pan and brush with butter.
- Cook pancakes about a few minutes on each side or done
- Serve with additional butter and syrup.

126. Cranberry Wow Pancakes Recipe

Serving: 0 | Prep: | Cook: 30mins | Ready in:

Ingredients

- Pancake
- 1-3/4 cups buttermilk
- 3 eggs
- 2 tbs oil (olive oil preferred)
- 1 tsp vanilla extracts
- 1 tsp orange extract
- 1 cup fresh cranberries
- 2 cups rolled oats*, uncooked

- 1/2 tsp salt
- 1/2 tsp baking soda
- 2 tsp baking powder
- Cranberry-orange syrup
- 1 1/2 cups fresh cranberries
- 1 cup orange juice
- 1 cup maple syrup

Direction

- Pancakes
- Place the first 5 ingredients in a blender container and blend at high speed for 2 minutes. Add cranberries blend just until berries are mixed throughout. Add remaining ingredients and mix in thoroughly, but briefly, using blender or rubber spatula.
- Pour onto hot griddle.
- Syrup
- Mixed ingredients into medium sauce pan. Bring to boil. Boil on low until cranberries are tender. Mash berries continue to simmer 5 minutes.

127. Cream Cheese Pancakes Recipe

Serving: 2 | Prep: | Cook: 4mins | Ready in:

Ingredients

- 16 ounces cream cheese, room temperature
- 1 tbsp. sour cream
- 1 large egg
- 1 large egg yolk
- 3 tbsp. sugar
- 1/2 tsp. salt
- 1/4 tsp. vanilla extract
- 1/8 tsp. ground cinnamon
- 1/2 cup all purpose flour
- 1/4 cup milk
- butter

Direction

- Stir together the cream cheese, sour cream, egg, yolk, sugar, salt, vanilla and cinnamon in a large bowl until smooth. Stir in the flour and milk until well blended. Cover and refrigerate the batter at least 30 minutes.
- Melt about 1/2 tbsp. butter in a large skillet over medium heat, swirling to coat the bottom of the pan. Spoon 3 tbsp. of the batter for each pancake into the skillet. Cook about 2 minutes per side until the pancakes are light golden and cooked through. Repeat with the remaining batter, adding more butter to the skillet as needed.
- Makes about 1 1/2 dozen pancakes.

128. Creamy Pancakes With Peaches Recipe

Serving: 1 | Prep: | Cook: 6mins | Ready in:

Ingredients

- 4 ripe peaches
- 1 to 2 tsp fructose or brown sugar
- 1/4 tsp nutmeg, freshly grated if possible
- 1 cup sour cream
- 1 cup fine-curd cottage cheese
- 1-1/2 tsp pure vanilla extract
- 4 eggs, separated
- 1/2 cup whole wheat pastry flour
- 1/4 cup unbleached white flour
- 1/4 tsp salt
- 2 tsp sugar
- 2 to 3 tsp butter
- 1/2 cup maple syrup

Direction

- Dip peaches into boiling water for 30 seconds; drain and peel. Slice into a bowl; sprinkle with fructose (or brown sugar) and nutmeg. Cover and set aside.
- In a large bowl, thoroughly blend sour cream, cottage cheese, vanilla and egg yolks. Sift together dry ingredients and stir into the

creamy ones. Whip egg whites to soft peaks; fold gently into batter.
- Lightly rub a crepe or frying pan with butter; heat over medium-high. Cook pancakes, using about 1/3 cup batter for each. Brown pancakes on each side (1 to 3 minutes per side) and keep warm on a platter.
- When all cakes are made, serve with maple syrup and peach slices.

129. Crepes With Strawberry Filling Recipe

Serving: 810 | Prep: | Cook: 2mins | Ready in:

Ingredients

- 2 cups flour
- 2 1/2 cups whole milk
- 4 eggs
- 2 tbsp. butter (melted)
- Pinch of salt
- 1 tsp. vanilla extract (optional)
- vegetable oil (for pan)
- Filling
- 1 lb cream cheese
- 1 pt whipping cream
- 1/4 cp powdered sugar
- 1 tsp almond extract
- 1 qt. sliced strawberries

Direction

- 1. Sift flour and mix with salt in a bowl.
- 2. Make a well and pour in eggs. Stir well.
- 3. Slowly pour in milk while stirring. Keep stirring batter until small bubbles form on the surface.
- 4. Stir in Butter.
- Voilà!
- The batter does not need to stand before using it. However, if you do let it stand, you will most likely want to add 1 tbsp. of water before cooking with it. General rule of thumb: if it seems thicker than cream, add a little more water, and/or a little more milk.
- 1. Pour a little vegetable oil on a folded paper towel, and wipe the pan evenly. Keep paper towel at hand while preparing crepes, in case you want to give it another wipe.
- 2. Pour in 2 - 3 tbsp. of batter and quickly move pan around, so that batter spreads evenly, covering the whole surface with a thin layer.
- 3. Let cook for about 1 minute. Then, flip with a metal spatula, and cook other side for about 30 seconds.
- Repeat these steps until you are out of batter, stacking cooked crepes on a plate. Yum!
- Beat cream cheese till light and fluffy. Add cream and continue to beat till very light and fluffy. Beat in sugar and extract. Spread on crepes. Spoon strawberries in center. Roll up and serve. Heavenly.

130. D Bomb Buttermilk Pancakes Recipe

Serving: 3 | Prep: | Cook: 10mins | Ready in:

Ingredients

- 3 eggs, separated, minus one yolk (so 2 yolks and 3 whites)
- 1 and 2/3 cups buttermilk
- 1 tsp baking soda
- 2 tsps baking powder
- ½ tsp salt
- 1 and a 1/2 cups AP flour
- 2 TBSP caster sugar
- 1-2 TBSP maple syrup
- 3 TBSP melted butter
- 2 TBSP vanilla extract

Direction

- In a medium sized bowl beat the yolks until pale and smooth.

- Beat in the buttermilk and baking soda and mix well.
- Sift in the flour, baking powder, salt and caster sugar, gently mixing as you add these.
- Add the melted butter, maple syrup and vanilla extract and mix well.
- In a small bowl beat the egg whites until stiff peaks form.
- Fold in the whites very gently until well incorporated.
- Let the batter sit on your cupboard for about 20 minutes.
- Make sure your griddle is on about 325 degrees. Wipe the griddle with an even layer of clarified butter using a folded up paper towel. Scoop batter onto griddle, flip when lots of bubbles form and the underside is golden brown.
- Serve with warm maple syrup and Brown Sugar Swiss meringue buttercream. MMMM…..Enjoy!

131. Daddys Baked Pancake Recipe

Serving: 4 | Prep: | Cook: 25mins | Ready in:

Ingredients

- 1/2 cup butter
- 2 eggs, beaten
- 1 cup flour
- 1/2 tsp. cinnamon
- 1 cup milk
- confectioner's sugar

Direction

- Melt butter in heavy 12 inch iron skillet or 8 by 8 baking dish.
- Mix eggs, flour, cinnamon, and milk to a rough consistency and pour mixture over butter in skillet. Bake in preheated 375% or 400% oven for 20 to 25 minutes.
- When done will be slightly brown and puffed in the pan. Remove from oven and immediately sift confectioner's sugar (I did this fairly heavy) all over the pancake. Then you may slice and put on breakfast plates. Very delicious.

132. Delicious Chocolate Chip Pancakes Recipe

Serving: 9 | Prep: | Cook: 7mins | Ready in:

Ingredients

- 2 eggs
- 2 cups all purpose flour
- chocolate chips
- 1 cup milk
- 1 tsp baking soda
- 2 tsp baking powder
- 1/2 tsp of salt

Direction

- Set an electric frying pan to about 350 degrees Fahrenheit and spray with cooking oil.
- Put all ingredients except for the Chocolate Chips (unless you like them mixed in) into a mixing bowl.
- Stir with a whisk until all dry clumps are gone. Add more milk if needed.
- Use a measuring cup to scoop out some of the batter and pour slowly over electric frying pan. Stop when reasonable size and pour more batter over another empty space in the pan.
- Sprinkle a handful of chocolate chips over the batter as soon as you're done pouring it in the pan.
- Flip every 3 minutes until it looks done and no wet batter can be seen and voila! A great chocolate chip pancake.

133. Duncan Estate Acadian Plogues Ployes Dated 1954 Recipe

Serving: 8 | Prep: | Cook: 10mins | Ready in:

Ingredients

- 1 cup white buckwheat flour
- 1 cup white flour
- 4 teaspoons baking powder
- 1 teaspoon salt
- 1-1/2 cups cold water
- 1/2 cup boiling water

Direction

- Mix dry ingredients.
- Add cold water and let stand for 10 minutes.
- Add boiling water and drop to make thin 6 inch pancakes on hot griddle.
- Bake on one side only until bubbled and firm.
- Serve on warm platter.

134. Dutch Apple Pancake Recipe

Serving: 4 | Prep: | Cook: 30mins | Ready in:

Ingredients

- 1 T. butter
- 1 large Granny Smith apple
- 3 T. sugar
- 1/2 t. cinnamon
- Batter:
- 3 eggs
- 3/4 c. all-purpose flour
- 3/4 c. milk
- 1 T. sour cream
- 1/8 t. salt
- 1 t. lemon zest

Direction

- Preheat the oven to 400 degrees F. Spray a 9-inch pie pan with a non-stick spray.
- Peel, core and cut apple into 1/2-inch slices. In a non-stick sauté pan over medium heat, melt the butter. Add the apple, granulated sugar and cinnamon and sauté, stirring constantly, until the apple begins to soften and brown lightly, 3 to 5 minutes.
- Remove from heat and set aside.
- Batter:
- In a large bowl, whisk the eggs until lightly frothy. Add the flour, milk, sour cream, salt and lemon zest and whisk just until a smooth batter forms.
- Assembly:
- Immediately pour the batter into the prepared pie pan. Put the apple mixture over the pancake batter, trying to keep the apple slices on top of the batter.
- Bake until the pancakes are puffed and golden brown, 25 to 30 minutes.
- Dust with confectioners' sugar and serve immediately.

135. Dutch Baby Casserole Recipe

Serving: 6 | Prep: | Cook: 20mins | Ready in:

Ingredients

- 1/3C butter
- 4 eggs, room temperature
- 1C milk, room temperature
- 1C flour
- 1T sugar
- 1/4t cinnamon or nutmeg or both
- 1t vanilla
- lemon wedges
- powdered sugar
- fresh fruit
- syrup

Direction

- Preheat oven to 425F.
- Melt the butter in a 9x13 glass casserole as the oven preheats. Don't burn the butter.
- Combine the eggs, milk, flour, sugar, cinnamon, and vanilla: until liquid is a uniform consistency. A blender works great.
- Pour mixture into the casserole with melted butter.
- When oven is properly preheated, insert the casserole.
- Bake until puffy and well browned, 20 to 25 minutes.
- Serve at once. Sprinkle with powdered sugar and lemon juice. Could also top with different fresh fruit. Serve with any syrup you want (maple syrup, pancake syrup, honey).

136. Dutch Baby Pancake Recipe

Serving: 4 | Prep: | Cook: 20mins | Ready in:

Ingredients

- 2 Tablespoons unsalted butter, room temperature
- 3 large eggs
- 3/4 cup whole milk
- 1/2 cup all purpose flour
- 1/4 teaspoon salt
- 1/2 teaspoon vanilla extract
- 1/4 c sugar

Direction

- Preheat oven to 425. In a medium cast iron or non-stick skillet, melt 2 tablespoons butter over medium heat.
- In a blender, combine eggs, milk, flour, salt, vanilla, and sugar. Blend until foamy for about a minute. Pour batter into skillet.
- Bake until pancake is puffed and lightly browned, about 20 minutes.

137. Dutch Baby Recipe

Serving: 4 | Prep: | Cook: 25mins | Ready in:

Ingredients

- 4 Tbsp. butter
- 3 eggs
- 1/2 cup milk
- 1/2 cup bread flour (works the best) can use all-purpose
- 1/4 tsp salt
- 1/8 tsp vanilla
- 1/8 tsp nutmeg or cinnamon or both
- confectioners' sugar
- lemon juice

Direction

- Heat oven to 425 degrees
- In a 10 in. cast-iron skillet, put in the butter.
- Place in oven until butter melts & starts to sizzle.
- Meanwhile, combine eggs, milk, flour, salt, cinnamon, nutmeg until almost smooth, should be sl. lumpy.
- When butter in frying pan is hot & starting to sizzle, either carefully remove pan from oven or (very carefully), pour in batter while in oven.
- Bake until puffed & golden brown about 15 or 20 min.
- Take out & serve immediately after sprinkling with confectionary sugar and drizzle lemon juice on top. Can use maple syrup, pancake syrup or fruit topping if desired
- Makes 3 or 4 servings

138. Dutch Pancake Recipe

Serving: 4 | Prep: | Cook: 22mins | Ready in:

Ingredients

- 3 eggs
- 1/2 cup milk
- 1/2 cup flour
- Dash of salt
- 7 tsp butter
- 1/8 tsp pure vanilla extract
- Toppings:
- Freshly squeezed lemon juice
- Powdered or confectioners sugar
- maple syrup
- ricotta cheese, Gjetost cheese, or another desert cheese.
- fruit
- ham, sausage or vegetables (leave out the vanilla if you make the savory version)

Direction

- Preheat oven to 400 degrees and place an iron skillet or oven safe frying pan or 10 inch cake pan in the oven.
- In a bowl beat the eggs until they are thick and frothy.
- Fold in the milk, vanilla, salt, and flour. (If you like you could also add chocolate chips, cinnamon, dried fruits or nuts).
- The batter will be thin but creamy looking. Once the Oven is heated, Drop the butter into the pan and spread it around with a fork.
- Pour the batter into the Pan and close the oven.
- Bake for 20-25 minutes. The pancake will puff up as it cooks and it's done when it starts to brown a bit.
- Take the Dutch pancake out of the oven and cut into wedges and place on plates. Add toppings and eat.

139. Dutch Puff Pancakes Recipe

Serving: 8 | Prep: | Cook: 35mins | Ready in:

Ingredients

- 2/3 cup water
- 1/4 cup margarine or butter
- 1 cup baking mix
- 4 eggs
- 1 to 2 cans fruit pie filling
- cinnamon sugar or confectioner's sugar

Direction

- Heat oven to 400 F. Generously grease 13 x 9 x 2 baking pan or two 9" pie pans.
- Heat water and margarine to boiling in 2 qt. saucepan.
- Add baking mix all at once. Stir vigorously over low heat until mixture forms a ball, about 1 minute. Remove from heat.
- Beat in eggs, 2 at a time, beating until smooth and glossy after each addition.
- Spread in pan(s); do not spread up the sides.
- Bake until puffed and dry in the center, 30 to 35 minutes. Immediately after baking, spread pie filling over pancake; sprinkle with cinnamon sugar or confectioner's sugar.
- Serve immediately.

140. Easy Cinnamon Vanilla Pancakes Recipe

Serving: 4 | Prep: | Cook: 10mins | Ready in:

Ingredients

- 2 cups all-purpose baking mix (such as Bisquick)
- 1 cup Fat Free cinnamon vanilla Crème or cinnamon vanilla Crème Flavor NESTLÉ coffee-MATE Liquid coffee creamer
- 1/2 cup LIBBY'S® 100% Pure pumpkin
- 2 large eggs
- maple syrup

Direction

- COMBINE baking mix, Coffee-mate, pumpkin and eggs in large bowl; stir until blended.

- GREASE griddle or large, non-stick skillet. Heat over medium-high heat. Pour about 1/4 cup pancake batter onto hot griddle for each pancake; cook for 2 to 3 minutes on each side or until golden. Repeat with remaining batter. Serve with syrup.

141. Easy Coconut Flour Banana Pancakes Recipe

Serving: 3 | Prep: | Cook: 20mins | Ready in:

Ingredients

- 3 egg
- 3 tbsp butter
- 3 tbsp Classic coconut milk
- 2 tsp honey
- 1/4 tsp baking powder
- 1 medium banana
- 1/4 tsp Real salt
- 4 tbsp coconut flour

Direction

- Whisk together eggs, coconut milk, butter, honey, baking powder, salt and the banana. Blend until smooth and uniform. Whisk in coconut flour – add slowly (coconut flour thickens stuff quickly).
- Using a ladle, pour the batter onto a medium heat griddle sprayed with PAM. Watch closely, will cook quickly. Flip after ~ 1.5 minutes/side.

142. Easy Elegant Buckwheat Pancakes Recipe

Serving: 4 | Prep: | Cook: 30mins | Ready in:

Ingredients

- 1 egg yolk
- 2/3 cup vanilla, low-fat yogurt
- ¼ cup flour
- ¾ cup buckwheat flour
- 1 cup low-fat milk
- 2 tbsp sugar
- 1 tsp salt
- 2 tsp baking powder
- 2 tbsp apple sauce
- 3 egg whites

Direction

- Beat egg yolk and yogurt until creamy.
- Add flours and milk, beat smooth.
- Mix in the remaining ingredients.
- Beat egg whites until white and foamy, stir in.
- Let stand 5 minutes.
- Heat a fry-pan over medium heat and drop spoonfuls of batter in.
- Cook about 3 minutes per pancake, flipping ½ way through cooking.

143. Easy Simple Basic Vegan Pancakes Recipe

Serving: 3 | Prep: | Cook: 10mins | Ready in:

Ingredients

- 1 cup whole wheat pastry flour
- 1 tablespoon baking powder (aluminum-free recommended)
- 1/2 teaspoon salt
- 3/4 cup soy milk (or any other plant milk)
- 1/4 cup applesauce

Direction

- Combine dry ingredients well in a bowl.
- In another container, combine the applesauce and soy milk.
- Pour the liquids into the dry ingredients and combine till all the flour is very moist but still a little lumpy.

- Heat up a pan -- I recommend an iron skillet with some spray oil on it -- and get it good and hot. Have a plate ready to catch completed pancakes.
- Take a 1/4 cup measure (like the one you used for the applesauce) and scoop up some batter and pour into the pan. You should hear it sizzle. (Don't pour any more in!)
- Wait until the pancake becomes bubbly and the bubbles look like they might want to stay, then turn the pancake over.
- Cook the other side for 30-45 seconds.
- Put the completed pancake onto the plate and repeat the batter pouring process until you run out of batter.

144. Eggless Banana Pancakes Recipe

Serving: 2 | Prep: | Cook: 10mins | Ready in:

Ingredients

- 1 cup flour
- 1 t brown sugar
- 1 tsp baking powder
- ¼ tsp salt
- 1 dash cinnamon
- 2/3 cup milk or buttermilk (more if needed)
- ½ banana (very ripe and mashed)
- 1 tsp vanilla
- 1 tsp vinegar

Direction

- Mix flour, sugar, baking powder, salt and cinnamon together.
- In another bowl, combine all other ingredients.
- Add wet ingredients to dry ingredients and stir well.
- Add more soy milk if batter is too thick.
- Cook on medium-high heat till browned on both sides.

145. Eierkuchen Puffy German Egg Cakes Recipe

Serving: 4 | Prep: | Cook: 8mins | Ready in:

Ingredients

- 1/2 cup flour
- 3/4 tsp baking powder
- 1/4 tsp baking soda
- 1/2 cup buttermilk
- 6 large eggs, separated
- 1 tsp vanilla
- 1/2 tsp cream of tarter
- 1 Tbs sugar
- Topping:
- 1 cup sweetened whipped cream or sour cream or parts of both blended together
- powdered sugar and fresh berries on the side

Direction

- Mix all dry ingredients together except cream of tartar and sugar.
- In another bowl mix buttermilk, yolks and vanilla.
- Blend into dry ingredients till well mixed.
- Beat whites with cream of tater till foamy.
- Gradually beat in sugar till still but moist peaks.
- Fold into batter
- Heat electric griddle to 350F or over medium heat on stove griddle.
- When hot, brush griddle lightly with some melted butter.
- For each pancake spoon on about 1/2 cup batter.
- Turn cake over when bottom is golden brown, cooking golden on second side and edges feel dry.
- This takes about 7 minutes or so.
- Make sure griddle is proper temp as too cooking too hot or too low will not produce these puffy cakes
- Serve pancakes at once (about 3 per person).

- Dust with powdered sugar or offer topping with berries on the side.

146. Enhanced Pancake Mixes Recipe

Serving: 4 | Prep: | Cook: 10mins | Ready in:

Ingredients

- 2-3 tablespoons of your favorite instant pudding flavor
- any pancake mix in portion you want
- 1/4 cup granulated sugar
- 1 tsp. vanilla extract (other extract flavors are also great: maple, almond, cocoanut, lemon, etc.)

Direction

- Put pancake mix in bowl.
- Add sugar, dry pudding mix & blend. Don't overdo the pudding mix, as it will make your pancakes so light that they will fall apart when trying to flip them over. Of course, who am I to tell you how you like them.
- Add extract & liquid ingredients as directed on box (i.e., water, eggs, oil, etc.).
- Stir according to directions on box and cook on griddle as usual.

147. Extra Special Oatmeal Pancakes Recipe

Serving: 14 | Prep: | Cook: 6mins | Ready in:

Ingredients

- 4 pouches instant oatmeal, maple and brown sugar or cinnamon spice
- 1 1/4 c. flour
- 1 tbsp. baking powder
- 1/3 c. oil
- 1 egg, beaten
- 2 c. milk

Direction

- Mix dry ingredients together. Add combined oil, egg and mild. Stir until just combined. Let stand 5 min. before cooking. Use 1/4 c. batter per pancake, and cook on griddle till bubbles form. Flip, and continue cooking till golden.
- Makes 14

148. Fabulous Buttermilk Pancakes Recipe

Serving: 810 | Prep: | Cook: 10mins | Ready in:

Ingredients

- 2 large eggs
- 3 cups buttermilk
- 1 teaspoon baking soda
- 3 cups all purpose flour
- 2 teaspoons baking powder
- 1 teaspoon salt
- 2 teaspoons sugar
- 4 tablespoons melted butter
- 1 teaspoon vanilla extract
- butter for frying

Direction

- Whisk together eggs and buttermilk.
- Add the soda and whisk.
- Add flour, baking powder, salt and sugar and whisk.
- Stir in the melted butter.
- Pour batter into pitcher.
- Place butter on med heated griddle, when butter begins to foam.
- Pour pancake the size to your liking.
- For my grandchildren, chocolate chips are mandated but optional for anyone else along with banana slices or blueberries.

149. Fat Free Low Sugar Pumpkin Pancakes Recipe

Serving: 1 | Prep: | Cook: 10mins | Ready in:

Ingredients

- 1/3 c whole-wheat or buckwheat flour
- 2 tsp dark brown sugar
- 2 tablespoons Splenda granular (or sugar)
- 1 1/2 tsp baking powder
- 1 tbsp pumpkin pie spice
- pinch salt
- 1/3 cup canned pure pumpkin (not pie filling)
- 2 tsp maple extract
- 1 tsp vanilla extract
- boiling water, as needed

Direction

- Heat non-stick pan over moderate.
- Combine dry ingredients in a medium bowl.
- Add pumpkin and extracts, followed by enough boiling water to achieve a batter consistency.
- Spoon about 2 tbsp. batter per pancake onto hot pan, brown on both sides.
- Serve hot with maple syrup or (my favourite) home-made cranberry-orange sauce!

150. Favorite Homemade Pancakes Recipe

Serving: 16 | Prep: | Cook: 3mins | Ready in:

Ingredients

- 1 egg
- 1 1/4 cups buttermilk
- 1/2 tsp. baking soda
- 1 1/4 cups flour
- 1 tsp. sugar
- 2 Tbsp. soft shortening
- 1 tsp. baking powder
- 1/2 tsp. salt

Direction

- Heat a griddle slowly while mixing the batter. Beat the egg well and then beat in the buttermilk and 1/2 tsp. baking soda. Beat in flour and remaining ingredients with a mixer until smooth. Cook until golden brown. Makes about 16 pancakes.

151. Finnish Pancake Recipe

Serving: 6 | Prep: | Cook: 35mins | Ready in:

Ingredients

- 1/3 cup butter
- 5 eggs
- 1 tablespoon sugar
- 2 cups milk
- 1 cup flour
- 1 cup small curd cottage cheese
- 1 teaspoon baking powder
- Fresh berries/peaches & Confectioner's sugar (optional)

Direction

- Preheat oven 425 degrees, cut butter into small pieces & place in 10" cast iron skillet. Heat in oven until butter is melted.
- Combine eggs, & sugar in electric mixer and mix at high speed for 1 minute. Continue to mix while slowly adding milk, then flour, then cottage cheese, then baking powder. Pour blended mixture into hot skillet and bake for 35 minutes until pancake is puffed and beginning to brown.
- Remove from oven & let sit 5-8 minutes before cutting. (Pancake will fall)

- Sprinkle with confectioner's sugar and serve with fresh berries or peaches and warm maple syrup.

152. Fireside Pancakes Recipe

Serving: 2 | Prep: | Cook: 5mins | Ready in:

Ingredients

- 2 cups baking mix
- 1/2 cup instant dry milk
- 3 tsp. egg Replacer
- 1/2 - 1/3 cup water or margarine

Direction

- Put all dry ingredients in a Ziploc bag.
- Seal, write the amount of water to add on the outside of the bag.
- At campsite, add most of the water and mix to form a smooth batter. Add more water if needed.
- Cook over moderate heat in a lightly greased skillet until bubbles form and burst.
- Turn and cook the other side until brown.
- Do not press down on the pancake while it is cooking.

153. Fluffy Cottage Cheese Pancakes Recipe

Serving: 4 | Prep: | Cook: 10mins | Ready in:

Ingredients

- 1 cup flour
- 1/2 tsp. baking soda
- 1/4 tsp. salt
- 2 T. sugar
- 4 eggs
- 1 cup cottage cheese
- 1/2 cup milk
- 2 T. canola oil

Direction

- Sift together the flour, baking soda, salt and sugar in a small bowl.
- In a large mixing bowl, whisk together the eggs, milk, oil and cottage cheese.
- Add the dry ingredients.
- Stir until completely blended.
- Add a small amount of oil or butter to griddle/skillet over medium heat.
- Drop mixture by the 1/4 cup on the griddle and cook until bubbles form on top.
- Flip and cook on the other side until golden brown.
- Serve with your favorite syrup.

154. Fluffy Free Pancakes Recipe

Serving: 6 | Prep: | Cook: 1hours | Ready in:

Ingredients

- 3 eggs
- 1 1/2 cups oat flour
- 2 teaspoons baking powder
- 1/2 teaspoon salt
- 1/2 teaspoon xanthan gum
- 1 tablespoon brown sugar
- 1/2 teaspoon lemon zest
- 1/2 teaspoon turmeric
- 1/3 cup brown rice protein
- 1 1/2 cups water

Direction

- Measure all dry ingredients in to a large bowl and stir to combine
- Make a well in the dry ingredients and add the water. Do not combine just yet.
- Separate the eggs, leaving the whites in a medium bowl and the yolks added to the water in the larger bowl.

- Using a fork vigorously combine the ingredients in the larger bowl
- Whip the egg whites in the medium bowl until fluffy and doubled in bulk
- Fold the egg whites in to the batter
- Brush a griddle with a little oil at medium heat
- A half cup batter at a time, grill your pancakes one side at a time

155. Fluffy Pancakes Recipe

Serving: 4 | Prep: | Cook: 25mins | Ready in:

Ingredients

- recipe makes 8 pancakes
- 1-1/2 cup milk
- 1/4 cup white vinegar
- 2 cups all-purpose flour
- 1/4 cup white sugar
- 2 teaspoon baking powder
- 1 teaspoon baking soda
- 1 teaspoon salt
- 2 eggs
- 1/4 cup butter, melted
- cooking spray

Direction

- Combine milk with vinegar in a medium bowl and set aside for 5 minutes to "sour".
- Combine flour, sugar, baking powder, baking soda, and salt in a large mixing bowl. Whisk egg and butter into "soured" milk. Pour the flour mixture into the wet ingredients and whisk until lumps are gone.
- Heat a large skillet over medium heat, and coat with cooking spray. Pour 1/4 cupfuls of batter onto the skillet, and cook until bubbles appear on the surface. Flip with a spatula, and cook until browned on the other side.

156. Fluffy Pecan Pancakes Recipe

Serving: 0 | Prep: | Cook: 5mins | Ready in:

Ingredients

- • 2 cups flour
- • 2 tablespoons brown sugar
- • 1/2 teaspoon salt
- • 1 teaspoon baking powder
- • 1/2 teaspoon baking soda
- • 3/4 cup finely chopped pecans, toasted if desired
- • 1 cup buttermilk
- • 3/4 cup milk
- • 2 large eggs, separated
- • 1/4 cup melted butter
- • vegetable oil
- • pecan halves or fruit for garnish, optional

Direction

- In a mixing bowl, combine the flour, sugar, salt, baking powder, soda, and chopped pecans.
- In another bowl, whisk together buttermilk and milk, egg yolks, and melted butter. Blend into the dry ingredients just until all ingredients are moistened.
- Beat egg whites in another bowl until stiff peaks form. Fold into the batter until well incorporated.
- Heat a small amount of oil in a large skillet over medium heat. When skillet is hot enough for a drop of water to sizzle, scoop pancake batter onto the skillet in about 1/4-cup portions, spreading slightly. When edges are rather dry and bubbles are popping and bottoms are nicely browned, about 2 to 3 minutes, turn over and cook the other side until browned, about 2 minutes longer.
- Serve hot with butter and syrup and garnish with pecan halves or fruit, if desired.

157. Fluffy Eggless Pancakes Recipe

Serving: 6 | Prep: | Cook: 10mins | Ready in:

Ingredients

- 1 1/2 cups flour
- 4 tsp baking powder
- 1 tsp salt
- 1 tbsp sugar
- 1 tsp white vinegar
- 4 tbsp melted butter
- 1 1/3 cups milk

Direction

- In a large bowl sift together the dry ingredients.
- Add the milk, vinegar, and melted butter.
- Whisk until there are only a few lumps.
- Ladle onto a medium hot skillet.
- Flip when the first side is golden brown.
- Remove when the second side is golden brown.

158. French Ports Baked Pancakes Recipe

Serving: 6 | Prep: | Cook: 60mins | Ready in:

Ingredients

- 1 stick butter plus 3 table spoons melted
- 4 tablespoons sugar
- 3 eggs plus 2 eggs
- 2 cups flour
- 1 1/2 teaspoons baking powder
- 1 1/4 cup milk
- 3 cups small curd cottage cheese
- 1 teaspoon salt
- 1 - 21 oz can blueberry pie filling
- 3/4 cup blueberry syrup about 1/2 of a 12 oz bottle
- 1 cup sour cream
- 1 teaspoon vanilla extract
- 2 tablespoons powdered sugar

Direction

- Preheat oven to 350. Spray a 9x13 baking pan with non-stick cooking spray. Combine the 1 stick of butter and sugar in a large bowl. Add 3 eggs; beat well. Combine flour and baking powder. Mix flour mixture and milk alternately into butter mixture. Pour 1/2 of batter in pan.
- Mix cottage cheese, 2 eggs, the 3 tablespoons melted butter and salt in a medium bowl. Spread over the batter in the pan. Top with remaining batter. Bake for 60 min or until golden brown.
- Mix and heat blueberry pie filling and syrup together in a saucepan make a blueberry sauce. Mix sour cream, vanilla and powdered sugar together in a small bowl to make a sour cream sauce. When pancake is done pour syrup over top, swirl sour cream mixture over and serve.

159. Fresh Corn Cakes Recipe

Serving: 6 | Prep: | Cook: 10mins | Ready in:

Ingredients

- 2½ cups corn kernels. Fresh
- 2 eggs
- 2 tablespoons all-purpose flour
- ½ teaspoon salt
- 1 tablespoon sugar
- bacon drippings

Direction

- Husk, silk, and wash fresh ears of corn. Cut kernels off, then cut again close to the cob, scraping to remove all kernels and corn milk. In a medium mixing bowl, beat the eggs. Add the dry ingredients and blend. Stir in the fresh corn.

- Heat a skillet with a small amount of bacon drippings to oil the surface. Drop batter by spoonfuls into the hot skillet. Fry until the edges are crisp; then turn and brown the other side. Serve with Corn Cakes Butter.
- Corn Cakes Butter:
- 1 tsp. hot sauce
- ½ cup butter, softened
- Combine butter and hot sauce, and mix until well blended. Serve on Fresh Corn Cakes.

160. Friendly Monster Portrait Recipe

Serving: 2 | Prep: | Cook: 15mins | Ready in:

Ingredients

- 1 cup prepared liquid pancake batter
- 1 can (5 1/2 ounces) pineapple chunks
- 1 can (16 ounces) peaches
- 1 pint strawberries
- 1 kiwi fruit (or banana, if desired)
- 1 container (4 ounces) whipped topping
- 1 package (3 ounces) cream cheese, softened

Direction

- Use pancake mix to cook one large pancake on griddle. Remove to plate and set aside to cool. Drain pineapple chunks and peaches. Rinse and hull strawberries. Peel and slice kiwi fruit. In bowl, mix together whipped topping and softened cream cheese. Spread mixture onto cooled pancake. Arrange fruit on pancake to create a friendly monster face. You can use pineapple chunks for teeth, peaches for ears, kiwi for eyes and strawberries for nose and hair. You may add other fruits to make your monster scarier.
- Nutritional Information per Serving:
- Calories 600; Total fat 29g; Cholesterol 90mg; Sodium 370mg; Carbohydrate 78g; Fiber 8g; Protein 8g

161. Fruit Glazed Oatmeal Mini Cakes Recipe

Serving: 30 | Prep: | Cook: 40mins | Ready in:

Ingredients

- Glaze
- 1 packet Knox Gelatine
- 1/2 cup (130g) fruit juice split in half (I used slim cranberry twist)
- 1 tablespoon (17g) honey
- 1 tablespoon (13g) lemon juice
- Decoration
- 1/2 cup (45g) semi-sweet chocolates (Chipits in my cupboard)
- 1 cup (160g) frozen blueberries, defrosted partway
- lemon zest
- Pancake
- 1 1/4 cup (110g) white flour
- 1/4 cup (30g) minute oatmeal, dry
- 1 cup (180g) Kefir
- 1 egg (40g)
- 1 tablespoon (16g) truvia
- 1/2 teaspoon (20g) salt
- 1 teaspoon (20g) vanilla extract
- 1/3 cup (25g) whey protein isolate
- up to 120 g water to a batter consistency
- 2g lemon zest
- 1 tablespoon (12g) baking powder
- For the griddle
- 2 tablespoons (10g) canola oil

Direction

- Glaze
- Sprinkle gelatine over 1/4 cup cold fruit juice to soften, one minute.
- Bring the remaining juice to boil in a small saucepan.
- Add boiling juice, honey and lemon juice and stir until dissolved, three minutes.
- Leave bowl of glaze to set in refrigerator, twenty minutes.

- Pancakes
- Whisk together all ingredients except the baking powder and half the water. Whisk more water until a batter consistency is reached.
- Let rest in refrigerator for at least twenty minutes.
- Preheat cast iron griddle on medium low heat. Brush with oil.
- Take the batter bowl out of the refrigerator and quickly whisk in the baking powder.
- My twelve inch griddle can take four pancakes at a time, a tablespoon of batter each. Make sure there is enough room to flip.
- When batter is firm enough to flip, do so and cook the second side.
- Arrange on a plate, decorate with fruit, and spoon on the fruit glaze.
- Makes about thirty mini pancakes.

162. Fruit Yogurt Pancake Recipes Recipe

Serving: 68 | Prep: | Cook: 5mins | Ready in:

Ingredients

- 2 cups flour
- 5 Tbsp. sugar
- 2 tsp. baking powder
- 1 tsp. baking soda
- 1/2 tsp. salt
- 4 eggs; slightly beaten
- 1 cup fruit flavored yogurt
- 1 cup water
- 4 Tbsp. melted butter

Direction

- Combine dry ingredients in large bowl. Whisk together remaining ingredients and add to flour mixture. Preheat griddle, oil lightly, and ladle 1/4 cup batter onto griddle for each pancake. Cook until bubbly, turn and cook until light brown.

163. German Apple Pancake

Serving: 2 | Prep: | Cook: 15mins | Ready in:

Ingredients

- PANCAKE:
- 3 large eggs, room temperature
- 1 cup whole milk
- 3/4 cup all-purpose flour
- 1/2 teaspoon salt
- 1/8 teaspoon ground nutmeg
- 3 tablespoons butter
- TOPPING:
- 2 tart baking apples, peeled and sliced
- 3 to 4 tablespoons butter
- 2 tablespoons sugar
- Confectioners' sugar

Direction

- Preheat a 10-in. cast-iron skillet in a 425° oven. Meanwhile, in a blender, combine the eggs, milk, flour, salt and nutmeg; cover and process until smooth.
- Add butter to hot skillet; return to oven until butter bubbles. Pour batter into skillet. Bake, uncovered, for 20 minutes or until pancake puffs and edges are browned and crisp.
- For topping, in a skillet, combine the apples, butter and sugar; cook and stir over medium heat until apples are tender. Spoon into baked pancake. Sprinkle with confectioners' sugar. Cut and serve immediately.
- Tips:
- Many fruits can be used in place of the apples. Pears, berries, peaches or plums are all delish. If you use berries, just skip the precooking step.
- For extra flavor, try adding a splash of almond or vanilla extract to the batter.
- Nutrition Facts

- 1 serving: 192 calories, 12g fat (7g saturated fat), 107mg cholesterol, 273mg sodium, 18g carbohydrate (8g sugars, 1g fiber), 5g protein

164. German Apple Pancake Recipe

Serving: 4 | Prep: | Cook: 15mins | Ready in:

Ingredients

- 1/2 cup all-purpose flour
- 1/2 teaspoon salt
- 3 eggs, room temperature
- 1/2 cup Half and Half OR whole milk
- 2 tablespoons unsalted butter
- 2 tart apples, peeled, cored and thinly sliced
- 1 tablespoon firmly packed dark brown sugar
- 1/4 teaspoon ground cinnamon
- Pinch of grated nutmeg

Direction

- Preheat oven to 475 degrees F (250 degrees C).
- Whisk together flour and salt in a medium bowl.
- Whisk together eggs and milk in a small bowl.
- Gradually mix the wet ingredients into the flour until just blended.
- DO NOT OVERBEAT.
- Melt butter in an ovenproof skillet over medium heat.
- Add apple slices and brown sugar.
- Sauté apples until tender, about 3 to 5 minutes.
- Stir in cinnamon and nutmeg.
- Pour batter over apples and place pan in oven.
- Bake until puffy and golden, about 10 to 15 minutes.
- Remove from oven.
- Place serving platter over skillet and quickly invert pancake onto platter.
- You may also serve the pancake directly from the skillet.
- Squeeze the juice of 1 lemon WEDGE over pancake.
- Dust with confectioners' sugar.
- Slice and serve immediately.

165. German Pancake Recipe

Serving: 4 | Prep: | Cook: 25mins | Ready in:

Ingredients

- 4 eggs
- 2/3 c. flour
- 1 tsp. salt
- 2/3 c. milk
- 3 tbsp. butter

Direction

- Butter a heavy 10" oven proof skillet (cast iron)
- Pre-heat oven to 450 degrees.
- Beat the eggs with a fork to blend.
- Slowly add flour, beating constantly.
- Stir in salt and milk.
- Pour the batter into the skillet & drop the butter by teaspoonfuls into the batter, spreading evenly.
- Bake at 450 degrees for 15 mins.
- Reduce heat to 350 degrees and bake another 10 mins.
- Remove from oven and sift powdered sugar over the top.
- Serve with heated maple syrup!

166. German Pancake With Sweet Apple Filling Recipe

Serving: 8 | Prep: | Cook: 20mins | Ready in:

Ingredients

- Filling

- 1/4 cup of Melted butter
- 3/4 cup light brown sugar
- 1 1/2 Tbs cornstarch
- 1/2 cup of milk
- 4 apples (Granny Smith and or honey Crisp) cubed
- Batter
- 5 Large eggs (at room temperature)
- 1 cup of milk (at room temperature)
- 1/4 tsp vanilla extract
- 1 tsp ground cinnamon
- 1/4 tsp ground nutmeg
- 1/4 tsp salt
- Garnish
- juice of half a lemon
- icing sugar

Direction

- Mix the sauce for the Filling in a pan over medium heat until thickened.
- Add in the cubed apple.
- Stir and heat for 5-10 minutes on low to medium heat.
- Put two pans (I use a 10 inch cast iron skillet and a ceramic pie plate) in the oven and pre heat them to 450 degrees.
- Mix in a bowl the batter ingredients until smooth.
- Take pans out of the oven and coat each with 2 tbsp. of butter.
- Split the batter between the two pans and place in the 450 degree oven.
- Bake for 12 minutes (you will see that the pancakes grow into a tall odd shape which is fine.
- Open door and turn the pans for even heat.
- (Start to re-heat the filling on the stovetop).
- Bake for 5 more minutes till edges are golden brown and center just starting to brown.
- Pull out of oven and sprinkle with Lemon Juice.
- Transfer to serving plates.
- Add the Apple filling.
- Sprinkle with Icing Sugar.
- Devour and ask for more.

167. German Pancakes Recipe

Serving: 2 | Prep: | Cook: 7mins | Ready in:

Ingredients

- 1 cup flour
- 1 cup milk
- 2 eggs
- 2 tablespoons sugar
- 1 teaspoon baking powder

Direction

- Mix all ingredients well.
- Melt butter in large iron skillet or griddle.
- Pour in approximately 1/2 cup batter; tilt skillet to coat bottom.
- When top of pancake is set, turn and brown other side.
- Remove from pan.
- Fold pancake in half, then half again.
- Stack on platter until all batter is cooked.
- Serve topped or filled with fresh or frozen berries.

168. German Pancakes With Buttermilk Syrup Recipe

Serving: 8 | Prep: | Cook: 20mins | Ready in:

Ingredients

- Pancakes
- 6 eggs
- 1 cup milk
- 1 cup flour
- 1/2 teaspoon salt
- 2 tablespoons melted margarine
- buttermilk syrup
- 1 1/2 cups sugar
- 3/4 cup buttermilk
- 1/2 cup margarine

- 2 tablespoons corn syrup
- 1 teaspoon baking soda
- 2 teaspoons vanilla

Direction

- Place the eggs, milk, flour and salt in a blender.
- Cover and process until smooth.
- Pour the butter into an ungreased 9 X 13-inch pan, then add the batter.
- Bake uncovered at 400 for 20 minutes.
- Meanwhile, in a saucepan, combine the first five syrup ingredients and bring to a boil.
- Boil for 7 minutes.
- Remove from the heat and stir in vanilla.
- Serve pancake immediately with the syrup.

169. German Puff Pancakes With Spiced Apples Recipe

Serving: 12 | Prep: | Cook: 30mins | Ready in:

Ingredients

- You will need #12- 12 oz. individual soufflé/serving bowls (High temperature Oven-Proof)
- Ingredients: egg Mixture
- 1 1/2 cups flour
- 1 1/2 cups milk
- 9 eggs
- 3 tsp. vanilla
- apple Mixture
- 7 medium apples (any variety-mixed red and green look more attractive)
- 3/4 cup brown sugar
- 1 tsp. each cinnamon, nutmeg and ginger
- 1/2 cup mincemeat (dried condensed/canned)
- 4 tbs. butter/margarine
- 1/4 cup water
- Extras...
- 12 pats of butter/margarine
- ground nutmeg for garnish
- whipped topping for garnish
- 12 sliced apple wedges for garnish

Direction

- Directions: Whip milk, flour, eggs and vanilla. Set aside. Place pat of butter in each bowl. Preheat bowls in 400 degree oven for 10-15 minutes or until butter is popping hot. In the meantime, cut apples into chunks and place in fry pan with butter. Cook for 15 minutes or until apples are moderately soft. Add a bit of water if apples become too dry while cooking.
- When cooked, add cinnamon, nutmeg, ginger, brown sugar and mincemeat to apples. Continue cooking another 5-10 minutes or until well mixed and hot. When butter in dishes is popping hot, add an even measurement of pancake batter to each dish. Turn up oven to 425 degrees for 10 minutes then back down to 400 for another 5 minutes or until pancakes are puffed up and slightly brown on edges.
- Remove from oven, place an even measure of apples in center of each pancake. Top with dollop of whipped topping and sprinkle with fresh nutmeg. Place a wedge of apple on top as garnish and serve on a cloth doily on plate. Be careful, these are extremely hot and may crack plates if doilies are not used! Can also be made in a large iron skillet and cut into wedges and served on a plate, if desired.

170. Ginger Pancakes Recipe

Serving: 4 | Prep: | Cook: 20mins | Ready in:

Ingredients

- adapted from The Homesick Texan blog
- and the Magnolia Cafe in Austin, Tx.
- 6 tablespoons unsalted butter, melted
- 1 1/2 cups Half & Half
- 3 eggs
- 1 tablespoon plain yogurt

- 1/4 cup brown sugar
- 2 1/2 cups flour
- 1/2 tsp baking powder
- 1 teaspoon baking soda
- 1 teaspoon ground cloves
- 1 tablespoon cinnamon
- 1 tablespoon ginger
- 1/2 tablespoon nutmeg

Direction

- Melt the butter.
- Add the Half & Half, the eggs, the yogurt, and sugar and mix well. Sift together the dry ingredients. Combine the two gently and then judge if the batter is too thick. It should be thick but have some movement. I ended up adding another 1/2 cup of Half & Half.
- Cook them on a hot griddle or pan. I make a landing place of a cooling rack on a cookie sheet with a clean tea towel to keep them warm and I put them in an oven that was heated to the lowest temp and then turned off.
- Serve with maple syrup and toasted pecans. Enjoy.

171. Gingerbread Man Pancakes Recipe

Serving: 4 | Prep: | Cook: 5mins | Ready in:

Ingredients

- 1 cup flour
- 1 tablespoon sugar
- 1 teaspoon baking powder
- 1 teaspoon ground ginger
- 1/2 teaspoon salt
- 1/2 teaspoon baking soda
- 1/2 teaspoon cinnamon
- dash of ground cloves
- 2 tablespoons molasses
- 1 tablespoon vegetable oil
- 1 cup buttermilk
- 1 egg lightly beaten

Direction

- Combine dry ingredients in a bowl and set aside.
- In another bowl whisk molasses, oil, buttermilk, and egg until blended
- Pour liquid into flour mixture and stir until mixed
- Grease griddle and heat to medium low.

172. Gingerbread Pancakes Recipe

Serving: 4 | Prep: | Cook: 5mins | Ready in:

Ingredients

- 1 3/4 cups flour
- 1/2 cup whole wheat flour
- 1 1/2 tsp baking powder
- 1 1/2 tsp pumpkin pie spice
- 1/2 tsp ginger
- 1/4 tsp soda
- 1/4 tsp salt
- 1 1/4 cups skim milk
- 3/4 cup applesauce
- 1/3 cup molasses
- 1/4 cup cooking oil
- 1 egg
- softened butter

Direction

- In mixing bowl stir together flours, powder, pie spice, ginger, soda and salt. Make a well in the center of the flour mixture, set aside.
- In another mixing bowl, whisk together milk, applesauce, molasses, oil, and egg. Add milk mixture all at once to flour mixture. Stir, batter will be lumpy.
- Spoon about 1/4 cup batter onto hot griddle. Cook over medium heat about 3 minutes,

turning to second sides when pancakes have bubbly surfaces and edges are slightly dry.
- Serve with softened butter and syrup.

173. Gingerbread Pancakes Topped With Apples And Whipped Cream Recipe

Serving: 6 | Prep: | Cook: 10mins | Ready in:

Ingredients

- 1 cup flour
- 1-1/2 teaspoons baking powder
- 1/2 teaspoon cinnamon
- 1/2 teaspoon ginger
- Dash of cloves
- 3/4 cup milk
- 2 tablespoons molasses
- 1 tablespoon vegetable oil
- 1 egg, lightly beaten
- apple pie filling (home-made or canned)
- whipping cream
- 1/2 cup whipping cream
- 1 tablespoons sugar

Direction

- Mix all dry ingredients in bowl. In smaller bowl, mix all other ingredients. Combine until smooth. Pour 1/3 cup of batter on hot griddle. Turn once. Serve topped with apple pie filling, maple syrup and whipped cream.
- For whipped cream, mix whipping cream with sugar and beat until fluffy.

174. Gluten Free Gingerbread Pancakes Recipe

Serving: 6 | Prep: | Cook: 2mins | Ready in:

Ingredients

- 2 cups baking mix, Pamela's Ultimate or other gf pancake mix
- 3 tablespoons sugar
- 1 1/2 teaspoons cinnamon
- 1 1/2 teaspoons ginger
- 3/4 teaspoon allspice
- 1/2 cup crystallized ginger
- 2 eggs
- 1 1/2 cups milk
- 4 tablespoons butter, melted

Direction

- In a bowl, whisk baking mix, sugar, spices and crystallized ginger. In separate bowl, beat eggs. Add milk and butter to eggs and mix well. Pour wet ingredients into dry ingredients and gently stir until just combined.
- Cook on griddle.

175. Gluten Free Dairy Free German Apple Pancakes Recipe

Serving: 10 | Prep: | Cook: 5mins | Ready in:

Ingredients

- 6 eggs
- ¼ cup sugar
- 1½ cups rice flour
- ⅓ cup tapioca starch
- 2 teaspoons baking powder
- ½ teaspoon salt
- 2 cups milk, soy milk, rice milk or apple juice
- 2 tablespoons unsalted butter, melted, or vegetable oil
- 2 McIntosh, Cortland or other cooking apples, peeled and very thinly sliced
- ½ cup raisins, optional
- butter, oil or vegetable spray
- 2 tablespoons confectioner's sugar, for garnish

Direction

- Beat eggs with sugar until foamy.

- Add rice flour, tapioca starch/flour, baking powder and salt. Beat until smooth.
- Add milk and butter (or oil).
- Fold in apple slices and raisins, if desired.
- In medium skillet, heat butter or oil or coat with vegetable spray. Ladle ¼ cup batter into pan and cook until top is set, about 3 to 5 minutes. Flip with spatula and cook another 2 to 3 minutes.
- Turn pancakes onto a warm serving plate. Roll them up like crepes and keep them warm. Repeat with remaining batter until all is used. Lightly dust pancakes with powdered sugar. Serve warm.

176. Gluten Free Dutch Babies Recipe

Serving: 3 | Prep: | Cook: 18mins | Ready in:

Ingredients

- 1/4 cup (1/2 stick) butter
- 3 eggs
- 1/2 cup milk or nondairy liquid (i use rice milk)
- 1/4 cup GF Mix (mix follows below)
- powdered sugar for dusting
- GF Mix: 2 parts white rice flour, 2/3 part potato starch flour, 1/3 part tapioca flour (Mix & this recipe, except sauce, developed by Betty Hagman - The gluten-Free Gourmet - buy her book!)
- Sauce:
- Frozen berries (blue/rasp/strawberries or a mix)
- orange juice or lemon juice, less for thick sauce, more for runny sauce
- arrowroot or corn Starch (mix small amt in water first)
- Sweetener - sugar, maple syrup, honey or agave

Direction

- Preheat oven to 425 degree F.
- Melt butter in glass pie pan - make sure not to brown it!
- Meanwhile, mix eggs and milk in a blender.
- Add flour and blend again.
- Pour into pie pan.
- Bake 18 mins.
- Serve with sauce, syrup, jam, or crushed fruit.
- Dust with powdered sugar (a mini-strainer works great for this!)
- For sauce: Mix everything together in a small sauce pan, except starch, over low heat. Feel free to add spices (e.g. mint or cinnamon as desired) at this time. While stirring, mix starch into sauce and turn heat to high for 1 minute till almost bubbling. Keep stirring, turn heat down to low and sauce will thicken.
- Supposedly makes 4 servings, but I make this for my 2 year old and he eats 1/4th of this, and I usually can eat the rest!

177. Gluten Free Pumpkin Pancakes Recipe

Serving: 5 | Prep: | Cook: 20mins | Ready in:

Ingredients

- 1 cup sorghum flour
- 1/4 cup + 2 tbsp tapioca flour
- 3 tbsp almond flour
- 3/4 tsp salt
- 1/4 tsp ground ginger
- 1/4 tsp ground cardamom
- 1 tbsp baking powder
- 1/2 cup pumpkin puree
- 1 1/3 cup soy or nut milk
- 3 tbsp cane sugar
- 1 tbsp vegetable oil

Direction

- In a large bowl, sift or whisk together the flour, salt, spices, and baking powder.

- In a medium bowl, whisk together the pumpkin, milk, sugar and oil until well combined.
- Slowly incorporate the wet ingredients in with the dry, whisking until combined.
- Let the batter rest for a few minutes before cooking.
- Using a 1/4 cup measure, ladle out the batter and fry in a lightly oiled pan over medium-low to medium heat.
- Cook for around 2 1/2 minutes on the first side, 2 minutes on the second.
- (Makes around 10 pancakes.)

178. Good Morning Pumpkin Pancakes Recipe

Serving: 8 | Prep: | Cook: 20mins | Ready in:

Ingredients

- 2 cups biscuit mix
- 2 tablespoons packed light brown sugar
- 2 teaspoons ground cinnamon
- 12 ounces evaporated milk undiluted
- 1 teaspoon ground allspice
- 1/2 cup solid pack pumpkin
- 2 tablespoons vegetable oil
- 2 eggs
- 1 teaspoon vanilla extract

Direction

- In a large mixer bowl combine biscuit mix, sugar, cinnamon and allspice.
- Add evaporated milk, pumpkin, oil, eggs and vanilla then beat until smooth.
- Pour 1/4 cup batter onto heated and lightly greased griddle.
- Cook until top surface is bubbly and edges are dry.
- Turn and cook until golden.
- Keep pancakes warm.
- Serve with syrup or honey.

179. Grandmas Pancakes Recipe

Serving: 4 | Prep: | Cook: 20mins | Ready in:

Ingredients

- 1 1/2 cups flour
- 1 tsp soda
- 1 tsp salt
- 2 tsp sugar
- 2 eggs
- 2 cups buttermilk
- 1/3 cup vegetable oil

Direction

- Mix together the flour, soda, salt and sugar. Add in the eggs, buttermilk and oil. Beat until smooth. Use 1/4 cup of batter for each pancake on 400 degree griddle.

180. Grizzly Bears Pancake Recipe

Serving: 46 | Prep: | Cook: 40mins | Ready in:

Ingredients

- 2 eggs
- 2 cups milk
- 1 cup flour
- 2 tablespoons sugar
- 2 tablespoons butter
- 2 tablespoons sour cream
- mixed berries (optional)
- bananas, sliced (optional)
- peaches (optional)
- maple syrup (optional)

Direction

- Preheat oven to 350. Divide butter into 2 9" cake pans and melt in oven while it preheats.

- Mix together eggs and milk until blended. Add flour and 1 T sugar.
- Divide batter evenly between pans, right on top of melted butter.
- Sprinkle with remaining sugar.
- Bake at 350 for 40 minutes.
- Remove from pan. 1/2 cake per person.
- Serve warm with optional fruit, maple syrup and 1 T sour cream per pancake dolloped in the center.

181. Guilt Free Oatmeal Pancakes Recipe

Serving: 4 | Prep: | Cook: 10mins | Ready in:

Ingredients

- 2 cups rolled oats
- 2 cups milk
- Mix above 2 ingredients and refrigerate overnight.
- 2 eggs slightly beaten
- 1/8 cup canola oil
- 1/4 cup currants
- 1/2 cup flour
- 1 tsp. baking powder
- 1 tsp. baking soda
- 1 tsp. cinnamon
- 2 Tablespoons sugar

Direction

- The next morning, preheat the griddle to a medium high setting.
- Stir eggs, oil and raisins into the oatmeal until well blended.
- In another bowl mix flour sugar, baking powder, soda, and cinnamon. Add to oats mixture and mix.
- Batter will be thick. Drop by large spoonfuls on griddle.
- Serve with butter and warm maple syrup. Apple or other fruit toppings are good as well.

- Served with large portion of mixed fresh fruit in season.
- Good with turkey sausage.

182. Healthy Flax Pancake Mix Recipe

Serving: 3 | Prep: | Cook: 15mins | Ready in:

Ingredients

- Makes 6 cups, enough for 3 batches of pancake
- ----------------------
- 2 1/2 cups whole-wheat flour
- 1 cup buttermilk powder (see Ingredient notes)
- 5 tablespoons dried egg whites, such as Just Whites (see Ingredient notes)
- 1/4 cup sugar
- 1 1/2 tablespoons baking powder
- 2 teaspoons baking soda
- 1 teaspoon salt
- 1 cup flaxseed meal (see Ingredient notes)
- 1 cup nonfat dry milk
- 1/2 cup wheat bran or oat bran

Direction

- Whisk flour, buttermilk powder, dried egg whites, sugar, baking powder, baking soda and salt in a large bowl. Stir in flaxseed meal, dry milk and bran. Store in an airtight container.
- NUTRITION INFORMATION: Per cup: 485 calories; 10 g fat (1 g fat, 2 g mono); 14 mg cholesterol; 71 g carbohydrate; 29 g protein; 15 g fiber; 1331 mg sodium; 730 mg potassium.
- TIP: Ingredient Notes: Buttermilk powder, such as Saco Buttermilk Blend, is a useful substitute for fresh buttermilk. Look in the baking section or with the powdered milk in most supermarkets.
- Dried egg whites, such as Just Whites, reconstituted, can be substituted for fresh egg whites.

- You can find flaxseed meal at some natural-foods markets or mail-order it (try www.bobsredmill.com). It is highly perishable, so store it in the refrigerator or freezer. To make your own flaxseed meal, grind 2/3 cup whole flaxseeds to yield 1 cup.
- MAKE AHEAD TIP: Refrigerate in an airtight container or zip lock bag for up to 1 month or freeze for up to 3 months.

183. Hearty Poppy Seed Pancakes Recipe

Serving: 0 | Prep: | Cook: 15mins | Ready in:

Ingredients

- 1 cup Bob's Red Mill whole wheat pastry flour
- 1/2 cup oatmeal
- 1 1/2 tbsp dry poppy seeds
- 1 tsp baking powder
- 1 cup sugar substitute
- 1 eggwhite
- 1/2 cup non-fat plain yogurt
- 3/4 cup skim milk
- 1 tsp almond extract

Direction

- In a medium bowl, mix all dry ingredient thoroughly.
- Create a cavity in the mixture.
- Add egg white, yogurt, milk and extract in the cavity.
- Thoroughly blend ingredients all together.
- Pour 1/3 cup of batter on a sprayed non-stick griddle and griddle for about 2-3 minutes on each side or until thoroughly done.
- Serve with favorite topping!!

184. Herbed Potato Pancakes Recipe

Serving: 6 | Prep: | Cook: 20mins | Ready in:

Ingredients

- 1 teaspoon salt divided
- 2 tablespoons white vinegar
- 1 1/2 cups shredded potatoes from three small potatoes
- 3 grains white pepper
- One inch sprig fresh rosemary
- 1/4 teaspoon cream of tartar
- 1 egg
- 1/2 cup oat flour
- 1/2 teaspoon baking powder
- 2 teaspoons bacon fat or vegetable oil

Direction

- Pour the vinegar and half the salt in a large bowl.
- Peel the potatoes and swirl around in the vinegar after freshly peeled
- In a mortar crush the pepper grains, add the rest of the salt, cream of tartar, and rosemary. Crush finely.
- Remove the potatoes from the bowl and crack an egg in to the remaining vinegar, add 1/4 cup water, and whip together well.
- Preheat the griddle with a teaspoon of bacon fat.
- Shred the potatoes and stir in to the wet ingredients.
- Pour the crushed herbs over the potatoes.
- Pour the oat flour and the baking soda over all.
- Stir to moisten.
- Spoon a portion of the batter on to the prepared griddle (3 tablespoons each)
- Brown on each side.
- Serve as you like. Presented with yogurt and a sprig of rosemary.

185. Highland Mountain Dutch Apple Pancakes Recipe

Serving: 12 | Prep: | Cook: 45mins | Ready in:

Ingredients

- (1 1/2 recipe)
- Peel 9 large granny smith apples and cut into bite-sized pieces
- Add 1 1/2 cups sugar
- 2 Tbsps ground cinnamon
- 1 tsp cloves
- 1/2 tsp nutmeg
- Cover with Saran Wrap. Cook 8 minutes in microwave, stir and cook another 8 minutes in microwave.

Direction

- In the morning.
- When making coffee, turn oven on to 500 degrees (High altitude cooking).
- 45 minutes before serving:
- Place 4 Tbsps. butter in microwave to melt.
- Place apples again in microwave and cook for 5-8 minutes.
- Place 4 Tbsps. butter in skillets and place in oven to melt.
- In bowl, place 9 large eggs and the following:
- 4 tsps. vanilla extract
- 2 Tbsps. sugar
- 1 1/2 cup Bisquick
- 1 1/4 cup juice from apples
- 1/4 cup milk
- Mix. Take skillets out of oven and spray sides with Pam. Cover bottom of skillets with apples. Cover apples with flour mixture. Cook approximately 30 minutes.
- Cut into 8 slices, cover with powdered sugar, and garnish with parsley at edges and middle.
- Serve with smoked chicken, turkey and artichoke sausage. Maple syrup.
- Note: Use the largest and smallest iron skillets. For 6-8 people just use large skillet and take 1/3 measurements off.

186. Holiday Pancakes Recipe

Serving: 8 | Prep: | Cook: 10mins | Ready in:

Ingredients

- Off the shelf pancake batter, enough for eight to 12 servings
- one cup of fresh chopped cranberries (nothing from a can!)
- one table spoon of vanilla extract
- one and a half teaspoons of pumpkin pie spice

Direction

- Mix all of the ingredients into the pancake batter and grill.
- Serve hot with maple syrup or any topping of your choice.

187. Homemade Buttermilk Pancake Mix Recipe

Serving: 6 | Prep: | Cook: | Ready in:

Ingredients

- 4 cups All Purpose flour
- 1/4 cup sugar
- 1/2 cup dry buttermilk Powder
- 2 tsp baking soda
- 4 tsp baking powder
- 1 tsp salt

Direction

- Combine all the ingredients and whisk together to distribute evenly.
- Store your buttermilk pancake mix in a sealed container in a cool place and use it within three months.
- If you would like to keep the mix longer, store it in the freezer.
- To use your mix:

- Measure the desired mix into a large bowl.
- In a smaller bowl, whisk one egg for every 1 to 1 1/2 cups of mix.
- Add 1 1/2 tablespoons melted butter or oil to the egg for every one cup of mix.
- Add 2/3 cup water to the egg mixture for every one cup of mix.
- Add the liquid mixture to the mix and stir until just combined.
- If the batter is too dry add more water to reach the desired consistency.
- Cook on griddle.
- Mix can be doubled as needed.

188. Homemade Pancakes Recipe

Serving: 8 | Prep: | Cook: 3mins | Ready in:

Ingredients

- 2 eggs (separated)
- 1 teaspoon sugar
- 1/2 teaspoon salt
- 2 teaspoons baking powder
- 1/4 cup oil
- 1 cup milk (plus some for consistency)
- 1 1/3 cup flour
- 1 tsp. vanilla (opt.)

Direction

- Beat egg whites until stiff - set aside.
- Beat egg yolks, add sugar and salt, beat in.
- Add baking powder, beat until just mixed in well.
- Add flour, milk, and oil. Beat until smooth (not too much otherwise the baking powder won't react correctly) add vanilla.
- Add egg whites to batter and FOLD gently. Let batter sit for 15-30 minutes prior to cooking.
- Pour about a 1/2 cup of batter into a buttered greased frying pan or skillet and brown these lightly on both sides (watching for the bubbles, you will know when to turn them by the amount of bubbles that have popped and by the rising of the pancake).
- Good Luck and Enjoy!

189. Hotel Pancakes Recipe

Serving: 4 | Prep: | Cook: 3mins | Ready in:

Ingredients

- 2 Cups flour
- 1-1/4 Tsp baking soda
- 3/4 Tsp baking powder
- 1 Tsp kosher salt
- 1/4 Cup sugar
- 2 eggs, Unbeaten
- 1 Tsp vanilla
- 1/2 Cup melted butter
- 2 Cups buttermilk (Or 2 cups milk with 2 tsp vinegar or lemon. Let it sit about 10 minutes before using)

Direction

- Mix Dry ingredients thoroughly.
- Add remaining ingredients and stir lightly just to moisten dry mixture.
- Mixture will be thick and lumpy.
- I use 1/4 cup per pancake. You may have to spread mixture with the back of a spoon.
- Turn cakes when top is bubbly.

190. Individual Baked Pear Pancakes Recipe

Serving: 6 | Prep: | Cook: 30mins | Ready in:

Ingredients

- 6 eggs
- 1 cup whole milk
- 1 cup flour

- 4 tablespoons melted butter
- 1/2 teaspoon almond extract
- 2 teaspoons lemon zest
- 3 large baking pears
- 2 tablespoons powdered sugar
- 3 tablespoons lemon juice
- 6 individual au gratin dishes sprayed with cooking spray

Direction

- In blender mix eggs and milk then stir in flour and while stirring add melted butter.
- Add extract and zest then preheat oven to 425.
- Peel and core pears then halve and slice.
- Mix sugar and lemon juice in a bowl then toss slice pears and juice and mix well.
- Layer 6 slices into each dish then pour 1/2 cup batter over pears then bake 20 minutes.
- To serve sprinkle with powdered sugar then decorate with fresh berries.

191. Irish Pancakes Recipe

Serving: 4 | Prep: | Cook: 2mins | Ready in:

Ingredients

- 1 cup plain flour
- pinch of salt
- 2 eggs
- 1 cup milk
- 1 tbsp melted butter

Direction

- Put all the ingredients in a blender (wet ingredients first) and blend for about 30 seconds.
- Let the batter stand for about 30 minutes (enough time to make bacon, or cut fruit).
- Pre-heat your pan or griddle to medium heat.
- Grease the pan with a little butter or shortening.
- Pour about two tablespoons or so out onto the griddle, carefully tilt the griddle to thin these out, and cook them.
- If they are thin enough, they can go without flipping, especially if you serve them rolled up.
- Stuff them with fruit, bacon and eggs, butter, whatever you like. Sprinkle with powdered sugar, maybe drizzle a little syrup on them. Go nuts!

192. Irish Potato Pancakes Boxty Recipe

Serving: 4 | Prep: | Cook: 5mins | Ready in:

Ingredients

- "Boxty on the griddle,
- boxty in the pan,
- if you can't make boxty,
- you'll never get a man."
- 1 lb. of potatoes, grated
- 3-3/4 cups all-purpose flour
- 1 cup milk, preferably 2% or Homogenized
- 2 Tablespoons warm water
- 1 teaspoon baking soda
- 2 Tablespoons butter or margarine
- 1 cup mashed potatoes
- salt and pepper to taste
- Note: I always make these when there are leftover mashed potatoes. By doing so it cuts down on prep time.

Direction

- Soak grated potatoes overnight in cold water to remove the starch.
- Mix all ingredients together EXCEPT the flour.
- Mix All-purpose flour in a little at a time with a wooden spoon or your hands.
- Add extra milk if it seems too stiff.
- Lightly grease an iron skillet or griddle.
- Drop the mixture onto the skillet by rounded teaspoons.

- Brown the bottom slightly, then flatten the tops a little bit with a spatula.
- Depending on what you prefer they can be thick or thinner and crispy.
- Cook until golden brown. Served with butter or sour cream.
- Note: Herbs such as parsley can be added.

193. Jumbo Pancake Roll Recipe

Serving: 6 | Prep: | Cook: 20mins | Ready in:

Ingredients

- 2 eggs beaten
- 3 cups sour milk
- 2 tablespoons melted shortening or salad oil
- 3 cups flour
- 1 teaspoon salt
- 2 teaspoons baking powder
- 1/2 teaspoon baking soda
- 2 tablespoons sugar
- orange juice
- sugar

Direction

- Combine eggs, milk and shortening.
- Add sifted dry ingredients and beat until smooth.
- Make pancake full griddle size by pouring and tipping to spread batter and make cake round.
- Bake until brown on bottom and top surface is bubbly.
- Do not turn.
- Slip under broiler a second or two to dry.
- Sprinkle lightly with orange juice and sugar.
- Roll 1 cake jellyroll fashion using 2 forms then bake a second cake and roll around the first.
- Sprinkle with grated orange peel and sugar.
- Garnish with orange sections.

194. Latkes Minus The Potato Recipe

Serving: 14 | Prep: | Cook: 8mins | Ready in:

Ingredients

- 1 cup regular or lowfat cottage cheese
- 3 eggs, separated
- 1 cup all purpose flour
- 2 tablespoons sugar
- 1/2 cup heavy cream
- Pinch salt
- Grated zest of 1/2 lemon
- 1/2 cup oil, for frying
- apple sauce and sour cream on the side

Direction

- Beat cottage cheese, egg yolks, flour, sugar, cream, salt and lemon zest until smooth.
- Beat egg whites until stiff but not dry and fold into cheese mixture.
- In a large frying pan over medium-high heat, heat oil until hot.
- Drop 4 tablespoons batter into the pan to form each latke.
- Fry until golden, about 4 minutes per side.
- Use more oil for each batch as needed.
- Drain on paper towels and keep warm in a 250 degree F. oven until ready to serve.
- Serve with apple sauce and sour cream.

195. Latkes My Way Recipe

Serving: 14 | Prep: | Cook: 6mins | Ready in:

Ingredients

- 5-6 medium - large sized potatoes, grated
- Note: I prefer Yukon Gold
- 2 onions, thinly sliced or grated
- 2 garlic cloves, minced
- 1-2 large eggs
- 1/4 to 1/2 cup all-purpose flour

- 1 tsp. baking powder
- 2 Tbsp. fresh parsley, chopped
- salt and pepper to taste
- 2-1/2 cups of vegetable or sunflower oil for frying
- Garnish with grated nutmeg if desired

Direction

- Using a box grater or food processor, grate peeled potatoes.
- Place grated potatoes on several sheets of paper towel and press down to remove all moisture.
- Thinly slice/grate onion.
- Whisk eggs and add to onions, garlic and potatoes.
- Stir in flour, baking powder, parsley, salt and pepper and blend evenly.
- If you feel the mixture is too dry, add a tablespoon or 2 of milk.
- Pour enough oil into a large deep frying pan to measure 1-1/2 to 2 inches and place over medium-high heat.
- When the oil is hot enough, form potato mixture into pancake type shapes with hands.
- Carefully place latkes into oil and cook for at least 5-6 minutes per side.
- Do not over-crowd the frying pan.
- When the latkes are cooked, remove from oil and place on a plate lined with paper towel or a cookie rack to drain.
- Have either a separate plate or a cookie sheet handy to place latkes on and keep warm in a 325 degree oven until ready to serve.
- Condiments are sour cream and applesauce.

196. Lazy Day Pancakes Recipe

Serving: 6 | Prep: | Cook: 4mins | Ready in:

Ingredients

- 2 eggs
- 3 tablespoons sugar
- 1 tablespoon baking powder
- 1 teaspoon soda
- 1 teaspoon salt
- 2 cups flour
- 3 cups buttermilk
- 3/4 stick butter, melted

Direction

- In a large bowl, whisk eggs.
- Add sugar, baking powder, soda, salt, flour and buttermilk.
- Beat well (electric hand mixer is perfect).
- Stir in butter.
- Have griddle hot.
- Pour 1/2 cup batter onto griddle.
- Cook until top of pancake is bubble and the edges are light browned.
- Turn and cook until the other side is lightly browned.
- Have plates ready, serve with your favorite syrup that has been warmed (I always add a little butter to the syrup while it is heating).
- Enjoy!

197. Lemon Pancakes With Fresh Berries Recipe

Serving: 8 | Prep: | Cook: 6mins | Ready in:

Ingredients

- 2 1/3 C. all-purpose flour
- 1/3 C. powdered sugar
- 1 1/2 tsp. baking soda
- 1 tsp. baking powder
- 1 C. milk
- 1 C. sour cream
- 2 eggs
- 2 Tbs. butter, melted
- 2 Tbs. lemon juice
- 1 Tbs. freshly grated lemon peel
- 1/2 C blueberries (optional)

- TOPPING INGREDIENTS
- Any fruit you desire such as... fresh or frozen (thawed) strawberries or fresh or frozen blueberries, thawed

Direction

- Combine flour, powdered sugar, baking soda and baking powder in large bowl.
- Combine all remaining pancake ingredients in small bowl; mix until smooth.
- Stir sour cream mixture into flour mixture until well mixed (batter will be thick).
- Fold in the blueberries if using.
- Heat lightly greased griddle or frying pan to 350°F or until drops of water sizzle.
- For each pancake, spoon 1/4 cup batter onto hot griddle; spread to form 4-inch circle.
- Cook until bubbles form on top (1 to 2 minutes).
- Turn pancakes; continue cooking until browned (1 to 2 minutes). Keep warm.
- Repeat with remaining batter.
- Top with maple or blueberry syrup and your choice of fruit.

198. Lemon Poppyseed Pancakes Recipe

Serving: 4 | Prep: | Cook: 2mins | Ready in:

Ingredients

- 2 cups Bisquick® baking mix
- 1 cup sour cream
- 1/2 cup milk
- 1 tablespoon poppy seeds
- 2 teaspoons lemon zest
- 2 teaspoons fresh lemon juice
- 2 eggs
- juice of 1 lemon
- pancake syrup

Direction

- Beat ingredients with wire whisk until well blended. Make pancakes as usual.
- For syrup: Squeeze juice from one lemon and add to usual pancake syrup, stirring well. Perfect lemony syrup!

199. Lemon Souffle Pancakes Recipe

Serving: 6 | Prep: | Cook: 10mins | Ready in:

Ingredients

- 1 cup low-fat cottage cheese
- 1 T pure maple syrup plus additional as an accompaniment
- 2 T fresh lemon juice
- 2 tsps freshly grated lemon zest
- 2 T vegetable oil
- 3 large eggs, separated
- 2 tsps double-acting baking powder
- 1/2 cup all purpose flour
- 1/4 tsp salt

Direction

- In a food processor blend together the cottage cheese, 1 T of maple syrup, the lemon juice, the zest, the oil, the egg yolks, the baking powder, the flour, and the salt for 1 minute and transfer the mixture to a bowl. In another bowl with an electric mixer beat the egg whites until they just hold stiff peaks and fold them into the cottage-cheese mixture gently but thoroughly. Heat a greased griddle over moderate heat until it is hot enough to make drops of water scatter over its surface. Working in batches, pour the batter onto the griddle by 1/3-cup measures and cook the pancakes for 2 minutes on each side, or until they are golden and cooked through. (The pancakes will be thick). Transfer pancakes as they are cooked to a heated platter and serve them with additional maple syrup.
- Makes about 15 pancakes.

200. Lemon Ricotta Pancakes Recipe

Serving: 15 | Prep: | Cook: 20mins | Ready in:

Ingredients

- 1 cup all purpose flour
- 3/4 tsp baking powder
- 3/4 tsp baking soda
- 1/4 tsp ground nutmeg
- 1/4 tsp salt
- 2 eggs, separated
- 1 cup buttermilk
- 2/3 cup whole-milk ricotta cheese
- 2 tbsp sugar
- 1 tbsp grated lemon peel

Direction

- Heat oven to 200 degrees F. Whish flour, baking powder, baking soda, nutmeg, and salt in a large bowl. Whisk egg yolks, buttermilk, ricotta cheese, sugar and lemon peel in medium bowl until blended.
- Beat egg whites in medium bowl at medium high speed until soft peaks form. Stir ricotta mixture into flour mixture just until combined. Fold in egg whites.
- Heat griddle or large non-stick skillet over medium heat until hot, oil griddle. Ladle batter by scant 1/4 ladleful onto griddle, spreading to 4 inch rounds. Cook 2 minutes or until bubbled break surface and around edges of pancake. Turn; cook for 1 minutes or until golden brown. Place in oven to keep warm while cooking remaining pancakes.

201. Light And Fluffy Pancakes Recipe

Serving: 12 | Prep: | Cook: 3mins | Ready in:

Ingredients

- 1-3/4 cups white flour
- 1 tsp baking powder
- 1 tsp baking soda
- 1/2 tsp salt
- 1 1/2 cups buttermilk
- 3 eggs, lightly beaten
- 2 tbsp vegetable oil
- 1 tbsp honey or 3 tbsp white sugar(your choice)
- orange honey Butter:
- 1/2 cup butter, softened
- 1/3 cup honey
- 2 tbsp orange juice, concentrate

Direction

- In a mixing bowl combine flour, baking powder, baking soda and salt.
- Combine buttermilk, eggs, oil and sugar (or honey); add to dry ingredients and mix well.
- Pour batter by 1/4 cupfuls onto lightly greased hot griddle; turn when bubbles form on top of pancakes.
- Serve with butter and maple syrup or try this...
- For Orange Honey Butter:
- Combine butter and honey in a medium bowl; beat well.
- Stir in orange juice concentrate until smooth. Serve with pancakes.

202. Make Ahead Pancake And Waffle Batter Recipe

Serving: 8 | Prep: | Cook: 3mins | Ready in:

Ingredients

- 4-1/2 cups flour
- 1/4 cup sugar
- 1 tsp. salt
- 1 pkg. dry yeast
- 4 cups milk
- 1/2 cup butter
- 6 eggs

Direction

- In large bowl, combine flour, sugar, salt and yeast. Heat milk and butter over low heat until warm and add along with eggs to flour mixture. Beat at medium speed until smooth. Cover and refrigerate for up to 4 days, stirring in 2 additional tablespoons sugar after second day.
- For pancakes, lightly grease griddle and pour about 1/4 cup batter onto hot surface for each pancake. Turn when edges look cooked and bubbles begin to break on surface.
- For waffles, bake in a hot waffle iron until steaming stops.

203. Mango Pancakes Recipe

Serving: 6 | Prep: | Cook: 5mins | Ready in:

Ingredients

- 1 cup unbleached all-purpose flour
- 1 tablespoon baking powder
- 1/2 teaspoon baking soda
- 1/4 teaspoon salt
- 1 1/2 cups low-fat buttermilk
- 1/2 cup low-fat ricotta cheese
- 3/4 teaspoon honey
- 3/4 teaspoon canola oil
- 1 teaspoon freshly grated orange zest
- 1/4 teaspoon vanilla extract
- 1 egg white, beaten
- 1/2 cup mango, diced
- 1/2 cup strawberries, diced
- juice of one orange

Direction

- In a bowl, combine flour, baking powder, baking soda and salt. In another bowl, whisk buttermilk, ricotta, honey, oil, orange zest and vanilla. With wire whisk, fold wet ingredients into flour mixture until just blended. Using rubber spatula, gently fold egg white into batter until just blended. Fold the mango, strawberries, and orange juice into the batter until just blended. Spoon batter into heated skillet and cook pancakes on both sides until golden brown. Serve warm.
- 6 servings

204. Maple Wholewheat Pancakes Recipe

Serving: 2 | Prep: | Cook: 10mins | Ready in:

Ingredients

- 1 1/2 cups whole wheat flour
- 1/2 cup all purpose flour
- 3 teaspoons baking powder
- 3/4 teaspoon salt
- 1 3/4 cups milk
- 1/3 cup maple syrup
- 1 large egg
- 1/4 cup butter or margarine, softened

Direction

- Combine the whole wheat flour, all-purpose flour, baking powder, and salt in a large bowl.
- Whisk to blend thoroughly.
- In a separate bowl, whisk together the milk, maple syrup, egg, and the melted butter.
- Make a well in the dry ingredients and pour in the egg mixture.
- Stir until well moistened.
- The batter will contain some lumps.
- Set the batter aside.
- Place griddle over medium heat.

- Brush the surface with vegetable oil or rub with a strip of uncooked bacon as the griddle warms.
- When the griddle is hot, stir the batter, adding more milk if necessary to create a consistency like thick heavy cream.
- Since the batter is thick only take up about 1/4 cup of the batter when pouring onto the hot griddle.
- Cook until the bubbles that have formed around the outside edge are broken.
- Turn pancakes over and cook the other side.
- Stir in additional milk as needed to maintain a pourable consistency.

205. Marlboro Three Grain Pancakes Recipe

Serving: 4 | Prep: | Cook: | Ready in:

Ingredients

- 1/2 cup quick cooking oatmeal
- 1/2 cup yellow cornmeal
- 2 cups buttermilk
- 1 egg, beaten
- 1 TBS oil
- 1 cup whole wheat flour
- 2 TBS light brown sugar
- 1 tsp shredded orange peel
- 1 tsp baking soda
- 1/2 tsp salt
- 1/2 cup pecan pieces
- butter Stewed Fruit:
- 3 lg or 4 sm pears or apples, core and chop
- 1/4 cup orange juice
- 2 TBS butter
- 1/4 cup dried blueberries
- 1/2 cup light brown sugar
- dash salt

Direction

- Butter Stewed Fruit: Sprinkle pears or apples with orange juice. Melt butter in a skillet, add the fruit and blueberries. Cook over medium heat until orange juice boils. Sprinkle with brown sugar and salt. Cook over low heat, uncovered, until tender and liquid is reduced, about 12 minutes. Fruit may be stewed ahead of time and kept covered and refrigerated for up to 3 days. Makes 3 cups.
- Pancakes: Combine oatmeal and cornmeal in mixing bowl; stir in buttermilk and let stand 10 minutes, stirring occasionally. Stir in egg and oil.
- Combine flour, brown sugar, orange peel, baking soda and salt. Add to first mixture and stir until smooth. Add pecans.
- Heat griddle over medium heat; lightly coat with oil. Pour 1/3 cup of batter for each pancake, spreading to make a 4-5" circle. Cook until edges lose their wet and shiny look, about 1 minute; flip pancake. Cook second side until brown and baked through, about 1 minute. Continue until all batter is used.

206. Marshmallow Milk Pancakes Recipe

Serving: 8 | Prep: | Cook: 3mins | Ready in:

Ingredients

- marshmallow milk Pancakes
- 1 ¼ cups all purpose flour
- 4 big marshmallows
- 2 tsp. baking powder
- 1 beaten egg
- 1 cup of milk
- 1 Tbsp. cooking oil
- ½ tsp. salt
- 1 tsp. vanilla
- 1 or 2 big marshmallows cut in small pieces

Direction

- In a small saucepan put the milk and marshmallows until melted.
- Stir together flour, baking powder and salt.
- Combine egg, marshmallow milk, vanilla, and oil.
- Mix or blend perfectly with the flour mixture.
- Pour about ¼ cup batter onto a hot lightly greased skillet, this is very important.
- Wait about 1 minute, just when it´s almost ready and sprinkle the marshmallow pieces.
- Turn to cook on the other side.
- Ready, enjoy!!

207. Matzah Brei Light And Airy Pancakes Recipe

Serving: 1 | Prep: | Cook: 5mins | Ready in:

Ingredients

- For each person use:
- 1 matzah board
- 1 egg, beaten
- fry pan with oil to fry and you may need to keep adding oil for making several batches.
- Toppings:
- syrup
- maple syrup
- jelly
- pie filling
- brown sugar and cinnamon
- Okay, ketchup, heinz of course.

Direction

- Break matzos in a large bowl and pour hot water over them.
- After a couple of minutes, pour water off, squeeze surplus water out, add other ingredients and mix well.
- Place oil in fry pan to heat, add mixture all at once and flatten out into a large cake. You can cut it in the pan while it is cooking, or make small individual ones. I always make individual ones. Per one serving you get maybe 3 cakes.
- Flip it when it starts getting crusty and I like mine very brown and crispy underneath.
- Don't worry if you can't flip the whole thing at once, I can't either. Why I make small ones. Like 3 to a pan
- Cook through until well done but still soft but crunchy.
- Serve immediately with maple syrup. Or just brown sugar or cinnamon on top, fruit topping, jelly or my favorite Ketchup! I KNOW I KNOW.
- I love this stuff, almost as much as potato pancakes.

208. Metabolism Boosting Healthy Pancakes Recipe

Serving: 6 | Prep: | Cook: 36mins | Ready in:

Ingredients

- 2 cups blueberries
- ½ cup maple syrup
- 1 cup almond milk
- 1 cup nonfat plain yogurt
- ½ cup rolled oats (not instant)
- 1 1/3 cups whole-wheat flour
- ¼ cup buckwheat flour
- ½ teaspoon aluminum-free baking powder
- ½ teaspoon baking soda
- 1 teaspoon ground cinnamon
- ¼ teaspoon salt
- 2 large eggs
- 2 tablespoons agave syrup, maple syrup or honey
- 1 tablespoon virgin coconut oil, melted and cooled, plus more for the pan
- 1 teaspoon vanilla extract

Direction

- 1. In a small saucepan, place the berries and maple syrup and bring to a simmer over medium-low heat. Simmer until the blueberries pop, approximately three minutes. Keep warm.

- 2. Whisk the almond milk and yogurt together in a medium bowl. Add the oats and mix well. Let stand for at least 15 minutes.
- 3. Combine the flours, baking powder, baking soda, cinnamon and salt in a large bowl.
- 4. Crack the eggs into a small bowl and lightly whisk. Add the agave syrup, oil and vanilla and whisk to combine. Pour mixture into the oat mixture.
- 5. Pour the egg mixture into the flour mixture and use a wooden spoon or rubber spatula to stir together just enough to combine. Be careful not to over mix; some lumps are fine.
- 6. Preheat the oven to 175 degrees.
- 7. Place a cast-iron griddle or large skillet over medium heat and melt 1 teaspoon oil. The pan is ready if a few droplets of water dropped on the surface jump and spit. If the water steams slowly, the pan is too cold, and if the water boils and evaporates immediately, the pan is too hot.
- 8. Spoon a heaping tablespoon of batter onto the griddle for each pancake. Cook for one-and-a-half to two minutes, until tiny bubbles appear on the surface of the pancake and a few of them burst. Flip pancake and cook for one-and-a-half to two minutes, or until browned. Place the cooked pancakes directly on a rack in the oven to keep warm. Repeat until all of the batter is cooked, using another teaspoon of coconut oil to re-grease the griddle if necessary. The batter should make 18 pancakes.
- 9. Place three pancakes on a plate. Spoon the berries and syrup on top, dividing evenly among the plates. Serve six.

209. Milk Egg Wheat Gluten Corn Free Buckwheat Pancakes Recipe

Serving: 3 | Prep: | Cook: 20mins | Ready in:

Ingredients

- 1 cup buckwheat flour
- 1 tsp gluten and corn free baking powder
- 2 Tbsp sugar
- 1/2 tsp salt
- 2 Tbsp potato starch
- 1 cup + a little more coconut milk
- 2 Tbsp olive oil

Direction

- Heat the skillet to medium heat while you are preparing the batter. (You don't want the skillet too hot; due to the thickness of the batter, they take a little while longer to cook than regular pancakes, so too hot will result in burning the edges and a raw middle.)
- Combine the dry ingredients.
- Mix in the coconut milk and oil until the batter is smooth.
- Make sure that the skillet is hot, water will sizzle and jump if you put just a drop on.
- Pour pancakes to the size that you prefer. I use a serving spoon or a ladle to do this. Because this batter is thick, you may have to even out the cake with the back of your spoon, this also makes it difficult to get perfectly round cakes. . .
- When bubbles start forming around the edges, cover the cakes with a lid for thirty seconds to a minute; this will stiffen up the top of the batter just enough so it doesn't drizzle off when you flip it.
- When the pancake has bubbles throughout, flip it. Depending on how thick your cake is, you might not get a lot of bubbles.
- Cover with the lid again for at least part of the time, so that you ensure cooking throughout.
- When cut, the cakes will be dense, but should not be sticky in the middle.
- Serve and enjoy!

- If you are making a larger batch to serve, you can put the cakes on a cookie sheet and cover with tin foil and keep them in an oven set to warm.

210. Miniature Dutch Apple Pancakes Recipe

Serving: 4 | Prep: | Cook: 20mins | Ready in:

Ingredients

- 1 tablespoon unsalted butter
- 1 large granny smith apple peeled, cored and cut into 1/2" slices
- 3 tablespoons granulated sugar
- 1/2 teaspoon ground cinnamon
- 3 large eggs
- 3/4 cup all purpose flour
- 3/4 cup milk
- 1 tablespoon sour cream
- 1/8 teaspoon salt
- 1 teaspoon grated lemon zest
- Confectioner's sugar for dusting

Direction

- Preheat oven to 400.
- Spray two 6-1/2 inch tapas pans with non-stick cooking spray.
- In a non-stick sauté pan over medium heat melt the butter.
- Add apple, granulated sugar and cinnamon and sauté stirring constantly for 5 minutes.
- Remove from heat and set aside.
- In a large bowl whisk the eggs until lightly frothy.
- Add flour, milk, sour cream, salt and lemon zest and whisk just until a smooth batter forms.
- Immediately divide the batter between the prepared pans.
- Divide the apple mixture between the pans trying to keep the apple slices on top of the batter.
- Bake until the pancakes are puffed and golden brown about 20 minutes.
- Dust with confectioners' sugar and serve immediately.

211. Mixed Flour Dosa Recipe

Serving: 0 | Prep: | Cook: 30mins | Ready in:

Ingredients

- wheat flour - 1 cup
- rice flour - 1/2 cup
- gram flour - 1/2 cup
- curd - 1/4th cup
- cumin seeds - 3/4th Teaspoon
- Tymol seeds - 1/4th Teaspoon
- ginger garlic paste - 1 teaspoon
- Few coriander leaves
- salt for taste
- water required to mix for a smooth paste
- oil - 1 teaspoon for each dosa

Direction

- 1. Mix all the above ingredients in a vessel to make a smooth paste/batter. Keep aside for 20-25 mins.
- 2. Heat the pan.
- 3. Make thin dosas by spreading the paste/batter on the pan.
- 4. Spread oil all around the dosa and when the edges turn golden brown, flip the dosa. Wait for jus few seconds.
- 5. Delicious dosa is ready to be served.
- 6. Can be readily eaten or also served with pickles.

212. Mixed Berry Pancakes Recipe

Serving: 8 | Prep: | Cook: 2mins | Ready in:

Ingredients

- 1 cup (250g) self-raising flour
- 1 egg
- 1 1/2 cups (375ml) buttermilk (see note)
- 40g butter
- 200g frozen mixed berries
- 1 cup (250ml) maple syrup
- 1 vanilla bean, split
- mixed berries, extra, to serve

Direction

- Place the flour in a large bowl and make a well in the centre. Add the egg and buttermilk and stir until well combined. Set aside for 30 minutes to rest.
- Melt half the butter in a large non-stick frying pan over medium heat. Spoon 1/4 cup (60ml) of pancake mixture into the pan and sprinkle with mixed berries. Cook for 1 minute or until bubbles appear on the surface and pancakes are golden underneath. Turn and cook for 1 minute or until golden underneath. Transfer to a plate and cover with foil. Repeat with remaining batter and mixed berries, greasing pan between each batch.
- Place the maple syrup in a small saucepan. Use a small, sharp knife to scrape the vanilla seeds into the maple syrup and add the bean. Place over low heat and cook, stirring, for 2 minutes or until heated through.
- Place pancakes on serving plates and top with extra berries. Drizzle with maple syrup and serve immediately.

213. Momma Jans Buttermilk Pancakes Recipe

Serving: 6 | Prep: | Cook: 10mins | Ready in:

Ingredients

- 2 cups all-purpose flour
- 1 tsp baking powder
- 1tsp salt
- 1 tsp baking soda
- 2 tsp sugar
- 2 eggs
- 2 cups buttermilk
- 1/4 cup melt butter
- 1 tsp vanilla

Direction

- In a large bowl, mix together dry ingredients; flour, baking powder, salt, baking soda and sugar.
- In a small bowl, mix together wet ingredients; eggs, buttermilk, melted butter and vanilla.
- Pour liquids into dry mix, stirring completely until smooth. Let stand for 10-15 minutes before using.
- Using a scoop or a small measuring cup to distribute batter. Pour batter on to hot heated skillet or griddle that's been buttered or sprayed with a non-stick.
- Cook until bubbles form on top surface of batter and able to lift with a spatula, should look golden brown. Flip, cook for a 1-2 minutes more.
- Pancakes cook fast. Please watch closely as they can burn.
- Makes roughly 12 pancakes

214. Moms Rhubarb Pancakes Recipe

Serving: 5 | Prep: | Cook: 30mins | Ready in:

Ingredients

- 2 cups flour
- 3Tbsp sugar
- 3 tsp baking powder
- 1/4 tsp salt
- 1 cup milk
- 4 eggs
- 4-5 cups rhubarb, cut up finely
- couple Tbsp veg.oil

Direction

- If possible, the night before you want to make these, cut up your rhubarb and lay it on a cookie sheet lined with paper towel. This makes for a better batter. I know some of you have a hard time finding rhubarb, and I don't know if frozen will work. Have never tried it. Beg from someone who has a plant :o)
- Combine dry ingredients.
- Beat eggs with milk.
- Add wet to dry and beat till mixed. Batter will be stiff, but if too stiff to mix in fruit, thin with a bit of milk
- Stir in rhubarb.
- Heat a thin layer of oil in large frying pan over med heat. About 2-3 glub, glubs, you know, how the oil goes glub, glub, when you pour it. Mom used to practically deep fry these when we were younger. She got better with her oil after my Dad had triple by- pass. They do need more than just a brushing of oil though.
- Get a big serving spoon and drop a flapjack amount of batter into the pan and smooth it out so it's not too thick. Cook ' till browned on bottom and starting to dry on edges, then flip over and cook through. If your heat is too high you will get burned on the outside and raw in the middle. They need to cook gently. Add more oil as needed, letting it heat up before adding batter.
- Place on baking sheet in just turned on oven to keep warm as you make them.
- Serve sprinkled with sugar, and cinnamon (optional).

215. Multigrain Hot Cakes Recipe

Serving: 6 | Prep: | Cook: 10mins | Ready in:

Ingredients

- 1 cup all-purpose flour
- 3/4 cup whole wheat flour
- 1/4 cup wheat bran
- 1/4 cup wheat germ
- 3/4 cup oat bran
- 1/2 cup powdered buttermilk
- 3 cups water
- 1 tsp vanilla extract
- 2 eggs, slightly beaten

Direction

- Mix buttermilk powder with water and eggs.
- Slowly stir in other ingredients. Add extract lastly.
- Stir by hand or mixer until all lumps are gone.
- Ladle out 1/4 cup at a time onto a lightly greased, medium hot griddle. Turn when bubbles stay on top.
- Note: 3 cups of regular buttermilk can be substituted, but eliminate the water.

216. Multigrain Pancakes Recipe

Serving: 16 | Prep: | Cook: 4mins | Ready in:

Ingredients

- 3/4 cup whole wheat flour
- 1/2 cup oatmeal
- 2 tsp. baking powder
- 1/2 tsp. salt or to taste
- 2 eggs or equivalent egg substitute
- 4 tbsp. honey
- 1/2 cup unbleached all-purpose flour
- 1/4 cup yellow cornmeal
- 1 tsp. baking soda
- 4 tbsp. canola oil
- 2 (2 1/4 cups) low-fat buttermilk
- 1/2 cup chopped pecans

Direction

- Combine whole wheat and all-purpose flours, oatmeal, cornmeal, baking powder, baking

soda and salt in a food processor and process only to blend.
- Blend oil, eggs, 2 cups of buttermilk and honey together in a large bowl.
- Add flour mixture and stir just until blended.
- Fold in pecans.
- Heat a griddle or large skillet over medium-high heat.
- Brush with oil.
- Ladle a 1/4 cup-measure of batter onto griddle for each 4-inch pancake.
- Cook until golden brown on the bottom and small bubbles form on surface, about 1 minute.
- Turn and cook second side until brown.
- Adjust heat to keep pancakes from burning before cooking through.

217. Natural Cereal Pancakes Recipe

Serving: 4 | Prep: | Cook: 10mins | Ready in:

Ingredients

- 1 cup pancake mix
- 1 cup milk
- 1 egg
- 1 tablespoon liquid or melted shortening
- 1/3 cup Quaker 100% natural cereal
- Warm maple syrup

Direction

- Preheat griddle to hot.
- Combine pancake mix, milk, egg and shortening then mix until smooth.
- Stir in cereal.
- For each pancake pour 1/4 cup batter onto hot lightly greased griddle to make 8 pancakes.
- Turn pancakes when tops are covered with bubbles and edges look cooked turning only once.
- Serve with warm maple syrup.

218. No Oil Banana Pancakes Recipe

Serving: 4 | Prep: | Cook: 15mins | Ready in:

Ingredients

- 2 eggs
- 2 mashed bananas
- 1 cup milk
- 1-1/2 cups flour
- 1-1/2 teaspoons baking powder
- 1/4 teaspoon salt

Direction

- Mix eggs, bananas and milk well.
- Add flour, baking powder and salt.
- You may have to add extra milk to make the batter the right consistency.
- Pour out onto hot griddle in desired portions.
- Cook until browned on both sides.

219. Not Your Mammas Blueberry Ricotta Pancakes Recipe

Serving: 8 | Prep: | Cook: 35mins | Ready in:

Ingredients

- SERVING SIZE IS 2 PANCAKES
- 3 eggs, yolks and whites separated
- 3/4 cup ricotta cheese
- 1/4 cup plus 1 tablespoon sugar
- 3/4 teaspoon salt
- 1 tablespoon plus 1/2 teaspoon vanilla
- 2 1/4 cups milk
- 1 3/4 cups flour
- 1 1/4 teaspoons baking powder
- 1 1/2 pints blueberries

Direction

- In a large bowl, whisk together the egg yolks and ricotta cheese so that there are no large lumps of cheese, but make sure the mixture does not become too smooth (this will make the pancakes wet and grainy). Whisk in the sugar, salt and vanilla, then the milk.
- In a separate bowl, whisk together the flour and baking powder. Fold this into the egg batter just until no lumps remain.
- Separately, whip the egg whites to medium-stiff, shiny peaks, about 4 minutes. Gently fold these into the batter just until uniformly combined.
- Ladle a generous one-fourth cup of batter onto a medium-hot, lightly greased griddle for each pancake. Place 10 to 12 blueberries on each pancake and cook, about 2 minutes per side, until the cakes are golden-brown and cooked through. Serve immediately with maple syrup on the side.
- Each serving: 276 calories; 10 grams protein; 41 grams carbohydrates; 2 grams fiber; 8 grams fat; 4 grams saturated fat; 98 mg. cholesterol; 369 mg. sodium.

220. Nutella Pancakes Recipe

Serving: 2 | Prep: | Cook: 30mins | Ready in:

Ingredients

- 1 1/4 cups all purpose flour
- 1 tsp baking soda
- 1/4 tsp salt
- 1 tbsp sugar
- 2 tbsp nutella
- 1 large egg
- 1 1/2 cups buttermilk

Direction

- In a large bowl, whisk together flour, baking soda, salt and sugar.
- In a medium bowl, whisk together Nutella and the egg. When smooth, beat in buttermilk.
- Pour the wet ingredients into the dry ingredients and stir until just combined.
- Heat a griddle or frying pan over high heat until a drop of water on the surface skips around.
- Lightly grease it with butter or oil and drop batter into 3-inch rounds. The color is a bit hard to judge with chocolate pancakes, but they are ready to flip when the edges look slightly dry and the center of the pancake stops producing bubbles. Turn over and cook for another minute or two in the other side.
- Serve immediately, with more Nutella or maple syrup.

221. Nutty Breakfast Rolls Recipe

Serving: 4 | Prep: | Cook: | Ready in:

Ingredients

- 1/2 cup Skippyy Creamy, Super Chunky or roasted honey Nut peanut butter
- 8 hot cooked pancakes
- 2 medium bananas, halved lengthwise, then crosswise

Direction

- Evenly spread Skippy Creamy Peanut Butter on hot pancakes, then top with bananas; roll up. Serve, if desired, cut in pieces with maple syrup.
- VARIATIONS:
- Apple Cinnamon: Stir in 1/4 cup applesauce and 1/2 teaspoon ground cinnamon to Peanut Butter.
- Cinnamon: Stir in 1/2 teaspoon ground cinnamon to Peanut Butter.
- Chocolate Chip: Stir in 1/4 cup semi-sweet chocolate chips to Peanut Butter.
- Cinnamon Raisin: Stir in 1/2 teaspoon ground cinnamon and 1/4 cup raisins to Peanut Butter.

222. Nutty Breakfast Rolls For Kids Recipe

Serving: 4 | Prep: | Cook: 5mins | Ready in:

Ingredients

- 1/2 cup peanut butter of your choice
- 8 hot cooked pancakes
- 2 medium bananas, halved lengthwise, then crosswise

Direction

- Prepare pancakes according to package directions or use your own favorite recipe.
- Evenly spread peanut butter on hot pancakes, then top with cut up bananas; roll up. Serve cut pieces with maple syrup if desired.
- VARIATIONS:
- Apple Cinnamon - stir 1/4 cup applesauce and 1/2 tsp. ground cinnamon into peanut butter
- Cinnamon - stir 1/2 tsp. cinnamon into peanut butter
- Chocolate Chip - stir 1/4 c semi-sweet chocolate chips into peanut butter (can also mix into pancake batter and cook).
- Cinnamon Raisin - Stir i1/2 tsp. ground cinnamon and 1/2 c raisins into peanut butter.

223. Oatmeal Buttermilk Pancakes Recipe

Serving: 4 | Prep: | Cook: 20mins | Ready in:

Ingredients

- 1-1/2 cup uncooked oatmeal
- 2 cups buttermilk
- 3 egg whites
- 1 cup whole wheat flour
- 2 teaspoon baking soda
- 2 tablespoons brown sugar or less or none

Direction

- Combine oatmeal, buttermilk and egg whites.
- Let stand for at least 1/2 hour or refrigerate up to 24 hours.
- Add remaining ingredients and stir batter just until the dry ingredients are moistened.
- Bake on a hot lightly oiled griddle.

224. Oatmeal Cottage Cheese Pancakes Recipe

Serving: 12 | Prep: | Cook: 15mins | Ready in:

Ingredients

- 1/2 cup oatmeal
- 1/2 cup cottage cheese
- 1 tsp vanilla (omit if making savory)
- 2 egg whites
- 1 whole egg
- Optional:
- orange/lemon/lime zest
- black pepper/red pepper flakes
- minced chive/garlic/shallot
- bacon crumbles

Direction

- Put all ingredients in blender, blend until well incorporated and almost smooth, about 5 minutes.
- Heat up a skillet on medium heat, lightly smear with the oil of your choice.
- Pour a scant tablespoon for each pancake, silver dollar size. Cook until bubbles form and it's nice and brown, turn.
- Eat them with maple syrup, jam, honey, agave, lemon and powdered sugar, or, if savory, sour cream or yogurt, greens, crème fraiche or just drizzled with a tasty oil.

225. Oatmeal Pancake Mix Recipe

Serving: 8 | Prep: | Cook: 6mins | Ready in:

Ingredients

- 4 cups quick cooking oats
- 2 cups all-purpose flour
- 2 cups whole wheat flour
- 1 cup brown sugar
- 1 cup non-fat dry milk
- 2 tablespoons cinnamon
- 5 teaspoons salt
- 3 tablespoons baking powder
- 1/2 teaspoon cream of tartar

Direction

- Combine all ingredients and stir to mix well. Store in refrigerator.
- Makes about 8 cups.
- Directions for cooking pancakes:
- In a medium mixing bowl, beat 2 eggs. Beat in 1/3 cup of vegetable oil gradually. Alternately beat in 2 cups pancake mix and 1 cup of water. Pour in large spoonfuls into a lightly greased skillet over medium-high heat, and cook until the tops show broken bubbles, about 2 to 3 minutes. Turn and cook about 2 to 3 minutes more, until golden brown. Makes about 12 5-inch pancakes.

226. Oatmeal Pancakes Recipe

Serving: 4 | Prep: | Cook: 15mins | Ready in:

Ingredients

- 1 1/3 cups water
- 1/2 cup old-fashioned oats
- 5 tablespoons butter, diced, plus more for frying
- 1 1/3 cups all purpose flour
- 1 cup (packed) golden brown sugar
- 2 large eggs
- 1 teaspoon ground cinnamon
- 1 teaspoon baking powder
- 1/4 teaspoon (generous) salt
- 1/4 teaspoon (scant) ground nutmeg

Direction

- Preheat oven to 250°F. Place large baking sheet in oven. Stir 1 1/3 cups water, oats, and 5 tablespoons butter in heavy medium saucepan over medium-high heat until mixture comes to boil. Cook until mixture is very thick, stirring constantly, about 5 minutes. Transfer to large bowl and cool 15 minutes. Stir in flour, sugar, eggs, cinnamon, baking powder, salt, and nutmeg.
- Heat griddle or 2 large non-stick skillets over medium-high heat. Brush with butter. Drop batter onto griddle or skillets by generous 1/2 cup for each pancake; spread batter to 4- to 5-inch rounds. Cook pancakes until brown and cooked through, about 4 minutes per side. Place on baking sheet in oven to keep warm. Repeat with remaining batter

227. Oatmeal Pancakes From Pancake Recipes On The Net Recipe

Serving: 4 | Prep: | Cook: 4mins | Ready in:

Ingredients

- 2 eggs
- 2½ cups milk
- 2 tablespoons vinegar
- ½ cup sugar or 1 tablespoon sweetener
- 1 cup oatmeal

- 1 teaspoon soda
- 2½ cups flour (more if needed)
- 1 tablespoon salad oil
- 2 handfuls of raisins (optional)
- 1 teaspoon cinnamon (optional)

Direction

- Blend together and fry on well-greased griddle over medium heat.

228. Oatmeal Pancakes With Butter Milk Syrup Recipe

Serving: 8 | Prep: | Cook: 15mins | Ready in:

Ingredients

- 1 Cup whole wheat flour
- 1 Cup old fashioned oats
- 1/4 Cup wheat germ
- 1/4 Cup dry milk Powder
- 1 Tablespoon brown sugar
- 1 teaspoon baking soda
- 2 eggs
- 2 Cups buttermilk
- 1/4 Cup oil
- Syrup:
- 1 Cup sugar
- 1/4 Cup butter
- 1 Tablespoon light corn syrup
- 3/4 Cup buttermilk
- 1 teaspoon vanilla

Direction

- Mix dry ingredients, for the pancakes.
- In another bowl, beat eggs, buttermilk and oil, mixing well.
- Stir into dry ingredients, just until blended.
- Pour about 1/4 cup for each pancake onto hot, greased griddle, cook.
- For syrup:
- Combine sugar, butter and corn syrup in a saucepan, bring to boil and boil, stirring for about 5 minutes or until golden brown.
- Remove from heat and stir in buttermilk and vanilla, let stand about 5 minutes, stir and serve with pancakes(or) if any is left after breakfast, this syrup is good on crisp, buttered toast.

229. Oatmeal Spice Pancakes W/ Peach Compote Recipe

Serving: 18 | Prep: | Cook: 30mins | Ready in:

Ingredients

- 3 peaches
- 1 Tablespoon Splenda brown sugar Blend
- 1 Tablespoon lemon juice
- 1 Star Anise
- 1 Teaspoon vanilla extract
- 1 1/2 cups oat flour (I chop up my dry minute oatmeal in the blender)
- 2 Tablespoons Truvia (Stevia crystals)
- 1 Tablespoon baking powder
- 1/4 Teaspoon allspice
- 1/4 Teaspoon nutmeg
- 20 grams debittered brewer's yeast
- 2 Omega eggs
- 1/2 cup puréed peaches
- 1 1/2 cups 1% milk
- 3/4 cups white flour
- 2 Tablespoons liquid coconut oil

Direction

- For the compote.
- Roughly chop the three peaches.
- In a saucepan stir together the peaches, brown sugar, lemon juice, star anise, and vanilla extract.
- On medium heat bring the mixture to a steady simmer, stirring occasionally.
- Allow the compote to reduce to your desired richness, about ten minutes.

- The Pancakes
- Stir together the dry ingredients; oat flour, white flour, Truvia, baking powder, brewer's yeast and spices.
- In a separate bowl whisk together the eggs, peach purée and milk. Add quickly in to the dry mixture and mix until just combined. There will be lumps.
- Heat a griddle on medium low heat, and brush with a little coconut oil.
- Drop batter by heaping tablespoons on to the griddle, and flip when well browned. Allow the pancake to brown on the second side.
- Serve with peach compote and Greek yogurt.
- I sprinkled a little icing sugar.
- Heat cooking spray sprayed frying pan keep on medium heat.
- In a smaller bowl add berries and thaw and heat in microwave. Remove from microwave and stir in Splenda to sweeten.
- In another bowl combine liquids stirring well.
- Make a well in center of dry ingredients and pour in liquid stir well to mix.
- Drop by spoonfuls into hot skillet.
- Cook a few minutes each side.
- Serve with Splenda sweetened berries in place of syrup.
- With berry syrup it is 5 Weight watcher points if following the Flex Plan.
- If following The Core plan THESE Are Core.
- ENJOY.

230. Oatpancakes Recipe

Serving: 1 | Prep: | Cook: 35mins | Ready in:

Ingredients

- 1/2 cup Large flake oatmeal
- 3/4 tsp baking powder
- 1/8 tsp salt
- 1/4 tsp baking soda
- 3/4 tsp cinnamon
- 1/4 cup fat free plain yogurt (can use fat free vanilla ... if using vanilla yogurt leave out vanilla extract)
- 8 tsp fat free buttermilk (can use 1 tsp fat free sour cream and 7 tsp skim milk if out of Buttermilk)
- 1/2 tsp vanilla extract
- 1 extra large egg white
- syrup
- 1 cup frozen mixed berries
- 2 tsp splenda

Direction

- Process oats in food processor until fine, put in medium bowl. Add rest of dry ingredients combine well.

231. Old World Recipe Squash Latkes Recipe

Serving: 4 | Prep: | Cook: 10mins | Ready in:

Ingredients

- 3 medium Mexican squash, zucchini, or yellow squash (see picture of the Mexican squash, if you don't know what it is)
- 2 eggs
- 1/3 cup sugar
- pinch salt
- 1/2 tsp baking soda
- all purpose flour
- cooking oil

Direction

- Rinse the squash, chop off the navel and stem, if any.
- Shred the squash using a coarse grater
- Stir in eggs, salt, sugar, mix very well
- Add baking soda, stir some more
- Add flour in small batches until thick batter forms. It should be like buttermilk in texture, maybe a little thicker
- Heat 4-5 tbsp. oil in a skillet

- Spoon your latkes onto the skillet and fry over medium heat on both sides until pleasantly browned.
- Serve with sour cream or plain yogurt on the side.
- Alternatively, dust some confectioner sugar over before serving

232. Orange Cloud Pancakes Recipe

Serving: 12 | Prep: | Cook: 5mins | Ready in:

Ingredients

- 3/4 cup (6 ounces) cottage cheese or ricotta
- 3 large eggs, separated
- 4 tablespoons (1/2 stick, 2 ounces) butter, melted
- 1 tablespoon orange juice
- 1/2 cup (2 ounces) King Arthur white whole wheat flour
- 1 tablespoon sugar
- 1/2 teaspoon salt
- pinch of ground cinnamon
- 1 tablespoon orange zest or 1/8 teaspoon orange oil

Direction

- Place the cottage cheese, egg yolks, melted butter, and orange juice in a food process or blender, and process until the cottage cheese is smooth, about 30 seconds. Add the flour, sugar, salt, and cinnamon, and process again. Scrape the mixture into a medium bowl and stir in the orange zest or oil. Let this mixture rest for 10 minutes.
- In the bowl of your electric mixer, whip the egg whites until they're stiff but not dry. Use a rubber spatula to stir a spoonful of the whites into the batter to loosen it, and then gently fold in the rest of the whites. This batter doesn't need to rest; cook the pancakes right away, as directed below.
- Pour the batter in 1/3-cupfuls onto a preheated griddle. Cook the pancakes till golden brown on both sides. Serve immediately; they don't hold well in the oven.
- Yield: about a dozen 4" pancakes.

233. Orange Pancakes Recipe

Serving: 6 | Prep: | Cook: 10mins | Ready in:

Ingredients

- 2 cups biscuit mix (I prefer Bisquick)
- 1/2 cup orange juice
- 1/2 cup milk
- 2 eggs

Direction

- Mix all ingredients well, cook on a well-heated, buttered griddle. Enjoy!

234. Orange Ricotta Pancakes Recipe

Serving: 4 | Prep: | Cook: 20mins | Ready in:

Ingredients

- 2 large eggs (wet)
- 1/4 cup melted unsalted butter (1/2 stick) (wet)
- 1 cup milk (wet)
- 1 cup ricotta (wet)
- 1 medium-sized orange (juice and zest) (wet)
- 1/4 cup sugar (wet)
- 1/4 cup light brown sugar (wet)
- 1 1/4 cup unbleached all-purpose flour (dry)
- 1 tbsp. baking powder (dry)
- 1 tsp. cinnamon (dry)
- 1/4 tsp. clove (dry)
- 1/4 tsp. nutmeg (dry)

Direction

- Whisk the wet ingredients (yes, this includes the sugar) together in a small bowl. In a large bowl, whisk the dry ingredients together.
- Once they are thoroughly mixed, pour the wet ingredients on top of the dry. Using a rubber spatula or large spoon, mix until all of the dry stuff is wet and there are no large lumps. Tons of little lumps are great! (NOTE: You do not want to overstir this until it's smooth. If you do, gluten will form and the result will be a chewier, more bread-like pancake.)
- Place a non-stick griddle or large skillet over medium heat. Once hot, pour about a quarter cup of mixture onto the pan. (NOTE: You can tell how hot the griddle is by throwing a few drops of water on the surface. If the water dances — it shimmers and shakes — then it is hot enough. If the water sizzles fast and evaporates quickly, it's too hot. Turn it down and let it cool.)
- Cook about 4 minutes on one side. This is very tricky because the cook time will vary based on a number of things — but there are two visual cues to look for. First, is the amount of darkness on the side facing down. If it is starting to turn to a dark brown, go ahead and turn it. Second, bubbles on the surface side. If you have the right temperature bubbles will form. When they begin to set and are slow to disappear, the pancake is ready for turning. They should cook about 75% on the first side.
- Once flipped, cook them for another minute or until they take on a nice brown glow. They won't be nearly as pretty as the first side, but you can put that side face down!
- You can serve them right away, or cover with a towel and place in a warm oven until you are ready to serve. Once ready, coat with powdered sugar and eat with or without syrup of your choice. Enjoy!

235. Oven Apple Pancakes With Cider Sauce Recipe

Serving: 6 | Prep: | Cook: 20mins | Ready in:

Ingredients

- 1 1/2 cups flour
- 1/2 cup sugar
- 4 eggs
- 2 1/2 cups milk
- Put all ingredients in blender and whirl until smooth.
- Preheat oven to 425. Preheat 6 6" cast iron skillets in hot oven for 3 minutes.
- Remove and spray with Pam. Divide batter among 6 skillets and bake for 20 minutes.
- Remove pancakes from skillet, top with apples and cider sauce. Serves 6.
- Fried Apples:
- Melt one tablespoon of butter in a skillet. Peel and slice 4 apples. Fry apples in butter, adding brown sugar, cloves and cinnamon to taste.

Direction

- Cider Sauce:
- 1 cup sugar
- 2 tablespoons cornstarch
- 1/2 teaspoon pumpkin pie spice
- 2 cups apple cider
- 2 tablespoons lemon juice
- 1/4 cup butter
- Mix sugar, cornstarch and pie spice in a saucepan. Stir in cider and lemon juice. Cook, stirring constantly, until thickens and boils. Boil and stir for 2 minutes, remove from heat and add butter.

236. Oven Baked Pancakes Recipe

Serving: 6 | Prep: | Cook: 10mins | Ready in:

Ingredients

- 2 Cups package pancake mix
- 1 1/2 Cups milk
- 1 egg
- 2 Tbsp cooking oil
- 1/2 tsp. ground cinnamon
- 1/2 Cup blueberries, optional
- 1/4 Cup semisweet chocolate chips, optional
- 2 Tbsp cooked bacon pieces, optional
- butter & syrup

Direction

- Preheat oven to 425 degrees. In a medium mixing bowl stir together pancake mix, milk, egg, cooking oil & cinnamon. (Batter will have small lumps)
- Stir in the blueberries, chocolate chips or bacon if desired. Pour into a greased 15 1/2x10 1/2x1 inch baking dish.
- Bake about 10 minutes or until done. Cut into squares and serve with butter & syrup.

237. Oven Pancake Recipe

Serving: 6 | Prep: | Cook: 28mins | Ready in:

Ingredients

- 3 eggs
- 1/2 cup flour
- 1/2 cup milk
- 1/4 tsp salt
- 2 T melted butter

Direction

- Preheat oven to 450°.
- Beat the eggs with a fork to blend.
- Slowly add flour, beating constantly.
- Stir in salt, milk, and butter.
- Grease a 10", oven-proof skillet and pour batter in.
- Bake 18 minutes at 450°.
- Then lower heat to 350° and bake 10 minutes more.
- Serve with melted butter (or lemon juice) and powdered sugar, or fresh fruit and whipped cream.

238. Oven Pancakes Swedish American Recipe

Serving: 4 | Prep: | Cook: 30mins | Ready in:

Ingredients

- 3 eggs
- 3 cups milk
- 1 1/2 cups flour
- 2 Tablespoons sugar
- 1/2 t baking powder
- 1/2 t salt
- 2 Tablespoons butter or bacon drippings
- Use 2 large 4 1/2 by 9 inch loaf pans
- (or increase recipe by 1/3 again to fit a 9 by 13 inch pan)

Direction

- Beat eggs and salt.
- Gradually mix in remaining ingredients (except butter and bacon drippings.
- Preheat oven to 400 degrees F.
- Put pans in oven with butter or drippings in them; let them get hot, but don't brown butter.
- Add egg mixture and bake on lower rack for 15 minutes until they rise up in "bubbles."
- Then move to upper rack for 15 more minutes or until lightly brown.
- Serve hot with cranberry sauce, fruit syrup or jam on top. We use lingonberries cooked, or preserves from Sweden, found at some grocery stores in America.

239. P M S Pancakes Recipe

Serving: 6 | Prep: | Cook: 30mins | Ready in:

Ingredients

- 2 cups flour
- 1/4 cup cocoa
- 1/2 cup sugar, or other sweetener (with the use of applesauce   sweetener is not really needed, 1/4 cup honey would be great in this)
- 1 tablespoon baking powder
- 1/2 teaspoon sea salt
- 2 cups milk
- 1/2 cup apple sauce or 1/4 cup of sweet creamy butter, or 1/4 cup olive oil
- 1 teaspoon vanilla
- chocolate chips or I prefer chocolate chunks! Dark and White chocolate!

Direction

- Mix all dry ingredients.
- Make a well and add liquids.
- Mix well.
- Add more or less liquids to your desired consistency.
- Pour enough batter for a pancake on a preheated skillet.
- I use about 1/4 to 1/3 of a cup of batter and I have the most perfect pancake pan so they come out very nice,
- Sprinkle with chocolate chips.
- Flip when edge is dry-ish.
- Cook until done, careful the melted chocolate chips stick to your spatula.
- We served these with chocolate whipped topping that you get in the can and hot fudge topping or chocolate syrup.
- Maraschino Cherries are great on these also!
- -
- These are a heavier pancake due to the use of the apple sauce.
- Use butter or olive oil to make them lighter and fluffier.

240. Pancake Breakfast Muffin Recipe

Serving: 1 | Prep: | Cook: 5mins | Ready in:

Ingredients

- pancake mix
- Sasauge
- bacon

Direction

- Mix Pancake mix
- Then put all the sausage, bacon, etc. into muffin pan.
- Put the pancake mix in with the ingredients.
- Let bake till lightly brown!
- Eat up!
- Now comment on my page!

241. Pancake Breakfast For A King Recipe

Serving: 10 | Prep: | Cook: 3mins | Ready in:

Ingredients

- 2 and a half cups self rising flour
- 2 large eggs
- 1 fourth cup sugar
- 1 half teaspoon vanilla flavoring
- 1 and a half cup milk
- 4-6 eggs scrambled
- 1/2 to 1lb. bacon fried

Direction

- Preheat skillet.
- In medium to large bowl mix flour, eggs, sugar and vanilla flavoring.
- Add milk to the consistency you would like for pancake batter. Add more milk, about 1 tablespoon at a time for thinner pancakes.

Spray skillet with cooking spray, or butter. Pour batter onto skillet until it's rounded into 8" to 10". Cook for about 1 and a half minutes on both sides. You should have a nice golden brown color. When pancake is done lay 1 or 2 strips of cooked bacon onto center. Next add a heaping tablespoon of scrambled eggs on top of bacon. Roll up and it's ready to eat. You can add nuts, chocolate chips or fruit such as strawberries or blueberries to this recipe. Gourmet Sigon cinnamon adds a nice flavor as well

242. Pancake Snowmen Recipe

Serving: 68 | Prep: | Cook: 5mins | Ready in:

Ingredients

- 1 cup Hungry Jack buttermilk pancake mix
- 3/4 cup water
- 1/3 cup (1 small) mashed banana
- 1/4 cup chocolate chips
- 1 to 2 tsp. powdered sugar

Direction

- Heat griddle or large skillet to 375. Grease lightly with oil. Griddle is ready when small drops of water on griddle sizzle and disappear almost immediately. In medium bowl, combine pancake mix, water and banana. Stir just until large lumps disappear. Using about 1/4 cup batter for each snowman, pour 2 pancakes, one slightly smaller than the other, onto greased griddle with sides touching to resemble snowman. Cook 1 to 1-1/2 minutes. Turn when edges look cooked and bubbles begin to break on surface. Cook 1 to 1-1/2 minutes.
- While cooking second side, place chocolate chips on surface to resemble eyes, nose, mouth and buttons. Remove from griddle; sprinkle lightly with powdered sugar. 6-8 pancakes.

243. Pancakes From Scratch Recipe

Serving: 8 | Prep: | Cook: 15mins | Ready in:

Ingredients

- 2 cups flour
- 1-3/4 cup milk
- 2 heaping tablespoons baking powder
- 2 eggs beaten
- 1/4 cup melted butter
- 3 tablespoons sugar
- 1 teaspoon salt

Direction

- Mix dry ingredients.
- Combine eggs and melted butter to milk and slowly stir in the flour.
- Heat pan then pour batter in pan to desired size and cook until browned on both sides.

244. Pancakes Recipe

Serving: 4 | Prep: | Cook: 3mins | Ready in:

Ingredients

- 1 cup (140 grams) all purpose flour
- 1 1/2 teaspoons (7 grams) baking powder
- 1/4 teaspoon salt
- 2 tablespoons (28 grams) white sugar
- 1 cup (240 ml) milk
- 2 tablespoons (28 grams) unsalted butter, melted
- Extra melted butter for pan

Direction

- In large bowl whisk together the flour, baking powder, salt and sugar.

- In a separate bowl combine the egg, milk and melted butter.
- Add egg mixture to flour mixture and whisk until just combined.
- The batter should have small lumps.
- Do not overmix as the pancakes will be tough.
- Heat a frying or griddle over medium high heat until hot.
- Using a pastry brush, brush cooking surface with a little melted butter.
- Pour about 1/4 cup of batter into pan, spacing pancakes a few inches from each other.
- When bubbles appear on the top surface of the pancakes, 2 to 3 minutes, turn cakes.
- Cook until lightly browned, about 1 to 2 minutes.
- Serve immediately with butter and/or maple syrup.
- Makes about 8 3" cakes OR 3 8" cakes (I made 8"ers!)
- For blueberry pancakes, fold in blueberries.
- For bacon pancakes, fold in chipped up bacon.

245. Pancakes Never Fail I Promise Recipe

Serving: 2 | Prep: | Cook: 5mins | Ready in:

Ingredients

- 1 egg
- 1 tbs sugar I use half splenda
- 1/4 tsp salt
- 1 cup milk
- 1 cup all purpose flour
- 2 tsp baking powder
- 1 tbs melted butter or veg oil
- 1 tsp vanilla or almond or your favorite

Direction

- Beat together egg, salt, sugar, milk and flavoring. Sift together flour and baking powder and mix into liquid until almost smooth. Add melted butter. Cook. Makes 4.

- Serve with topping of choice. I enjoy these with melted chocolate chips first or sugar free jams.

246. Pancakes With Caramel Bananas And Pecan Nuts Recipe

Serving: 5 | Prep: | Cook: 7mins | Ready in:

Ingredients

- 2/3 cup all-purpose flour
- 1/2 cup whole wheat flour
- 1/2 cup rolled oats
- 1 teaspoon baking powder
- pinch of salt
- 2 T golden sugar
- 1 egg
- 1 T sunflower oil, plus oil for frying
- 1 cup low fat milk
- For the caramel bananas and pecan nuts
- 4 T butter
- 1 T maple syrup
- 3 bananas, halved and quartered
- 1/4 cup pecan nuts
- Makes 10

Direction

- Mix together the flours, oats, baking powder, salt and sugar.
- Make a well in center of flour mixture, add egg, oil and a quarter of milk.
- Mix well, gradually add rest of milk. Leave to rest for 20 minutes in refrigerator.
- Heat a large heavy frying pan. Using 2 T of batter for each pancake.
- Cook for 3 min. on each side or until golden. Keep warm.
- Wipe out bottom of pan and add butter. Heat slowly add syrup, add bananas and nuts.
- Cook 4 min. turning once.

- Place 2 pancakes on each warm plate, top with caramel bananas and pecan nuts.

247. Peach Pancakes With Peachy Berry Sauce Recipe

Serving: 10 | Prep: | Cook: 1hours | Ready in:

Ingredients

- Ingredients
- 1 cup all-purpose flour
- 2 Tablespoons cornmeal
- 1 Tablespoon sugar
- 1 teaspoon baking powder
- 1/2 teaspoon baking soda
- 1/2 teaspoon ground cinnamon
- 1/3 teaspoon salt
- 3/4 cup milk
- 2 peaches for 3/4 cup peach puree (see below)
- 1 egg, beaten
- 2 Tablespoons cooking oil

Direction

- Peachy-Berry Sauce:
- 1/2 cup maple syrup
- 1 cup fresh raspberries, blackberries, blueberries, or a combination
- 1 cup thinly sliced, peeled peaches or nectarines or a combination
- Peach Puree:
- Pit, peel, and quarter 2 large peaches.
- Place in a food processor bowl or blender container. Cover and process or blend until smooth.
- Pancake Batter:
- In a bowl, stir together flour, cornmeal, sugar, baking powder, baking soda, cinnamon, and salt.
- Make a well in center of dry mixture; set aside.
- In another bowl, combine milk, peach puree, egg, and cooking oil.
- Add milk mixture all at once to the dry mixture. Stir until just moistened (batter should be lumpy).
- Pour 1/4 cup of batter onto hot, lightly greased griddle or heavy skillet. Cook over medium heat for about 2 minutes on each side or until pancakes are golden brown, turning to second side when pancakes have bubbly surfaces and edges are slightly dry. Serve warm with peachy-berry sauce.
- Peachy-Berry Sauce:
- In a saucepan, bring maple syrup just to a simmer. Remove from heat. Stir in fruit. Serve over peach pancakes.
- Makes: 10 pancakes and 2-1/2 cups sauce

248. Peach Puff Pancake With Cherry Almond Sauce Recipe

Serving: 6 | Prep: | Cook: 25mins | Ready in:

Ingredients

- 6 eggs
- 1-1/2 cups milk
- 1 cup All Purpose flour (Not self-rising)
- 4 Tbsps sugar
- 1 tsp vanilla
- 1/2 tsp salt
- 1 tsp cinnamon
- 2/3 stick butter or margarine
- 12 canned peach Halves (approx.) sliced thin
- 4 Tbsps brown sugar
- *For Apple Pancake just substitute 4 peeled, sliced apples & serve with maple syrup
- (Makes 1 - 9" x 13" baking dish or 2 - 9" round pie plates)
- CHERRY ALMOND SAUCE for peach Puff Pancakes:
- 1 can cherry pie filling
- 1/2 stick butter or margarine
- 1/3 cup brown sugar
- 1/4 cup light corn syrup
- 1/2 tsp almond extract

- Cook all ingredients except almond extract, in saucepan till blended & bubbly. Remove from heat, add almond extract. Mix well and pour over peach Puff Pancake. (Optional - Garnish with slivered almonds)

Direction

- Preheat oven to 425 degrees. Slice butter into baking dish, add peach slices & place in oven till butter is melted and bubbly. Meanwhile, mix eggs, milk, flour, sugar, vanilla, salt & cinnamon till blended. Pour batter over peaches. Sprinkle with brown sugar. Bake approximately 25 minutes till brown & puffy. Serve immediately with Cherry Almond Sauce ladled over top.

249. Peach And Strawberry Pancakes Recipe

Serving: 4 | Prep: | Cook: 20mins | Ready in:

Ingredients

- 2 cups sifted all purpose flour
- 1/4 cup granulated sugar
- 4 teaspoons baking powder
- 1 teaspoon salt
- 2 eggs well beaten
- 1-1/2 cups milk
- 1/4 cup butter melted
- 2 peaches finely diced
- 1 teaspoon vanilla extract
- 2 cups fresh strawberries finely chopped

Direction

- Mix flour, sugar, baking powder and salt. Add eggs, milk, butter, peaches and vanilla. Stir until well blended and smooth then gently fold in strawberries. Spoon about 1/4 cup of batter for each pancake on preheated greased griddle. Turn only once.

250. Peachy Strawberry Oven Pancakes Recipe

Serving: 4 | Prep: | Cook: 30mins | Ready in:

Ingredients

- Pancake
- 2 Teaspoons of butter
- 1 and 1/4 cup buttermilk pancake and waffle mix (just add water type)
- 3/4 cup of water
- 2 Tablespoons of sugar
- 1 egg
- 1 Can (15 ounces) of sliced peaches drained and coarsely chopped
- Topping
- 1 cup of fresh strawberries
- whipped cream

Direction

- Heat oven to 375 degrees. Generously grease 9-inch pie pan with butter. In medium bowl, combine all ingredients except peaches; mix just until smooth. Do not over mix. Fold in peaches. Pour batter into greased pan.
- Bake at 375 for 22-30 minutes until golden brown and center springs back when lightly touched.
- Cut into wedges to serve.
- Top with whipped cream and strawberries.

251. Peanut Butter Chocolate Chunk Pancake Muffins Recipe

Serving: 6 | Prep: | Cook: 15mins | Ready in:

Ingredients

- -1 cup of pancake mix
- -1/4 Uncooked oats
- -3/4 cup water

- -1 Tsp. vanilla
- -2 Tsp peanut butter
- -Chopped into Chucks chocolate Hershey's Kisses*[optional]
- *You can pretty much use any type of milk chocolate

Direction

- Preheat oven to 350 degrees.
- Combine all ingredients in a medium sized bowl.
- The chocolate chunk you can add in or sprinkle on top.
- Mix well.
- Line your muffin pan with muffin liners, or just spray pan with non-stick spray.
- Bake for about 10-15 min or until light brown on top.
- Enjoy!

252. Peanut Butter Pancakes Recipe

Serving: 5 | Prep: | Cook: 20mins | Ready in:

Ingredients

- 1 1/2 cups all-purpose flour
- 6 tablespoons sugar
- 2 teaspoons baking powder
- 1/4 teaspoon salt
- 1 1/4 cups fat-free milk
- 1/4 cup chunky peanut butter
- 1 tablespoon roasted peanut oil or vegetable oil
- 1/2 teaspoon vanilla extract
- 2 large eggs, lightly beaten

Direction

- Lightly spoon flour into dry measuring cups; level with a knife. Combine flour, sugar, baking powder, and salt in a large bowl. Combine milk and remaining ingredients; add to flour mixture, stirring until smooth.
- Spoon about 1/4 cup batter onto a hot non-stick griddle or a large non-stick skillet. Turn pancakes when tops are covered with bubbles and edges look cooked.

253. Peanut Butter Pancakes With Strawberry Syrup Recipe

Serving: 12 | Prep: | Cook: 15mins | Ready in:

Ingredients

- Ingredients:
- 1 cup all-purpose flour
- 1 tablespoon baking powder
- 1/2 teaspoon salt
- 2 tablespoons sugar
- 1 egg
- 1 cup plus 2 tablespoons milk, plus extra if needed to thin
- 1/2 cup creamy peanut butter, melted
- 2 tablespoons oil
- 4 tablespoons butter
- strawberry syrup Ingredients:
- 2 pints strawberries, thinly sliced
- ½ cup sugar
- ½ cup water
- 1 lemon, zested

Direction

- Directions:
- Preheat a griddle. In a large bowl, whisk together dry ingredients. Slowly mix in egg, milk, peanut butter and oil until combined.
- Add a little extra milk if batter feels too thick. Let mixture sit 5 minutes. Melt 1 tablespoon butter on griddle and move around to coat entire griddle.
- Pour about 1/4 cup of batter per pancake on griddle to form 5-inch pancakes. Fill griddle without crowding pancakes. Flip when air pockets start to pop on the top and a quick

peek on the underside reveals a golden pancake. Repeat with remaining butter and batter.
- Strawberry Syrup
- Directions:
- In a saucepan over medium heat, combine all ingredients and bring to a boil, stirring until sugar is dissolved. Lower heat to a simmer and cook until liquid is reduced to a syrupy consistency, about 10 minutes. Remove from heat and serve warm on peanut butter pancakes.

254. Pear Ginger Almond Pancakes Recipe

Serving: 1 | Prep: | Cook: 20mins | Ready in:

Ingredients

- 1 small pear, sliced
- 1/3 cup all-natural buckwheat pancake mix
- 8 ounces nondairy "milk"
- 2 tablespoons sliced almonds
- 1/2 teaspoon fresh grated ginger
- 1 tablespoon lemon juice mixed with 1 tablespoon water

Direction

- Toss the pear slices with the lemon-water mixture and ginger, and microwave for four minutes. Stir 2 tablespoons water into the pancake mix; add more water if needed or desired. Cook pancakes on the stove top until golden, and transfer them to a plate. Top first with the pear-ginger mixture and then the almonds, and serve with a side of chilled "milk."

255. Pecan Pancakes Recipe

Serving: 6 | Prep: | Cook: 10mins | Ready in:

Ingredients

- 2 cups dry pancake mix
- 1/2 cup finely chopped pecans
- 1 teaspoons vanilla extract
- 1 teaspoon ground cinnamon
- 1/4 teaspoon nutmeg
- 1/4 teaspoon ground ginger
- For the oil called for in the mix, use melted butter
- water and egg as called for in the mix directions
- butter pecan syrup
- 2 cup granulated sugar
- 2/3 cups water
- 1/3 cup dark corn syrup
- 4 tablespoons butter
- 2 teaspoons vanilla extract or 1 teaspoon vanilla extract and 1
- teaspoon rum extract
- 1/2 cup finely chopped pecans

Direction

- In a small bowl, mix the nuts, spices, and extract together until the nuts are covered with spices. Prepared the pancake mix as directed on the package. Stir in the nut mixture, stirring no more than needed. Cook per the directions on the package.
- Syrup
- Mix the sugar, water and corn syrup together in a saucepan. Bring to a boil, stirring as needed. Add the butter, extract, and nuts and stir.
- Serve hot.

256. Perfect Buttermilk Pancakes Recipe

Serving: 3 | Prep: | Cook: 15mins | Ready in:

Ingredients

- 2 cups all purpose flous
- 2 tsp baking powder
- 1 tsp baking soda
- 1/2 tsp salt
- 3 tbsp sugar
- 2 large eggs, beaten slightly
- 1 tsp vanilla
- 3 cups buttermilk
- 4 tbsp melted butter

Direction

- Preheat griddle to 375.
- Whisk in medium bowl: flour, baking powder, baking soda, salt & sugar.
- Add beaten eggs, buttermilk, vanilla & melted butter.
- Batter should have small to medium lumps.
- Brush griddle with your choice: melted butter, bacon grease, oil.
- Wipe off excess.
- Using 1/2 cup scoop, pour batter on hot griddle 2" apart.
- When pancake have bubbles on top & slightly dry around edges, Flip (about 2 1/2 minutes).
- Cook until golden brown on bottom (about 1 minute).
- Continue cooking.
- To keep warm, put on plate in warm oven of 175 till ready to serve.

257. Perfect Pancake Recipe

Serving: 5 | Prep: | Cook: 15mins | Ready in:

Ingredients

- 1 1/4 c. of milk
- 2 tsp. of vanilla
- 3 tbsp. of butter, melted or vegetable oil
- 2 tsp. of baking powder
- 2 tbsp. of sugar
- 1 1/2 c. of all-purpose flour
- 3/4 tsp. of salt
- 2 large eggs

Direction

- First beat the eggs, milk, and vanilla until light and foamy, approx. 3 minute at high speed of a mixer.
- Now stir in butter or oil.
- Next you want to whisk the dry ingredients together and gently, but quickly, mix into the egg and milk mixture.
- Now you want to let the batter relax while griddle is heating (or overnight in refrigerator) the batter will thicken upon resting.
- Now you can butter and preheat griddle.
- Then you can drop ¼ cupfuls of the batter on the lightly greased griddle.
- Let this cook on one side until bubbles begin to form and break (this is the time to add anything like berries, choc. Chips, etc.), then you can flip the pancakes and cook the other side until golden (turning only once).

258. Pineapple Coconut Pancakes Recipe

Serving: 4 | Prep: | Cook: 30mins | Ready in:

Ingredients

- 1 cup Bisquick
- ¼ cup pineapple juice
- ¼ cup milk
- 12 pineapple chunks
- 1 tsp cane sugar
- shredded sweetened coconut

Direction

- Mash the pineapple chunks with a fork, and combine all ingredients except coconut.
- Spoon about batter onto a hot greased pan.
- Top with some shredded coconut and spread about 1 tbsp. batter over coconut.
- Flip and brown second side. Repeat for rest of batter.

259. Plump Pumpkin Pancakes Recipe

Serving: 8 | Prep: | Cook: 10mins | Ready in:

Ingredients

- 2 cups all purpose flour
- 2 tablespoons light brown sugar
- 1 tablespoon baking powder
- 1 teaspoon ground cinnamon
- 1 teaspoon ground nutmeg
- 2 egg whites
- 1-1/2 cups skim milk
- 1/2 cup canned pumpkin
- 1 teaspoon oil

Direction

- Combine flour, sugar, baking powder, cinnamon and nutmeg in mixing bowl. In separate bowl beat egg whites until stiff. Combine milk and pumpkin in large measuring cup. Add milk and pumpkin mixture to dry ingredients, mixing well. Fold egg whites into flour mixture.
- Heat griddle to medium and brush lightly with oil. Pour 1/4 cup batter onto griddle for each pancake. Cook until tops are bubbly then turn and cook until remaining side is golden brown.

260. Poffertjes Dutch Tiny Pancakes Recipe

Serving: 0 | Prep: | Cook: | Ready in:

Ingredients

- 125 grams (4 1/2 oz) flour
- 125 grams buckwheat flour
- 300 mls (1/2 pint) lukewarm milk
- 1 egg
- 10 grams (2 teaspoons) dried yeast
- 2 tablespoons corn or golden syrup (optional)
- pinch salt
- 75 grams (2 1/2 oz) melted butter
- icing (powdered) sugar

Direction

- Dissolve the yeast in a small portion of the milk.
- Sieve all the flour with the salt, make a hole in the middle and pour in the yeast mixture.
- Stir from the centre, slowly adding the remaining milk and later, the beaten egg and syrup.
- Leave mix to rise for about three quarters of an hour in a warm place.
- Heat the pan on high, butter each cup and pour in a small amount of the mix, filling it about half way.
- Cook till the poffertjes are golden and dry on the bottom.
- Turn them (with a small fork or toothpick) and cook the other side.
- A poffertjes pan usually makes about a dozen, enough for one person.
- Sprinkle generously with icing sugar and put a small lump of butter on top of the poffertjes.
- Serve hot.
- You will need a poffertjes pan. This was originally an enameled cast iron (one handle) fry pan with about a dozen small depressions covering the whole bottom of the pan.

261. Polynesian Banana Pancakes Recipe

Serving: 2 | Prep: | Cook: 15mins | Ready in:

Ingredients

- 1/2 cup self rising flour
- 1 tablespoon dark brown sugar
- 1/2 teaspoon cinnamon
- 1/4 teaspoon nutmeg
- 2 teaspoons rum extract
- 1/2 cup milk
- 1 egg, beaten
- 2 ripe, mashed bananas
- 1 tablespoon vegetable oil
- 1/3 cup shredded coconut

Direction

- Mix all ingredients together in a large bowl. In a skillet, heat 1 teaspoon vegetable oil over medium heat. *Be patient and don't use a higher heat because these will burn easily*
- Use about 1/3 cup batter per pancake. When the middle of the pancake bubbles and the edges are dry, flip it over to brown the other side.
- Repeat process until all the batter is gone.
- These are super good with an orange or a pineapple syrup!

262. Poppy Oat Pancakes Recipe

Serving: 4 | Prep: | Cook: 45mins | Ready in:

Ingredients

- 1 tbsp ground flax seed
- 3 tbsp hot water
- 1 1/4 cup whole wheat pastry flour
- 1/2 cup rolled oats
- 1 1/2 tbsp poppy seeds
- 2 tsp grated lemon zest
- 1 tsp baking powder
- 1/2 tsp baking soda
- 1 tbsp sugar
- 1 cup fat free, unsweetened soy milk (such as So Good Trim)
- 1/2 tbsp lemon juice
- 2-3 tbsp water (if needed)

Direction

- In a small dish, whisk together flaxseed and hot water. Set aside for 10 minutes.
- In a small bowl, mix sugar, soy milk and lemon juice, set aside.
- In a large bowl, whisk together flour, oats, poppy seeds, lemon zest, baking powder and baking soda.
- Stir in flaxseed and soy milk mixtures just until blended, adding water if the batter is too thick. A few lumps are OK.
- On a preheated griddle sprayed with non-stick cooking spray, drop batter by generous spoonfuls (about 1/4 cup) and cook 2-3 minutes per side.
- Variation:
- Use ½ cup orange juice in place of ½ cup soy milk, stir in the grated zest of 1 orange in place of the lemon zest and add 2 tsp. fresh-grated ginger.
- Stir in dried cranberries, currants or diced dates.

263. Potato Pancakes German Style Recipe

Serving: 4 | Prep: | Cook: 25mins | Ready in:

Ingredients

- 2 1/2 cup potatoes; (2 large) *
- 1 teaspoon lemon juice
- 1 egg; large, beaten
- 1/2 teaspoon salt
- 3 cup ; water
- 1 potato; boiled, mashed

- 2 tablespoon milk
- 1 vegetable oil; as needed

Direction

- Grate raw potatoes into water to which lemon juice has been added. Place potatoes in a strainer or cheese cloth and drain off liquid. Drain well. Beat raw and cooked potatoes with egg, milk, and salt to form a batter. Using 3 T oil for each batch, drop batter for 3 or 4 pancakes at a time in hot oil in a large fry pan. When firm on the bottom side, loosen edges and turn. Brown on other side. Remove, drain on paper towel, and keep warm. Continue until all batter is used. Serve immediately. NOTE: If potato cakes are served with meat, sprinkle with salt. Sprinkle with sugar if served with applesauce.

264. Protein Pancakes Recipe

Serving: 6 | Prep: | Cook: 30mins | Ready in:

Ingredients

- 1 egg
- 1 banana
- 1 scoop vanilla protein powder (I use either Grass-fed Whey or Vegan Protein Powder)
- 1 tbsp flour (coconut flour, GF all-purpose flour, Bob's Red Mill gluten-free pancake flour, etc.)
- ½ tsp baking powder
- Any add-ins you like!
- Optional: 1/4 tsp cinnamon, 1/2 tsp vanilla extract

Direction

- Mash banana and mix all the ingredients together in a bowl. Mix in add-ins.
- Pour onto sprayed pan and cook slowly on medium heat.
- Be patient! Cook it over low or medium heat in order for them to cook properly.

265. Puff Pancake Ala Orange Recipe

Serving: 2 | Prep: | Cook: 15mins | Ready in:

Ingredients

- 3 eggs
- 1/2 cup of pancake mix
- 1/2 cup of milk
- 1 tablespoon of butter
- 1 tablespoon of grated orange rind (lacking fresh oranges-a drop of orange oil or a little orange extract-kid friendly version)
- 3 oranges, segmented (as kids we used a can of mandarin oranges)
- 1/3 cup of firmly packed brown sugar
- Dairy sour cream
- nutmeg, fresh please, grate on your microplane!

Direction

- With the electric mixer beat the eggs on high speed until foamy.
- At medium speed, add pancake mix alternately with the milk until well blended.
- Preheat oven to 450 degrees.
- Put butter in an oven-proof skillet and put in the oven and melt and heat the pan for 3 minutes.
- Beat the egg mixture again while the skillet is heating up.
- Stir in orange peel. (Or extract)
- Pour into the skillet and bake 15 minutes.
- Cut oranges into bite size pieces and combine with the brown sugar.
- Spoon onto pancake directly from the oven.
- Serve directly from the pan.
- Top each serving with a dollop of sour cream and a light grate of nutmeg.
- Melt in your mouth goodness.

266. Puff Pancakes With Maple Baked Fruit Recipe

Serving: 4 | Prep: | Cook: 25mins | Ready in:

Ingredients

- Melt:
- 4 tsp. unsalted butter
- Whisk Together; Pour into Dishes:
- 1/2 cup all-purpose flour
- 1/2 cup whole or 2% milk
- 2 eggs
- 3 T. sugar
- 1/2 t. vanilla extract
- Pinch salt
- Serve with:
- Maple Baked fruit, right
- powdered sugar
- sour cream

Direction

- Preheat oven to 425degrees.
- Melt 1 teaspoon butter in each of the four 6" individual low-sided dishes (or 4 t. butter in one 10" glass pie plate) by placing in heated oven. Remove dishes from oven when butter has melted. Do not allow to cool.
- Whisk the remaining ingredients together until smooth. Pour 1/3 cup batter in each dish (or all of it into the pie plate). Do not stir batter in with melted butter. Bake until golden and puffed, 20-25 minutes for both the individual dishes or pie plate.
- Serve pancakes right from the oven with Maple Baked Fruit. Sprinkle with powdered sugar.
- Maple Baked Fruit
- Makes: 4 Cups; Total Time: 20 Mins.
- Pit and Slice:
- 1 lb. peaches or nectarines
- 1/2 lb. red plums
- Pour Over; Bake:
- 1/2 cup pure maple syrup
- Add:
- 1/2 cup fresh raspberries
- 1/2 cup fresh blueberries
- Preheat oven to 425degrees.
- Pit and slice peaches and plums; spread in a shallow dish.
- Pour syrup over fruit; toss gently to coat. Bake along with pancakes until bubbly, 20 min. Add berries and stir fruit gently. Spoon fruit inside puff pancakes.

267. Puffed Oven Pancake With Summer Fruit Recipe

Serving: 5 | Prep: | Cook: 20mins | Ready in:

Ingredients

- What better breakfast than this big, puffy pancake with cherries and peaches straight from the oven?
- 1/3 cup milk
- 1/3 cup flour
- 3 eggs
- 2 tablespoons sugar
- 1/4 teaspoon almond extract
- 4 tablespoons butter
- 1 yellow or white peach, pitted and sliced
- 1 cup pitted, halved bing cherries
- Confectioners' sugar

Direction

- Preheat oven to 425°F. Mix milk, flour, eggs, sugar and extract in a blender or in a large bowl with a whisk until well mixed. Place butter in a 9 or 10-inch frying pan (or ovenproof sauté pan). Place pan in hot oven to melt butter. Remove pan with an oven mitt and tilt to coat bottom and sides with butter. Spread fruit in pan and pour egg mixture over fruit. Immediately return to oven and bake for about 20 minutes or until puffed and golden. Remove from oven and sift confectioners' sugar over pancake. Cut into wedges and serve. Makes 4 to 6 servings.

268. Puffed Pancake Recipe

Serving: 6 | Prep: | Cook: 20mins | Ready in:

Ingredients

- 6 large eggs
- 1 cup milk
- 1/4 cup orange juice
- 1/2 cup sugar
- 1 cup flour
- I have also added different things to it such as sausage, bacon, ham, apples, pears, onions.... you get the idea. I just put them in the pan before I add the batter.

Direction

- Preheat oven to 425 degrees.
- Get a 9x13 baking pan or any metal or glass pan of comparable size (just be sure the sides are at least 3 inches high).
- Place 1/4 cup butter in the pan (or you can use cooking spray, that's what I use most of the time, and spray good).
- Put pan in the oven and let heat up and melt butter if you use it (just keep a close eye on it & don't let it burn).
- Place all ingredients in a blender (or you can use bowl & hand mixer) and blend until smooth.
- When pan is hot and butter is melted add any extras that you like ... or not.
- Then add batter.
- Bake 20 minutes.
- If you don't add anything to the batter it will rise up especially around the edges and start to curl in (this works better when using butter) and if you add things it will be more flat.
- We have often made this plain and added things after cooking. Some ideas are fruit, maple syrup, confection sugar, honey, jam.........you know what you like!
- *I have also cut this recipe in half and it does just fine .Just use a smaller pan and cut cooking time to 10 minutes.

269. Puffed Pancake With Blackberry Syrup Recipe

Serving: 2 | Prep: | Cook: 17mins | Ready in:

Ingredients

- Ingredients for pancake:
- /4 cup butter
- 3/4 cup whole milk
- 3 large eggs
- 3/4 cup all-purpose flour
- 1 tablespoon sugar
- 1 teaspoon orange zest
- Ingredients for Blackberry Syrup:
- 1 cup fresh blackberries
- 1/4 cup firmly packed brown sugar
- 1/2 cup orange juice
- 1/2 cup light corn syrup

Direction

- Directions for Batter:
- 1. Preheat oven to 450 degrees.
- 2. Melt butter in a 10-inch cast-iron skillet.
- 3. In the container of a blender, combine milk and eggs; process until smooth. Add flour, sugar, and orange zest; process until combined. Pour batter over melted butter in skillet. Bake for 12 to 15 minutes or until puffed and golden brown. Serve with warm Fresh Blackberry Syrup.
- Directions for Blackberry Syrup:
- 1. In a small saucepan, combine blackberries, brown sugar, and orange juice. Bring to a boil over medium-high heat. Reduce heat, and simmer for 10 to 12 minutes or until syrupy. Remove from heat, and stir in corn syrup. Serve warm.

270. Puffy Eggnog Pancake Recipe

Serving: 6 | Prep: | Cook: 20mins | Ready in:

Ingredients

- 6 large eggs
- 1 1/3 cups dairy eggnog
- 1 cup all-purpose flour
- 3/4 teaspoon freshly ground nutmeg
- 1/2 cup (1 stick) unsalted butter
- 1/2 cup sliced almonds
- 1 tablespoon granulated sugar
- syrup

Direction

- Preheat the oven to 425 degrees F and set the oven rack at the lower middle level. Mix the eggs in a large mixing bowl with an electric mixer. Add the eggnog, flour and nutmeg and mix until well blended, but do not overmix - batter will be lumpy.
- Place the butter in a 9 x 13-inch glass baking dish and put the dish in the oven until the butter is melted and sizzling - do not let it brown! Remove from oven and immediately pour the batter into the baking dish.
- Sprinkle the batter with the almonds and sugar. Return the pan to the oven and bake for 15 to 20 minutes, or until puffed and browned.
- Serve immediately with syrup.

271. Pumpkin Flax Pancakes Recipe

Serving: 8 | Prep: | Cook: 1hours | Ready in:

Ingredients

- 1 cup flour
- 1 cup oat flour
- 1 tsp salt
- 3 tbsp ground flax seed
- 1 tsp Pumpkin Pie Spice
- 4 tsp baking powder
- 1 cup pumpkin puree (homemade or canned)
- 3 eggs, beaten
- ¼ cup canola oil
- 3 tbsp raw sugar
- 1 ¾ cups unsweetened flax or soy milk

Direction

- In a large bowl, stir together the flours, salt, flaxseed, pumpkin pie spice and baking powder.
- In another bowl, whisk together the pumpkin, eggs, oil, sugar and milk.
- Add the wet ingredients to the dry ingredients and stir just until blended.
- Spoon onto a well-greased, hot griddle and cook until done.
- Serve with maple syrup or chunky applesauce.

272. Pumpkin Pancakes Recipe

Serving: 6 | Prep: | Cook: 30mins | Ready in:

Ingredients

- 4 large eggs
- 4 large egg whites
- 1 C. canned pumpkin
- 1/2 C. almond flour
- 1 tsp. baking powder
- 1/4 C. coconut milk
- 1 tsp. vanilla
- 1/2 tsp. nutmeg
- 1 tsp. cinnamon
- 1/2 C. pecans, crushed (optional)
- 1-2 Tbs. butter or coconut oil

Direction

- Mix all ingredients in a large bowl except optional pecans.
- Heat a griddle or large skillet to medium heat and coat griddle with butter or other fat source when hot.
- From here, traditional pancake rules apply with a slight modification. These will not bubble like your traditional pancakes. The batter is a bit thicker. On medium heat the first side takes about 2-3 minutes to brown then another 1-3 minutes on the other side.

273. Pumpkin Pancakes With Cran Pom Maple Syrup Recipe

Serving: 4 | Prep: | Cook: 5mins | Ready in:

Ingredients

- Pancakes
- 1 cup pancake mix (I used Arrowhead Mills buttermilk Pancake & Waffle Mix)
- 1 cup + 1 tbsp milk
- 1 tbsp canola oil (vegetable oil) + more for skillet or griddle
- 1 tsp pumpkin pie spice
- 1/2 cup pumpkin puree
- syrup
- 1/2 cup pomegranate-sauce.html">Cranberry Pomegranate Sauce
- 1 tbsp maple syrup (more to taste if you want your syrup sweeter)
- handful of pomegranate seeds for garnish

Direction

- Lightly coat skillet or griddle with oil and heat over medium to medium-high heat.
- Pancakes
- Combine ingredients and mix just until smooth. Measure 1/4 cup of batter and slowly pour into pan, be sure to leave a couple inches between each. Turn when bubbles form on surface and edges begin to dry and cook on other side for about 3 minutes or until golden brown. (This will probably need to be done in batches. I cooked about 4 at a time. I placed them on a plate tented in foil to keep warm.)
- Syrup
- Combine sauce with syrup and mix well to incorporate.
- Arrange desired number of pancakes on plate. Top with syrup and garnish with pomegranate seeds.
- *I made my pancakes silver dollar size. Feel free to make yours larger if desired.
- *For thicker pancakes, use less liquid. For thinner pancakes, use more liquid.

274. Pumpkin Pancakes Or Waffles Recipe

Serving: 2 | Prep: | Cook: 15mins | Ready in:

Ingredients

- 1 cup all-purpose flour
- 1 Tbsp sugar
- dash of salt
- 2 tsps baking soda
- 1 cup milk
- 2 Tbsps vegetable oil
- 1 egg
- 1/2 tsp cinnamon
- 1/2 cup canned pumpkin
- 1/2 cup sour cream
- ***honey-Pecan Butter***
- 1/2 cup pecans
- 1/2 cup butter
- 1/4 cup honey
- OR
- ***pumpkin Sauce***
- 1 cup maple syrup
- 1 1/4 cup pure pumpkin puree
- 1/4 teaspoon cinnamon
- OR
- ***HOT cider SAUCE FOR PANCAKES***

- Combine 3/4 cup apple juice or cider
- 1/2 cup brown sugar
- 1/2 cup light corn syrup
- 2 tablespoons butter
- 1/2 teaspoon lemon juice
- 1/8 teaspoon cinnamon
- 1/8 teaspoon nutmeg
- Bring to a boil
- Simmer about 15 minutes
- Makes 1 1/4 cups sauce

Direction

- Combine all ingredients.
- Batter will be lumpy.
- Spray grill or waffle maker with cooking spray.
- Bake pancakes on grill using medium heat until bubbles rise to the surface and edges are brown.
- Turn and bake until golden brown.
- Serve with Honey-Pecan butter
- Spread pecans on baking sheet and toast in 350 degree oven for 8 minutes.
- Chop nuts in food processor or blender.
- Beat butter and honey together until smooth.
- Add pecans.
- Serve with Pumpkin Pancakes or Waffles.
- Makes one cup.

275. Rage Of The Town Raspberry Pancaes Recipe

Serving: 4 | Prep: | Cook: 20mins | Ready in:

Ingredients

- 1-1/4 cups milk
- 2 tablespoons vegetable oil
- 1 egg yolk
- 1 cup flour
- 2 teaspoons baking powder
- 3 tablespoons granulated sugar
- 1/2 teaspoon salt
- 1/2 cup raspberries
- 1 egg white

Direction

- Mix milk, oil and egg yolk together.
- Combine dry ingredients then add to wet ingredients in large bowl.
- Mix together until dry ingredients are just wet then mix in raspberries.
- Beat egg white until it forms stiff peaks then fold egg white into mixture but do not over mix.
- Heat griddle until the point where a few drops of water put on pan immediately sizzle off.
- Pour pancakes by 1/4 cup on to heated griddle then flip pancakes when bubbles appear on edge.
- Serve warm with butter and your favorite syrup.

276. Raspberry Filled Dutch Pancake Recipe

Serving: 6 | Prep: | Cook: 20mins | Ready in:

Ingredients

- 1 tablespoon butter
- 3 eggs
- 1/2 cup milk
- 1/3 cup all purpose flour
- 3 tablespoons sugar divided
- 1/4 teaspoon salt
- 1-1/2 cups fresh raspberries
- 1/4 teaspoon ground cinnamon
- 1/2 cup sliced bananas
- Preheat oven to 450.

Direction

- Place butter in a pie plate then melt in oven 5 minutes tilting plate to coat evenly with butter.

- Meanwhile combine eggs, milk, flour, 1 tablespoon sugar and salt until smooth.
- Pour batter into plate and bake 8 minutes then reduce heat to 375 and bake 10 minutes longer.
- Combine raspberries with remaining sugar and cinnamon.
- Remove pancake from oven and scatter bananas over pancake then spoon blueberries over top. Cut into wedges and serve immediately.

277. Really The Best Pancakes Ever Recipe

Serving: 164 | Prep: | Cook: 4mins | Ready in:

Ingredients

- 1 1/2 cups all-purpose flou
- 3 T. sugar
- 1 3/4 T. baking powder
- 1 tsp. salt
- 1 1/2 cups milk
- 3 T. butter, melted
- 2 eggs
- 1/2 tsp. vanilla

Direction

- Whisk all the dry ingredients together in a large bowl.
- In a separate bowl combine all liquid ingredients.
- Add wet to dry and blend quickly, try to leave some of the lumps, but not any huge ones.
- Refrigerate for a few hours if you have time.
- Make sure your skillet or griddle is heated to where a few drops of water "dance" around in it. When bubbles have come to the surface and start to break flip it and cook on the other side.
- Enjoy!

278. Red Velvet Chocolate Chips Pancakes Recipe

Serving: 0 | Prep: | Cook: 2mins | Ready in:

Ingredients

- 1 cup all-purpose flour
- 1/4 cup granulated sugar
- 3 tablespoons baking cocoa
- 1 teaspoon baking powder
- 1/2 teaspoon baking soda
- 1/2 teaspoon salt
- 1 large egg
- 1 cup buttermilk/milk
- 2 tablespoons unsalted butter, melted
- 1 1/2 teaspoons vanilla extract
- 1 teaspoon red food coloring
- ½ cup chocolate chips
- garnishes: butter, powdered sugar, maple syrup and fresh berries

Direction

- COMBINE flour, sugar, baking cocoa, baking powder, baking soda and salt in large bowl; stir well.
- WHISK egg, buttermilk, butter, vanilla extract, chocolate chips and food coloring together in large bowl. Add to flour mixture; stir to combine.
- HEAT non-stick skillet or griddle over medium heat. Brush with a little oil or butter. Pour batter on to the skillet. Cook for about 2 minutes or until bubbles start to form on top. Gently lift and remove molds; flip and cook for 1 to 2 minutes or until bottom is lightly browned.
- Garnish with butter/maple syrup/ fresh berries or whatever suits your fancy

279. Revised Chocolate Chip Pancakes Low Calorie Recipe

Serving: 1 | Prep: | Cook: 8mins | Ready in:

Ingredients

- 2 egg whites
- 1/8cup whole wheat flour
- 1/2cup fat-free ricotta cheese (Sargento)
- 1/2 oz. semi-sweet chocolate chips
- 1/2 tsp vanilla extract

Direction

- Blend all the ingredients in a blender.
- Cook on a non-stick skillet, turning once.

280. Rhode Island Johnny Cakes Recipe

Serving: 46 | Prep: | Cook: 12mins | Ready in:

Ingredients

- 1 cup jonnycake meal (cornmeal)
- 1 tablespoon sugar, or to taste
- 1 teaspoon salt
- 1 cup boiling water
- 3 to 4 tablespoons milk

Direction

- Combine meal, sugar and salt in large mixing bowl. Add boiling water; mix well. Thin immediately with milk so mixture will drop easily from spoon. Additional milk may be needed.
- Drop by tablespoons onto hot greased griddle (you may use corn oil or bacon drippings). Do not let griddle get dry; add more oil as needed.
- Cook 5 to 6 minutes on each side, to desired brown. Enjoy!

281. Rice Bran Buttermilk Pancakes Recipe

Serving: 4 | Prep: | Cook: 20mins | Ready in:

Ingredients

- 1 cup rice flour
- 3/4 cup rice bran
- 1 tablespoon sugar
- 1 teaspoon baking powder
- 1/2 teaspoon baking soda
- 1-1/4 cups buttermilk
- 3 egg whites beaten
- vegetable cooking spray
- fresh fruit

Direction

- Sift together flour, bran, sugar, baking powder and baking soda into a large bowl. Combine buttermilk and egg whites in small bowl then add to flour mixture. Stir until smooth. Pour 1/4 cup batter onto hot griddle coated with cooking spray. Cook over medium heat until bubbles form on top and underside is lightly browned. Turn to brown other side then serve with fresh fruit.

282. Ricotta And Mozarella Corncakes Recipe

Serving: 15 | Prep: | Cook: 20mins | Ready in:

Ingredients

- 1 cup fresh kernel corn
- 2 eggs
- 2 cups milk
- 4 tsp. Melted butter
- 1 cup flour
- 3 tbsp. sugar
- 1 tsp. baking powder

- 1 tsp. salt
- 1 tsp. vanilla
- 125 gr. ricotta cheese
- Slices of Mozarella cheese

Direction

- Blend corn kernels in the blender.
- In a medium bowl mix dry ingredients (flour, sugar, salt, baking powder) in other bowl mix eggs, milk, butter, Ricotta cheese and vanilla, pour over dry ingredients and mix well and add corn.
- Grease a heated griddle, and spoon the batter. Turn pancakes as soon as they are puffed and full of bubbles, but before bubbles break. Turn and brown on the other side.
- Place a slice of Mozzarella cheese over each pancake until melts. Serve immediately.

283. Ricotta Cheese And Buttermilk Pancakes Recipe

Serving: 4 | Prep: | Cook: 6mins | Ready in:

Ingredients

- 1-1/2 cups all purpose flour
- 2 Tbsp. granulated sugar
- 1/2 tsp. salt
- 1/2 tsp. baking soda
- 1 tsp. baking powder
- 2 large eggs, separated
- 2 Tbsp. vegetable oil
- 1/2 cup ricotta cheese
- 1-1/4 cups buttermilk
- 1/4 cup orange juice
- 1 tsp. vanilla extract
- 2 cups strawberries, cut in quarters or berry or your choice

Direction

- Mix together flour, sugar, salt, baking soda, baking powder and set aside.
- In a separate bowl, combine the egg yolks, oil, buttermilk, ricotta cheese, orange juice and vanilla extract.
- Whisk together until smooth.
- Make a well in the center of the dry ingredients and pour in the liquid mixture.
- Mix together until ingredients are just blended.
- In a small bowl, beat egg whites until just barely stiff.
- Gently fold the beaten egg whites into the batter until blended.
- Allow to sit for about 15 minutes.
- Pour the batter into a heated, oiled frying pan and fry until you see bubbles forming on the top.
- Flip the pancakes over and fry until lightly golden in color.
- Place a dollop of butter on plated pancakes with a sprinkle of strawberries.
- Serve with warm maple syrup.
- Note: I also like to serve these pancakes with slices of apples or bananas that have been sautéed in butter and 1-1/2 tsp. cinnamon.

284. Ricotta Cheese Pancakes Recipe

Serving: 3 | Prep: | Cook: 15mins | Ready in:

Ingredients

- 1 c ricotta cheese
- 1 tsp baking powder
- 3 eggs
- 2 Tbsp melted butter
- 2 tsp sugar
- 1/2 c sifted flour
- 2/3 c milk

Direction

- Combine ingredients and blend until smooth.
- Cook on a greased, preheated grill in 2" rounds.

- Serve hot, topped with powdered sugar.

285. Ricotta Cinnamon Pancakes With Sauteed Apples Recipe

Serving: 4 | Prep: | Cook: 15mins | Ready in:

Ingredients

- apple Topping:
- 2 Tbsp. butter
- 4 c. Peeled and sliced apples (about 4 large apples)
- 1/4 c. brown sugar
- 1 tsp. vanilla extract
- Pancakes:
- 1 lb. part-skim ricotta cheese
- 4 large Brown eggs, preferably organic
- 1/4 c. honey
- 2 Tbsp. canola oil
- 1 tsp. lemon juice
- 1/2 c. whole wheat pastry flour
- 1/2 tsp. baking powder
- 1 pinch sea salt
- 1 tsp. cinnamon
- oil for pan
- Lite whipped cream (optional)

Direction

- Prepare Topping:
- In a large sauté pan, melt butter over medium heat.
- Add the apple slices and toss to coat with butter.
- Cook tossing and stirring, until the apples are softened and juicy.
- Sprinkle on brown sugar and vanilla and toss to mix.
- When the sugar has melted and bubbly, take the pan off the heat and keep warm.
- In a food processor or blender, process the ricotta eggs, honey, oil lemon juice, flour, baking powder, salt and cinnamon to mix.
- Pre-heat oven to 200F to hold the finished pancakes.
- Heat a griddle or a large non-stick (cast iron) pan over medium heat.
- Use a paper towel to coat the pan with oil.
- Pour 1/4 c. portions onto pan.
- When bubbles appear across the top of the pancakes and the edge looks firm and cooked, flip them.
- Cook the other side for a few minutes until golden brown.
- (The centers will rise up a bit.)
- Transfer to an oven safe platter and put in oven to keep warm.
- Reheat the apples in the pan and serve the pancakes topped with the apples and sauce.

286. Ricotta Hotcakes With Honeycomb Butter Recipe

Serving: 2 | Prep: | Cook: 5mins | Ready in:

Ingredients

- Hotcakes
- 2/3 cup ricotta
- 1/3 cup milk (plus an extra dash)
- 2 eggs, separated
- 1/2 cup plain (all-purpose) flour
- 1/2 teaspoon baking powder
- a pinch of salt
- 3 1/2 tablespoons butter
- honeycomb butter
- 1 cup unsalted butter, softened (half pound of butter is one cup)
- 3 1/2 ounces sugar honeycomb, crushed with a rolling pin
- 2 tablespoons honey
- To Serve
- _____
- 2 bananas

- 3 1/2 ounces honeycomb, broken into small pieces
- 2 tbsp clear honey
- (confectioners') sugar for dusting

Direction

- First make the honeycomb butter. I usually do this ahead of time. Put the butter, honeycomb and honey in a liquidizer and blend until smooth. Shape into a log on plastic wrap, roll, seal and chill in a refrigerator for 2 hours. (Store leftover honeycomb butter in the freezer – it's great on toast.)
- Place ricotta, milk and egg yolks in a mixing bowl and mix to combine.
- Sift the flour, baking powder and salt in a bowl. Add to the ricotta mixture and mix until just combined.
- Place egg whites in a clean dry bowl and beat until stiff peaks form. Fold egg whites through batter with a large metal spoon.
- Lightly grease a large non-stick frying pan with a small portion of the butter and drop 2 tablespoons of batter into the pan (don't cook more than 3 per batch). Cook over a low to medium heat for 2 minutes, or until hotcakes have golden undersides. Turn hotcakes and cook on the other side until golden and cooked through. Keep them warm while cooking in a very low oven.
- Transfer to a plate and quickly assemble other ingredients.
- Note – hotcake batter can be stored for up to 24 hours, covered with plastic wrap in the refrigerator.
- To serve, peel and slice the bananas and heat through with some of the honeycomb butter for a minute. Put the hotcakes on to warmed plates and spoon the bananas on top.
- Dust with powdered sugar (optional)

287. Ricotta Pancakes With Brown Sugar Cherry Sauce Recipe

Serving: 0 | Prep: | Cook: 2hours | Ready in:

Ingredients

- Sauce
- 1/2 cup (or more) water, divided
- 2 teaspoons cornstarch
- 1 tablespoon unsalted butter
- 2 cups halved pitted fresh bing cherries or other dark sweet cherries (about 14 ounces unpitted cherries)
- 2 tablespoons (packed) golden brown sugar
- 1 tablespoon fresh lemon juice
- Pancakes
- 3/4 cup unbleached all purpose flour
- 2 tablespoons sugar
- 1/2 teaspoon baking powder
- 1/4 teaspoon salt
- 1 1/3 cups whole-milk ricotta cheese
- 4 large egg yolks
- 1/2 cup whole milk
- 3 large egg whites
- vegetable oil (for brushing)
- Plain Greek-style yogurt or plain regular yogurt (optional)

Direction

- Sauce:
- Whisk 1/4 cup water and cornstarch in small bowl. Melt butter in medium non-stick skillet over medium heat. Add cherries, 1/4 cup water, and brown sugar; stir until sugar dissolves. Increase heat to medium-high; add cornstarch mixture and stir until mixture boils and thickens, adding water by tablespoonfuls if sauce is very thick, about 1 minute. Remove from heat; stir in lemon juice.
- Pancakes:
- Whisk flour, sugar, baking powder, and salt in small bowl. Using electric mixer, beat ricotta cheese and egg yolks in large bowl at medium-high speed until light and fluffy, about 1

minute. Reduce mixer speed to low; add flour mixture alternately with milk in 2 additions each, beating just until blended and scraping down sides of bowl as needed.

- Using electric mixer fitted with clean beaters, beat egg whites in medium bowl until stiff but not dry. Fold 1/4 of whites into ricotta mixture to lighten, then fold in remaining whites in 3 more additions.
- Heat griddle or large non-stick skillet over medium heat; brush griddle lightly with oil. Drop batter by generous 1/4 cupfuls onto griddle; spread each pancake with offset spatula to form 3 1/2-inch round. Cook until bubbles form on tops of pancakes and bottoms are golden, about 3 minutes. Turn pancakes over and cook until golden brown on bottoms, about 2 minutes.
- Transfer pancakes to plates. Top with cherry sauce and yogurt, if desired, and serve.

288. Ricotta Pancakes With Blueberry Compote Recipe

Serving: 2 | Prep: | Cook: 10mins | Ready in:

Ingredients

- 150g ricotta cheese
- 2 eggs Separated
- Pinch salt
- 90ml milk
- 100g Plain flour
- ½ Teaspoon baking soda
- 150g blueberries (100g for the Compote and 50g for the pancakes)
- 90g caster sugar
- 20g butter
- Some butter for cooking the pancakes.

Direction

- In a large bowl, mix together the ricotta, egg yolks and milk until it is lump free.
- Sift in the flour, baking soda and salt.
- In another bowl, whisk the egg whites until gently peaking.
- Fold into the ricotta/flour mixture.
- Gently fold in 50g of Blueberries.
- Leave the batter to rest whilst you make the Compote.
- In a small saucepan, gently heat together the remaining blueberries, butter and sugar until a smooth syrupy sauce forms and the blueberries just start to pop. Remove from the heat.
- In a large frying pan, heat 20g butter. Drop in tablespoons of the batter. Once bubbles start to appear on the surface, flip them over gently and cook for a minute or so more on the other side.
- Serve them stacked high and drenched with the compote.

289. Ricotta Lemon Pancakes Recipe

Serving: 4 | Prep: | Cook: 10mins | Ready in:

Ingredients

- Ricotta-Lemon Pancakes (originally published in Williams-Sonoma Essentials of Healthful Cooking).
- Serves 4 (Note: If they don't stick to the pan).
- 1 cup part-skim ricotta cheese
- 1/4 cup 1-percent milk
- 3 large eggs, separated
- 2 tablespoons granulated sugar
- 1/3 cup all-purpose flour
- 1 tablespoon grated lemon zest
- Kosher salt
- Pinch of cream of tartar
- 4 cups mixed berries such as whole blueberries and raspberries or trimmed and sliced strawberries
- 1 Tablespoon fresh lemon juice
- 1 teaspoon canola oil
- 1-2 tablespoons confectioners' sugar

Direction

- Preheat oven to 250 F (120 C).
- Place the ricotta in a large bowl. Add the milk, egg yolks, and granulated sugar and whisk together until blended. Add the flour, lemon zest, and 1/4 teaspoon salt, and using a rubber spatula, fold until just blended.
- In a separate bowl, combine the egg whites and the cream of tartar and, using a whisk or a handheld electric mixer set on medium speed, beat until soft peaks form. Using the rubber spatula, carefully fold the beaten whites into the ricotta mixture just until blended.
- In a bowl, combine the berries and lemon juice and stir gently to blend. Set aside.
- Place a large non-stick griddle or frying pan with low sloping sides over medium heat until hot enough for a drop of water to sizzle and then immediately evaporate. Brush the surface with a thin film of canola oil. For each pancake, ladle a scant 1/3 cup batter onto the hot surface. Reduce the heat to a medium-low and cook until small bubbles appear around the edges of the pancakes and the bottoms are lightly browned, 4-5 minutes. Carefully turn and cook until the other sides are lightly browned, 2-3 minutes longer. Transfer to an ovenproof platter and place in the oven to keep warm; do not cover the pancakes or they will get soggy. Repeat with the remaining batter. You will have enough batter to make 12 pancakes, each about 3 inches in diameter.
- Using a fine-mesh sieve, dust the warm pancakes generously with confectioners' sugar to taste. Serve the pancakes with the berries on the side.

290. Romantic Black Forest Pancakes Recipe

Serving: 2 | Prep: | Cook: 15mins | Ready in:

Ingredients

- PANCAKES
- 1-1/2 cups of pancake mix
- 3 tablespoons of unsweetened cocoa
- 1-1/2 tablespoons of sugar
- 1 cup plus 2 tablespoons of water
- CHERRY SAUCE
- 1/2 can cherries
- 2 tablespoons sugar
- 1 tablespoon cornstarch
- 1 tablespoon brandy flavoring
- 1/2 teaspoon almond extract
- whipped cream
- chocolate sprinkles

Direction

- Stir pancake ingredients together. Put a 1/4 cup of mixture onto hot greased griddle.
- Cook until edges begins to lightly brown and bubble, then flip and cook other side.
- For Cherry Sauce: drain cherries reserving liquid.
- Add enough water to liquid to make one cup liquid.
- Pour liquid into medium saucepan and add sugar and cornstarch.
- Bring to a boil stirring continuously. Boil for one minute or until thickened then remove from heat.
- Stir in drained cherries, Brandy and almond extract.
- Serve warm.
- To assemble the Black Forest Pancakes:
- Put pancakes on plate, top with Cherry sauce and add a dollop of whipped cream.
- You can then garnish with chocolate sprinkles.

291. Russian Blinys Pancakes Recipe

Serving: 8 | Prep: | Cook: 30mins | Ready in:

Ingredients

- 40g yeast
- 2 cups warm water
- 1kg buckwheat flour, sifted
- salt
- 2 tablespoons sugar
- 2 lightly beaten eggs
- 60g butter, melted
- 4-5 cups warm milk
- Topping
- sour cream
- Caviar

Direction

- Dissolve yeast in water and add 500g buckwheat flour.
- Mix until smooth.
- Cover with a cloth and set aside for about 1 hour or until the mixture becomes bubbly.
- Add salt, sugar, eggs and butter and mix thoroughly.
- Gradually add the remaining flour and beat until smooth.
- Add milk gradually, the batter should be quite runny.
- Cover with a cloth and set aside.
- When batter rises, beat it again and set aside to rise further.
- The batter should be set aside for at least 30 minutes before cooking.
- Heat a long handled fry pan, ensuring the bottom is perfectly smooth and clean.
- Rub over base of pan with 20g butter enclosed in a small clean cloth.
- Use a soup ladle to pour batter into pan.
- One ladle will be adequate for each blini.
- Cook for 1 minute and flip over.
- Cook 1 minute more.
- Slide out of pan on to a flat plate.
- Stack one on top of another to keep warm.
- Rub greased cloth over pan bottom before adding batter each time.
- Makes approximately 30.
- Serve with a dollop of sour cream and a teaspoon of caviar.
- Yummy.

292. Scandinavian Puff Pancakes Recipe

Serving: 6 | Prep: | Cook: 25mins | Ready in:

Ingredients

- 1/4 cup butter
- 3 eggs
- 1-1/2 cups milk
- 6 tbsp. sugar
- 3/4 cup flour
- 1/4 tsp. real maple syrup
- blackberries
- Sliced strawberries
- Sliced bananas

Direction

- Preheat oven to 425.
- On stove top Heat up a 12in. sauté pan with the butter till bubbly. (Do not burn butter)
- Meanwhile in a large bowl. Mix eggs, milk, sugar, flour and salt till smooth using an electric mixer
- Pour batter in to hot sauté pan then place pan in oven bake for 25-30 minutes till edges are golden brown and pancake is puffy pancake will settle once removed from oven let rest for 5 minutes
- Slice and serve with real Maple Syrup, dollop of butter and top with fresh, or frozen/thawed blackberries, sliced strawberries and sliced bananas. Enjoy.

293. Scottish Pancakes Recipe

Serving: 4 | Prep: | Cook: 10mins | Ready in:

Ingredients

- 2 oz. / 55g butter
- 15 fl. oz. / 450 ml warm buttermilk

- 10 oz. / 275g all purpose flour
- 3 oz. / 75g sugar
- 1 tsp. baking soda
- 1/2 tsp. salt
- 1 Tbsp. vinegar
- 2 eggs, well beaten

Direction

- Stir the butter into the warmed buttermilk until melted. Gradually pour the milk and butter into the flour and beat well. Allow the mixture to stand (for a few hours if possible) or at least 30 minutes.
- Stir the sugar, bicarbonate of soda, salt and vinegar into the beaten eggs. Pour this mixture into the flour and milk mixture and beat well to form a smooth batter.
- Heavily grease a hot griddle or hot stone and heat. Drop the batter, a tablespoon at a time onto the heated griddle and bake over a moderate heat until golden brown on both sides, then keep warm.
- Continue until all the batter is used up.
- Spread butter on each pancake and serve with preserves.

294. Shawn Boys Johnny Cakes Recipe

Serving: 4 | Prep: | Cook: 20mins | Ready in:

Ingredients

- 1 cup boiling water
- 1 cup corn meal
- 1 cup buttermilk
- 1 cup plain flour
- 3 tsp baking powder
- 1 tsp salt
- ¼ tsp soda
- 2 eggs, beaten
- 4 Tbsp bacon drippings
- 1 Tbsp brown sugar
- 1 tsp ground cinnamon
- ¼ tsp ground nutmeg

Direction

- Mix boiling water and corn meal to make a thick dough.
- Mix buttermilk and eggs thoroughly. Add milk/egg mixture to cornmeal dough and blend thoroughly.
- Sift together flour, baking powder, soda and salt. Add brown sugar, cinnamon and nutmeg to the dry ingredients and mix well. Add to cornmeal mixture and blend thoroughly.
- Stir in bacon drippings. (Note: If batter is a little thick or "stiff," add a little hot water and mix well to desired consistency.)
- Heat griddle to 375 and grease lightly.
- Ladle batter to make cakes approx. 4 inches diameter.
- Serve with softened butter and sorghum molasses or a good cane or maple syrup.
- (Note: Blackstrap molasses and sulphured molasses will spoil the flavor of Johnny Cakes

295. Simple Master Mix For Baking Recipe

Serving: 30 | Prep: | Cook: | Ready in:

Ingredients

- 4 C Whole-wheat flour, *
- 1 1/2 Tsp salt
- 2 Tbsp baking powder
- 1 C Powdered skim milk
- 1 C Powdered Whole egg
- 1 C margarine

Direction

- Thoroughly combine dry ingredients in a bowl. Cut in margarine as for pastry. Use mix within a week, or refrigerate for longer storage. Make about 8 1/2 cups. * May

substitute 4 cups sifted enriched, unbleached flour and 1/2 cup soy flour.
- ***BISCUITS 2 cups mix, 1/2 cup water. Makes about 15 2-inch biscuits, rolled or patted 1/4 inch thick. Bake in reflector oven, Dutch oven, or fry pan over slow fire, turning once.
- ***COFFEE CAKE 2 cups mix, 1/2 tsp. cardamom or coriander, 1/2 c sugar, 3/4 c water. Pour into greased pan, distribute topping, pour over 3 tbsp. melted margarine. Bake in oven. 350 F 40-50 Minutes until done, test with toothpick. Toppings: Jam 1/2 c brown sugar, 1/4 c sesame seeds or chopped nuts, 1/4 tsp. lemon peel. 1/2 c breakfast Gorp or Apple Jack Gorp.
- ***PANCAKES 2 cups mix, 1 cup water. Makes about 30 2-inch pancakes. Variations: Add 1/2 cup cornmeal and a little more water. Add 1/2 c chopped nuts or raisins.

296. Simple Anyberry Syrup Recipe

Serving: 8 | Prep: | Cook: 60mins | Ready in:

Ingredients

- 1 lb. berries of your choice (fresh or frozen are both perfectly acceptable)
- 3-4 cups water
- 1 cup sugar
- mason jars

Direction

- Get out your favorite medium pot and pour in the water to boil.
- While waiting for the water to boil, take your berries and divide them by half.
- Using a can or any other heavy blunt object, smash one half of the berries (just until they release their juices. I know it's fun, but don't overdo it.)
- Once the pot hits boiling dump the berries (and all their delicious juices) into the pot.
- Lower the heat to medium and let simmer until it has reduced by about half.
- Once the first reduction is done, stir in the sugar.
- Let reduce by about 1/3 or until it has thickened pretty noticeably.
- Pour syrup into any (clean) jar you have and let sit in the refrigerator for at least overnight before enjoying. :D

297. Simply Awesome Buttermilk Pancakes Recipe

Serving: 4 | Prep: | Cook: 36mins | Ready in:

Ingredients

- 1 1/2 flour
- 4 tsp. baking power
- 1 1/2 tsp. salt
- 1 tbs. sugar
- 1 1/4 cup milk
- 1 egg
- 3 tbp. oil
- Handful chocolate Chops (optional) (to taste)

Direction

- Stir together dry ingredients (flour, baking powder, salt, and sugar).
- Make a well in the center and pour in wet ingredients, mix together. Make sure it is blended well, no one likes clumps!
- Heat lightly oiled griddle or frying pan on medium heat. Pour or scoop batter unto griddle. Cook until golden on each side.
- Top with some soft butter, syrup, or fruit. Serve hot.

298. Smoky Corn Pancakes With Salsa Butter Recipe

Serving: 8 | Prep: | Cook: 20mins | Ready in:

Ingredients

- 1/2 cup boiling water
- 1/2 cup yellow cornmeal
- 1/2 cup flour
- 1/3 cup sugar
- 2 teaspoons baking powder
- 1-1/2 teaspoons salt
- 2 tablespoons melted butter
- 2 cups cooked corn kernels
- 2 eggs
- 1/4 cup milk
- 1/4 cup hot salsa
- 1 teaspoon finely minced jalapeno pepper
- 1/4 teaspoon liquid smoke
- 2 tablespoons cooking oil
- 4 tablespoons unsalted butter
- 1/4 cup salsa

Direction

- To make pancake batter start by pouring boiling water over the cornmeal.
- Let sit for 10 minutes while you measure and prepare the other ingredients.
- Place the dry ingredients in a bowl.
- Stir butter, corn, eggs, milk, salsa, jalapenos and liquid smoke into the cornmeal.
- Stir in the flour mixture.
- Heat the oil in a frying pan and when it has sizzled again ladle in the pancakes.
- Use about 1/4 cup batter for each cake so that the pancakes will be slightly larger than normal.
- Fry until dark golden brown edges develop and bubbles start to form and burst on top of the cakes.
- Turn each cake gently and fry on the other side.
- Continue frying pancakes adding more oil as necessary until all are cooked.
- To make the salsa butter melt the butter and remove from heat then whisk in the salsa.
- Serve on pancakes with a generous sprinkling of torn cilantro for garnish.

299. Soft N Fluffy Pancakes Recipe

Serving: 12 | Prep: | Cook: 20mins | Ready in:

Ingredients

- 3 egg yolk
- 1 2/3 cup thick buttermilk
- 1. tsp. vanilla
- 1 tsp. ground cinnamon (optional)
- 3 tbsp. vegetable oil or melted butter
- 1 1/2 cup flour
- 2 tbsp. sugar
- 1 tsp. baking powder
- 1 tsp. soda
- 1/2 tsp. salt
- 3 egg whites, siffly beaten

Direction

- - Beat egg yolks well with rotary beater and add vanilla.
- - Measure flour and cinnamon sifting.
- - Beat in buttermilk and mixed dry ingredients. Beat in butter.
- - Fold in beaten egg whites very carefully.
- - Pour batter into griddle.
- - When full of bubbles, turn pancakes.
- - Keep warm until serving time.

300. Sour Cream Blueberry Pancakes Recipe

Serving: 10 | Prep: | Cook: 30mins | Ready in:

Ingredients

- Pancakes:
- 2 cups all-purpose flour
- 1/4 cup sugar
- 4 teaspoon baking powder
- 1/2 teaspoon salt
- 2 eggs
- 1 1/2 cups milk
- 1 cup sour cream
- 1/3 cup butter-melted
- 1 cup fresh or frozen blueberries
- Topping:
- 1/2 cup sugar
- 2 tablespoon cornstarch
- 1 cup cold water
- 4 cups fresh or frozen blueberries

Direction

- Pancakes:
- In a large mixing bowl, combine flour, sugar, baking powder, and salt.
- Beat together eggs, milk, sour cream, and butter.
- Stir into flour mixture. Mix until just combined.
- Fold in blueberries.
- Pour batter by 1/4 cupfuls onto a greased hot griddle.
- Turn when bubbles form on top of pancakes.
- Cook until golden brown on both sides.
- Topping:
- In a large saucepan, combine sugar, cornstarch, and water until smooth. Add blueberries.
- Bring to a boil over medium heat.
- Cook for 2 minutes or until thickened, stirring constantly.
- Remove from heat and server over pancakes.

301. Sour Cream Pancakes Recipe

Serving: 20 | Prep: | Cook: 20mins | Ready in:

Ingredients

- 2 cups flour
- 1/4 cup sugar
- 4 tsp baking powder
- 1/2 tsp salt
- 2 eggs
- 1 1/2 cups milk
- 1 cup sour cream
- 1/3 cup butter, melted

Direction

- Combine the dry ingredients in mixing bowl.
- Add eggs, milk, and sour cream.
- Mix until blended, either by hand or with electric mixer on low.
- Stir in melted butter to combine thoroughly.
- The mixture will be very thick. At this point you can stir in fruit, nuts, chocolate chips or whatever you want in your pancakes.
- Pour batter by 1/4 cup onto greased, hot griddle.
- Cook on griddle until bubbles form on top, flip and cook until golden.
- Serve hot with syrup, fruit, whipped cream and butter.

302. Sour Milk Griddle Cakes Dated 1928 Recipe

Serving: 6 | Prep: | Cook: 10mins | Ready in:

Ingredients

- 2 cups flour
- 1/2 teaspoon salt
- 2-1/2 teaspoons baking powder
- 1 teaspoon baking soda
- 2 cups sour milk
- 1 beaten egg
- 2 tablespoons melted shortening
- 2 egg whites stiffly beaten
- 1 teaspoon vanilla extract

Direction

- Mix and then sift all of the dry ingredients then add well beaten egg to the liquid.
- Add liquid mixture to dry ingredients very gradually and stir quickly.
- Add melted shortening, egg whites and vanilla extract.
- Place on griddle and cook about 2 minutes on each side.

303. Sourdough Pancakes With Fruit Sauce Recipe

Serving: 8 | Prep: | Cook: 10mins | Ready in:

Ingredients

- Sourdough Pancakes with fruit Sauce
- The night before stir together:
- 2 cups flour
- 2 cups warm water
- 1 package yeast
- Cover with wax paper; let sit overnight on the counter. Next morning
- add:
- 1 egg
- 1 tbsp oil
- 1 tsp baking soda which has been dissolved in 1 tbsp water
- 1 tsp salt
- 1 tbsp sugar
- Mix well and cook on a hot griddle.
- fruit Sauce
- 1 apple chopped
- 1 pear chopped
- 1 cup orange juice
- 1/3 cup honey
- 1 tbsp cornstarch
- 1/4 cup water

Direction

- In medium saucepan, combine apple, pear, orange juice, honey. Over medium heat, bring mixture to a boil; stirring occasionally. Reduce heat; simmer 8 to 10 minutes, until fruit is tender. In small bowl, combine cornstarch and water, stirring until cornstarch is dissolved.
- Stir into hot mixture; cook and stir 1 to 2 minutes until mixture is thickened.
- Or just use fresh fruit, like Strawberries.

304. Soy Dessert Pancakes Recipe

Serving: 8 | Prep: | Cook: 15mins | Ready in:

Ingredients

- 1 egg beaten
- 1-1/3 cups milk
- 3 tablespoons melted shortening
- 1 cup flour
- 1/2 cup soy flour
- 3/4 teaspoon salt
- 4 teaspoon baking powder
- 3 tablespoon sugar
- 1 cup warmed cranberry sauce

Direction

- Combine egg, milk and shortening.
- Add sifted dry ingredients and beat until smooth.
- Bake on ungreased griddle.
- Pour batter from 1/2 cup measure.
- Spread with warm cranberry sauce.
- Stack 7 high then sprinkle with powdered sugar and serve in wedges.

305. Soynog Pancakes Recipe

Serving: 3 | Prep: | Cook: 5mins | Ready in:

Ingredients

- 1/2 c. soy flour

- 1/3 c. Bisquick
- 1 egg
- 1/3 c. egg nog, lite
- 1/4 c. milk, skim
- 1/2 tsp cinnamon

Direction

- Mix all ingredients until well blended.
- Cook over med/high heat.
- (They stick so be sure to use butter or cooking spray to coat pan!)

306. Spamcakes Recipe

Serving: 8 | Prep: | Cook: 20mins | Ready in:

Ingredients

- Spam
- 2 C Bisquick
- 2 eggs
- 1 C milk
- butter and syrup

Direction

- Cook as much or as little SPAM as you like. I cubed it up before cooking.
- Mix Bisquick, eggs and milk together to make pancake batter.
- Add cooked SPAM to pancake batter.
- Cook pancakes as you normally would.
- Butter and syrup to taste.
- Like I said this is a work in progress. I thought next time I may use slices of SPAM cooked, then coated in the batter and cooked as normal.
- I really liked the way the saltiness of the SPAM came through to cut the sweetness of the syrup. Would be interested to know if anyone else is willing to try this? HAHA! Enjoy!

307. Special Pecan Pancakes Recipe

Serving: 8 | Prep: | Cook: 10mins | Ready in:

Ingredients

- 1 egg
- About 1 1/2 cups of milk (or buttermilk, makes them extra fluffy)
- 2 cups of flour
- 1 tablespoon of whole-wheat flour
- 1 heaping tablespoon of fresh baking powder
- 1/2 tsp salt
- 2 tablespoons of sugar
- 4 tablespoons of vegetable oil (using buttermilk, use less)
- 1/2 cup of shelled pecans

Direction

- Beat together the egg and milk.
- Add the rest of the ingredients. Mix (can add more milk if needed).
- Pour 1/4 cup onto skillet heated at medium.
- Cook for a couple of minutes on one side (until edges are brown and bubbles form in batter).
- Flip and cook on other side a couple more minutes.
- Serve immediately.
- Don't forget: Mighty good on Saturday morning!
- Serve with Maple syrup, jam or topping of your choice!

308. Spice Pancakes Recipe

Serving: 6 | Prep: | Cook: 10mins | Ready in:

Ingredients

- 2 C All Purpose flour
- 1 T baking powder

- 1 T Splenda
- 1 t nutmeg
- 1/2 salt
- 1/2 t cinnimon
- 2 eggs
- 1/4 c butter, melted
- 1 3/4 c whole milk
- Smuckers sugar Free syrup
- fresh fruit or bananas

Direction

- Preheat griddle. Whisk first 6 ingredients in one bowl. In another bowl whisk eggs, melted butter and milk. Mix the liquid into the flour. Brush some butter onto the griddle and cook pancakes. Cover in fresh fruit and a huge dollop of syrup - serve immediately.

309. Spice Pancakes With Lemon Sauce Recipe

Serving: 68 | Prep: | Cook: 10mins | Ready in:

Ingredients

- 2 cups flour
- 1/2 cup oatmeal
- 2 tsps baking powder
- 1 tsp baking soda
- 2 tsps ground cinnamon
- 1/2 tsp ground nutmeg
- 1/4 tsp ground cloves
- Pinch salt]
- 2 large eggs, separated
- 2 1/2 cups buttermilk
- 2 Tbsps melted butter
- 1 Tbsp sugar
- 2 tsps dark molasses

Direction

- For lighter pancakes, separate eggs and beat egg whites in a deep bowl on high speed until they hold moist peaks.
- Beat egg yolks in a large bowl with buttermilk, butter, sugar and molasses. Add flour and spices. Beat until well mixed. Add whipped egg whites to the mixture by folding them gently into the batter until combined.
- Cook on a buttered griddle over medium heat by pouring out enough batter to form pancakes about 4-5 inches in diameter. Cook until the tops are full of bubbles and then flip and cook for another 1-2 minutes until golden brown.
- Serve with warm lemon sauce (see recipe below).
- Lemon Sauce
- In a small pan, mix one cup of sugar with 2-3 Tbsps. of corn starch. Add 2 cups of water and bring to boil over high heat. Remove from heat and add 4 Tbsps. butter, 2-3 Tbsps. grated lemon peel, and 1/4 cup lemon juice. Stir until the butter melts. Serve. May be stored in a container in the refrigerator for a week or so and re-heated

310. Spiced 2 Grain Pancakes Recipe

Serving: 4 | Prep: | Cook: 4mins | Ready in:

Ingredients

- 1 cup milk
- 1 large egg
- 1/2 stick butter, melted and cooled
- 1 cup old-fashioned oats
- 1/4 cup plus 1 Tbsp packed brown sugar
- 3/4 cup all-purpose flour
- 1/4 cup toasted wheat germ
- 1 tsp baking soda
- 1 1/4 tsps ground ginger
- 1 1/4 tsp ground cinnamon
- a scant 1/2 tsp ground cloves
- 1 tsp salt
- vegetable oil for griddle

- maple syrup, heated (butter pecan syrup is delicious, too!)

Direction

- In a blender, blend all ingredients except oil until just combined.
- Heat a griddle over moderate heat until hot enough to make a drop of water scatter over surface. Brush griddle with oil.
- Working in batches, drop scant 1/4 cup measures of batter onto griddle to form pancakes (4-inch) and cook until bubbles appear on surface and undersides are brown, about 2 minutes.
- Flip pancakes with a metal spatula and cook until undersides are golden brown and pancakes are cooked through, about 2 minutes.

311. Spiced Puffed Pancake With Fresh Fruit And Lemon Yogurt Sauce Recipe

Serving: 0 | Prep: | Cook: 22mins | Ready in:

Ingredients

- * 1/2 C all purpose flour
- * 3 tbsp sugar
- * 1/4 tsp salt
- * 1/4 tsp cinnamon
- * 1/8 tsp nutmeg
- * 1/8 tsp allspice
- * 1/2 C fat-free milk
- * 2 eggs
- * 2 tbsp butter
- * 1 C nonfat plain yogurt
- * 2-4tbsp honey depending on desired sweetness
- * 1 1/2 tsp lemon juice
- * 2 C fresh fruit
- * confectioner's sugar for dusting

Direction

- 1. Preheat oven to 400.
- 2. In a medium-sized bowl, whisk together the milk and eggs.
- 3. In a small bowl, whisk together the flour, sugar, salt, cinnamon, nutmeg, and allspice.
- 4. Pour the flour mixture over the egg mixture and whisk until no large dry spots remain. Do not over mix. The batter will be lumpy.
- 5. Place the butter in a 9 1/2 inch pie plate. Place pie plate in oven for 4-6 minutes or until butter is melted and bubbly.
- 6. Take out plate and pour batter into it. It is okay if the batter isn't perfectly even.
- 7. Bake for 20-25 minutes or until sides get tall and puffy.
- 8. While pancake is baking, mix together the yogurt, honey, and lemon juice in a small bowl for the sauce.
- 9. As soon as the pancake is out of the oven, dab the excess butter out of the center with a paper towel and pour sauce into the center. Decorate with fruit.
- 10. Try to serve the pancake as quickly as possible as the sides begin to fall as it cools.

312. Spiced Pumpkin Pancakes Recipe

Serving: 8 | Prep: | Cook: 25mins | Ready in:

Ingredients

- 1 cup pureed pumpkin
- 1/4 cup packed brown sugar
- 1/4 teaspoon ginger
- 1/4 teaspoon cinnamon
- 1/4 teaspoon salt
- 1 cup of milk
- 2 tablespoons butter, melted
- 1 egg lightly beaten
- 1 cup of flour
- 2 teaspoons baking powder

Direction

- In a mixing bowl, combine the pumpkin with the sugar, spices, and salt.
- Add the milk, melted butter, and egg, and beat until well blended.
- Combine the flour and baking powder, and add to wet ingredients.
- Stir until just mixed.
- Technique is everything in making pancakes.
- Make sure that the griddle or frying pan is hot enough that a drop of water skitters across the surface - about 375F degrees - or you won't get a wonderful crispy crust and fluffy interior.
- If you have one, use an electric skillet as you can then set the temperature for 375F.
- Grease the cooking surface lightly with butter or vegetable oil just before cooking the pancakes.
- Spoon or pour about 3 tablespoons of batter onto the griddle and spread it out with the back of a spoon to reach 3-4 inches in diameter.
- Cook until bubbles appear and break on the top, about 3 minutes.
- Flip and then cook for about 1 to 2 minutes.
- Keep pancakes warm in a 250F degree oven covered with a clean dish towel until they are ready to be served.

313. Steamed Semolina Savoury Cake Recipe

Serving: 4 | Prep: | Cook: 15mins | Ready in:

Ingredients

- 1 C semolina / rava
- few roasted cashew nuts chopped
- 1 tsp mustard seeds
- salt to taste
- 1 tsp curry leaves chopped
- 1 tsp green chillies chopped
- 1 tsp ginger flakes
- ....
- 1 tbsp chopped corriander leaves
- 1 tsp ghee (optional)
- 240 ml thick slightly sour yogurt / curd .

Direction

- Mix rava everything in a bowl.
- Add the coriander leaves and 80 ml of the curd.
- Mix well.
- Heat ghee and add to the mixture.
- Now add the 160 ml curd. Mix well.
- Set aside for a while until it is fully soaked.
- Grease idli moulds and scoop the batter in.
- Steam cook in small containers in a vegetable steamer until a pierced toothpick comes out clean.
- Serve hot with mixed vegetable curry / sambar.

314. Strawberry Pancake With Almonds Recipe

Serving: 4 | Prep: | Cook: 5mins | Ready in:

Ingredients

- 1 cup (125g) flour
- 1 cup (250ml) milk
- salt
- 3/4 cup (175g) sugar
- 5 eggs
- 1 cup (250g) low fat curd cheese
- 1 package vanilla sugar
- 2 egg yolk
- 1 tablespoon lemon juice
- 1 cup strawberries
- butter
- 1/4 cup almond slivers

Direction

- Mix flour, milk, 1/2 cup sugar, 5 eggs and a dash salt. Put all ingredients into blender and

blend until smooth. Let pancake dough rest for 30 minutes.
- Mix low fat curd cheese with the rest of sugar, vanilla sugar, 2 egg yolks and lemon juice. Put all ingredients into blender and blend until smooth. Wash strawberries and filter them through colander (put a few strawberries aside for decoration). Add strawberries to curd cheese mixture.
- Put butter into a pan and heat. Bake 8 pancakes. Spread strawberry cream onto each of the pancakes and roll them.
- Decorate the pancakes with almond splitters and strawberries.
- Serves: 4

315. Strawberry Pancakes Recipe

Serving: 5 | Prep: | Cook: 7mins | Ready in:

Ingredients

- 1 Cup Whole-wheat flour
- 1 Cup white flour
- 3 Tbsp. sugar
- 3 Tbsp. baking powder
- 1 tsp. sea salt
- 2 Cups of milk or Soy milk
- 1/2 Tsp vanilla extract
- 3 Tbsp. canola oil
- 1 Cup of Freshly Sliced strawberries
- whipped topping
- strawberry syrup

Direction

- Combine the dry ingredients in a bowl and sift together.
- Mix vanilla extract into the milk and pour into the dry ingredients.
- Add oil and mix until smooth.
- Ladle the pancake mix onto a hot griddle.
- Sprinkle with strawberries.
- Cook for 2 to 3 minutes per side.
- Place pancakes onto plates and top with whipped topping, strawberry syrup, and additional diced strawberries.

316. Sunday Morning Buttermilk Pancakes Recipe

Serving: 4 | Prep: | Cook: 4mins | Ready in:

Ingredients

- 1-1/4 cups flour
- 1/2 teaspoon baking soda
- 2 teaspoons baking powder
- 3/4 teaspoon salt
- 2 tablespoons sugar
- 1-1/4 cups buttermilk
- 3 tablespoons vegetable oil

Direction

- Stir together first 5 ingredients in a large bowl.
- Make a well in the center of mixture.
- Stir together egg, buttermilk, and oil.
- Add to dry ingredients, stirring until just moistened.
- Pour about 1/4 cup batter for each pancake onto a hot, lightly greased griddle.
- Cook until tops of pancakes are covered with bubbles, and edges look cooked.
- Turn and cook on other side.
- Serve with warm butter and warm maple syrup (or your favorite syrup).

317. Superb Sourdough Pancakes Recipe

Serving: 1 | Prep: | Cook: 8mins | Ready in:

Ingredients

- 1 cup whole-wheat sourdough starter

- 2 tsp sugar
- 1 tsp baking powder
- 1/4 tsp baking soda
- 1 egg
- 1 tsp canola oil

Direction

- Heat a griddle over medium heat.
- In a bowl or large measuring cup, combine all the ingredients, mixing gently.
- Grease the griddle and ladle 3-4 dollops into it.
- When the batter has air holes peeking through, flip the cakes over.
- When the steam is mostly gone, they should be ready.

318. Supper Pancakes Recipe

Serving: 6 | Prep: | Cook: 20mins | Ready in:

Ingredients

- 2 eggs
- 2-1/2 cups milk
- 3 cups flour
- 2 tablespoons baking powder
- 1-1/2 teaspoons salt
- 1/2 teaspoon dry mustard
- 1/3 cup melted shortening
- 1 cup all bran
- 15 thin slices boiled ham and cheese

Direction

- Beat eggs then add milk and mix well.
- Sift flour with baking powder, salt and mustard then add to first mixture.
- Stir until flour disappears.
- Add melted and cooled shortening then all bran.
- Dip slices of ham and cheese in batter and bake on hot griddle turning only once.

319. Swedish Oven Pancakes Recipe

Serving: 6 | Prep: | Cook: 25mins | Ready in:

Ingredients

- 3 cups milk
- 4 eggs
- 2 cups flour
- 4 T butter, melted
- 1 t salt
- 2 T sugar

Direction

- Beat eggs well.
- Add milk, melted butter, salt and flour.
- Bake in a greased 9 X 13 pan in 425F oven for 25-30 minutes.
- Cut into squares and serve immediately with butter and syrup.

320. Swedish Pancakes Recipe

Serving: 6 | Prep: | Cook: 10mins | Ready in:

Ingredients

- 3 eggs
- 1/2 teas salt
- 1 cup flour
- 1 cup oat flour (we grind oats in a grinder)
- 1/2 cups honey
- 3 cups milk
- 3Tablespoons melted butter

Direction

- Combine honey eggs and melted butter.
- Add salt, flour, oat flour, and milk, mix well.
- On a hot grill, drop about 1/4 cup of batter and spread to about a 4 inch round pancake.

- When bubbles form on top of cake, flip and cook other side until cooked.
- Butter and top with syrup or jam.

321. Sweet Chestnut Pancakes Regular And Gluten Free Recipe

Serving: 0 | Prep: | Cook: 5mins | Ready in:

Ingredients

- 4 ounces rice flour
- 3 eggs
- 1 tablespoon olive oil
- 1/2 pint milk
- 1/2 ounce sugar
- 4 ounces sweet-chestnut puree
- 4 ounces cornmeal
- 1/2 teaspoon tartaric acid
- 1/2 teaspoon baking soda
- salt to taste

Direction

- Beat eggs, oil, milk and puree. Mix dry ingredients. Quickly combine together. Spoon mixture onto iron griddle and cook over medium heat until both sides are golden brown. Serve hot with butter and jam.

322. Sweet Potato And Banana Pancakes Recipe

Serving: 5 | Prep: | Cook: 1hours | Ready in:

Ingredients

- 1 large sweet potato
- 1 1/2 cups bananas
- 6 eggs
- 1/4 teaspoon vanilla extract
- 1/3 cup coconut flour
- 1/3 cup almond flour
- 1 teaspoon baking powder
- 1 teaspoon ground cinnamon

Direction

- Preheat oven to 350 degrees F (175 degrees C). Place sweet potato in a baking dish.
- Bake in the preheated oven until flesh is easily punctured with a fork, 45 minutes to 1 hour. Allow sweet potato to cool until easily handled; peel.
- Mash sweet potato and bananas together in a bowl using a fork or electric mixer until smooth; add eggs and vanilla extract and mix well.
- Whisk coconut flour, almond flour, baking powder, and cinnamon together in a separate bowl; stir into sweet potato mixture until batter is well combined and thick.
- Heat a lightly oiled griddle over medium heat. Drop about 1/4 cup batter onto the griddle and cook until bubbles form and the edges are dry, 4 to 5 minutes. Flip and flatten pancake with spatula and cook until browned on the other side, 3 to 5 minutes. Repeat with remaining batter.

323. Sweet Potato Pancakes Recipe

Serving: 6 | Prep: | Cook: 4mins | Ready in:

Ingredients

- 1 ¼ cups flour
- ¼ cup chopped pecans
- 3 Tbsp yellow cornmeal
- ½ tsp salt
- ½ tsp cinnamon
- 1 cup milk (or buttermilk)
- 1 cup mashed cooked sweetpotato
- 3 Tbsp brown sugar
- 1 Tbsp canola oil
- ½ tsp vanilla

- 2 Large egg yolks
- 2 Large egg whites, lightly beaten

Direction

- Combine first 6 ingredients in a large bowl, stirring with a whisk.
- Combine milk, sweet potato, sugar, oil, vanilla and egg yolks, stirring until smooth. Add to flour mixture stirring until just combined. Beat egg whites with a mixer on high until soft peaks form; fold into batter. Let the batter rest for 10 minutes.
- Heat non-stick griddle or skillet over medium high heat. Coat with non-stick spray and evenly spoon out your pancake batter cook till done and serve with a nice crème fresh and a sprinkle of powdered sugar. Or go the traditional way and serve with butter and syrup.

324. Sweetcakes Pancake Mix Recipe

Serving: 1 | Prep: | Cook: 1mins | Ready in:

Ingredients

- Sweetcakes mix
- milk
- egg
- canola oil
- butter
- real maple syrup

Direction

- I mixed according to directions and made two pancakes, dotted with butter and drizzled with maple syrup. Fluffy and yummy.
- I have always like thin type pancakes so after I made the two pancakes I added two tablespoons milk to thin it a bit and cooked another batch. Either way is delicious.
- Definitely beats plain old pancake mix. Thanks for letting me try your mix.

325. Sweetstacks Pancakes Recipe

Serving: 6 | Prep: | Cook: 10mins | Ready in:

Ingredients

- 2 Cups SweetStacks Gourmet pancake mix (Full Batch)
- 2 eggs
- 1 1/3 cup of milk (For BEST results use whole milk)
- 6 TBLS vegetable oil

Direction

- Combine milk, eggs and vegetable oil.
- Add pancake mix to milk mixture and whip together with wire whisk.
- Pour pancake batter onto a griddle or pan on medium heat.
- Cook until surface bubbles are almost ready to burst then flip and cook on the other side. Do not overcook.
- A full batch yields approximately 16 pancakes. 4" diameter.
- Pancakes are made with 1/4 cup of batter.
- Add chopped fresh fruit or your favorite toppings! YUM!!

326. Swirl Springroll Recipe

Serving: 4 | Prep: | Cook: 5mins | Ready in:

Ingredients

- Batter :
- 6 tbsp flour
- 1 tsp sugar
- Pinch of salt and soda

- 1 egg, beaten (optional)
- Some water
- Filling:
- 6 tbsp fresh grated coconut
- 2 to 3 tbsp white sugar
- OR you can prepare your fave filling

Direction

- For the batter, mix everything, add water until it becomes somewhat a thin batter.
- Grease a pan.
- Pour a spoonful of batter in the middle and swirl it.
- Once cooked (1 min), flip and spread 2 tbsp. of filling in the middle.
- Once cooked, cover on both sides.
- Makes 4 pcs.

327. Tagine Estate Blueberry Sour Cream Pancakes Tried And True Recipe

Serving: 8 | Prep: | Cook: 20mins | Ready in:

Ingredients

- 1-1/3 cups flour
- 1-1/2 teaspoons baking soda
- 1 teaspoon salt
- 1 tablespoon brown sugar
- 1-1/2 teaspoons ground nutmeg
- 1 tablespoon cinnamon
- 1 egg beaten
- 1 cup sour cream
- 1 cup buttermilk
- 1 cup fresh blueberries rinsed

Direction

- Stir flour, soda, salt, sugar, nutmeg and cinnamon together thoroughly.
- Combine egg, sour cream and milk then add to dry ingredients stirring to combine.
- Add blueberries carefully blending just enough to mix them in.
- Drop batter by 1/4 cupfuls onto a hot greased griddle.
- Cook until surface is covered with bubbles then turn and cook other sides until browned.

328. Thanksgiving Latkes Recipe

Serving: 4 | Prep: | Cook: 10mins | Ready in:

Ingredients

- 2 turnips, grated
- 1 large sweet potato, grated
- 2/3 lb raw chestnuts, roasted and mashed
- 1 tbsp water
- 2 tbsp dried cranberries
- 1 tbsp brown sugar

Direction

- Mix all ingredients in a bowl until well blended.
- Shape into 4 patties, cover and chill 30 minutes.
- Preheat a spray of non-stick spray in a frying pan over medium heat.
- Fry patties until golden brown, flip and cook on the other side until golden also. Serve hot.

329. The Best Pancake Recipe

Serving: 4 | Prep: | Cook: 20mins | Ready in:

Ingredients

- 3/4 cup milk
- 2 tablespoons white vinegar
- 1 cup all-purpose flour
- 2 tablespoons white sugar
- 1 teaspoon baking powder

- 1/2 teaspoon baking soda
- 1/2 teaspoon salt
- 1 egg
- 2 tablespoons butter, melted
- cooking spray

Direction

- Combine milk with vinegar in a medium bowl and set aside for 5 minutes to "sour".
- Combine flour, sugar, baking powder, baking soda, and salt in a large mixing bowl. Whisk egg and butter into "soured" milk. Pour the flour mixture into the wet ingredients and whisk until lumps are gone.
- Heat a large skillet over medium heat, and coat with cooking spray. Pour 1/4 cupfuls of batter onto the skillet, and cook until bubbles appear on the surface. Flip with a spatula, and cook until browned on the other side.

330. The Spirit Of Apple Prune Pancake Recipe

Serving: 1 | Prep: | Cook: 8mins | Ready in:

Ingredients

- FILLING
- Boiled rosehip tea herbs (save the herb contents from your cuppa)
- 1/2 apple cut into quarter slices
- 1/2 cup water
- 4 pitted soft prunes
- PANCAKE
- 1 egg beaten
- 1/2 cup soy drink
- Approx 1/2 cup Gluten Free SR Flour (lighter, fluffier and healthier than wheat flour)
- 1/2 tablespoon peanut oil

Direction

- FILLING
- Stew apple and prunes until apples are semi soft (3 mins).
- 3 tablespoons fruity berry soy yogurt (or your choice).
- PANCAKE
- Pour mixture into hot frying pan
- Put lid on so top gets firm bubbles and is half cooked.
- Turn pancake over after bottom is golden brown 3 mins
- Cook for a further 2 minutes.
- Place the fruit filling onto the whole pancake.
- Place the yogurt onto 1/2 of the pancake.
- Fold in half.
- Sprinkle icing sugar on top and serve. Enjoy.

331. Thin New Hampshire Maple Syrup Pancakes Recipe

Serving: 4 | Prep: | Cook: 5mins | Ready in:

Ingredients

- 1 cup all purpose flour
- 1 1/2 teaspoons baking powder
- 1 tablespoon real maple syrup
- 1 egg, beaten
- 1 1/4 cups milk
- 3 tablespoons margarine or butter, melted

Direction

- In a large bowl, sift together the flour and baking powder.
- In a separate bowl combine the maple syrup, egg, and milk.
- Add the liquid mixture gradually to the dry ingredients.
- Stir until moistened.
- Add the margarine or butter.
- The batter should be fairly thin.
- Add more milk if necessary.

- Pour into a greased electric skillet or pan and cook until bubbles come to the surface and the edges are done.
- Turn and brown the other side.
- Makes 8 to 10 small pancakes

332. Top Of The World Pancakes Recipe

Serving: 4 | Prep: | Cook: 20mins | Ready in:

Ingredients

- 1 egg
- 4 T. vegetable oil
- 1/3 c. milk
- 3/4 c. water
- 2 t. vanilla extract
- 2 c. buttermilk pancake mix
- 4 T. sugar
- 1 t. baking powder

Direction

- With a whisk, mix egg, oil, milk, water and vanilla in a bowl. In another bowl, blend pancake mix, sugar and baking powder. Gradually add dry ingredients to liquid mixture, mixing well with a whisk.
- Cook pancakes on a lightly greased griddle over medium heat, using about 1/4 cup batter for each pancake. When top of pancake is dry, turn and cook 1 to 2 minutes longer.
- Note: This recipe makes thick pancakes. For thinner batter, increase water as needed.

333. Topsy Turvy Pancakes Recipe

Serving: 8 | Prep: | Cook: 25mins | Ready in:

Ingredients

- 3/4 Pound of Canadian-style bacon, sliced
- 1 Cup Maple flavored syrup
- 2 eggs
- 1&1/2 Cups all-purpose flour
- 1&1/2 Cups milk
- 1/4 Cup butter, melted
- 1 Tablespoon (plus)1&1/2 teaspoon baking powder
- 1 Tablespoon sugar
- 1/2 teaspoon salt
- 1 (15 oz) Jar Chunky applesauce

Direction

- Arrange the bacon slices, over lapping slightly, in ungreased 13x9x2 inch baking dish.
- Pour maple syrup over bacon.
- Beat eggs in bowl until foamy.
- Beat in remaining ingredients just until smooth, (Do not include the Applesauce at this point).
- Pour mixture over bacon and syrup.
- Bake uncovered in a 400 degree oven until golden brown and firm.
- 20 to 25 minutes.
- Cut pancakes into 8 pieces and invert on serving plates.
- Serve with heated applesauce.
- Enjoy.

334. Triple Coconut Pancakes Recipe

Serving: 4 | Prep: | Cook: 10mins | Ready in:

Ingredients

- 1 1/2 cups all-purpose flour
- 2 tablespoons sugar
- 2 tablespoons flaked sweetened coconut
- 1 teaspoon baking powder
- 1/2 teaspoon salt
- 1 (13.5-ounce) can light coconut milk
- 1 teaspoon coconut extract

- 1 tablespoon butter, melted
- 1 large egg, lightly beaten

Direction

- Lightly spoon flour into dry measuring cups and level with a knife. Combine flour, sugar, coconut, baking powder, and salt in a large bowl.
- Combine coconut milk, coconut extract, butter, and egg in a separate bowl and stir to combine well. Add coconut milk mixture to flour mixture, stirring until smooth.
- Pour about 1/4 cup batter per pancake onto a hot non-stick griddle or non-stick skillet. Cook 3 minutes or until tops are covered with bubbles and edges look cooked. Carefully turn pancakes over; cook 2 minutes or until bottoms are lightly browned.

335. Tropical Cakes With Golden Mango Sauce Recipe

Serving: 46 | Prep: | Cook: 15mins | Ready in:

Ingredients

- 1 ripe mango
- 1 cup all purpose flour
- 1/2 cup sugar
- 1 1/2 teaspoons baking powder
- 1 1/2 cups unsweetened coconut milk
- 2 large eggs
- 4 tablespoons unsalted butter, melted
- 2 tablespoons dark rum
- 1 1/2 teaspoons pure vanilla extract
- 1/2 cup shredded coconut
- Golden mango sauce, recipe follows
- Diced fresh mango, garnish

Direction

- Peel the mango and slice it in half lengthwise to remove the fruit from the pit. Cut each half lengthwise into thin slices and then cut the slices crosswise in half; set aside.
- In a medium bowl, whisk together the flour, sugar, and baking powder. In another bowl, whisk together the coconut milk, eggs, melted butter, rum, and vanilla extract. Pour the liquid ingredients and mix with the whisk, stopping when everything is just combined. (Don't worry if the batter is a bit lumpy.) With a rubber spatula, gently but thoroughly fold in the shredded coconut.
- If necessary, lightly butter, oil, or spray your griddle or skillet. Preheat over medium heat or, if using an electric griddle, set to 350 degrees F. If you want to hold the pancakes until serving time, preheat your oven to 200 degrees F.
- Spoon 1/4 cup of batter onto the griddle for each pancake, allowing space for spreading. Arrange a few slices of mango on each pancake. (If you have a leftover mango slices, you can dice them and use them for garnish.) When the underside of the pancakes are golden and the tops are speckled with bubbles that pop and stay open, flip the pancakes over with a wide spatula and cook until the other sides are light brown. Serve immediately, or keep the finished pancakes in the preheated oven while you make the rest of the batch.
- GOLDEN MANGO SAUCE
- 1 ripe mango
- Juice of 1 lime
- 2 tablespoons honey
- Place all the ingredients in a blender or a food processor fitted with the metal blade and whirl until the puree is perfectly smooth. Cover and refrigerate until ready to serve. The sauce will keep for about 4 days.

336. Vanentines Day Carrotcake Pancakes Recipe

Serving: 4 | Prep: | Cook: 15mins | Ready in:

Ingredients

- 1 1/4 cups all-purpose flour
- 1/4 cup chopped walnuts, toasted
- 2 teaspoons baking powder
- 1 teaspoon ground cinnamon
- 1/4 teaspoon kosher salt
- 1/8 teaspoon ground nutmeg
- dash of ground cloves
- dash of ground ginger
- 1/4 cup dark brown sugar
- 3/4 cup buttermilk
- 1 tablespoon canola oil
- 1 1/2 teaspoons vanilla extract
- 2 large eggs, lightly beaten
- 2 cups finely grated carrot
- 3 tablespoons butter, softened
- 2 tablespoons honey

Direction

- Combine flour, walnuts, baking powder, cinnamon, salt, nutmeg, cloves and ginger in large bowl.
- Stir with whisk.
- In separate bowl, combine brown sugar, buttermilk, canola oil, vanilla extract and eggs. Add sugar mixture to the flour mixture. Stir just until moist.
- Fold in grated carrots
- Heat a large non-stick skillet over medium heat.
- Coat pan with cooking spray.
- Spoon 1/4 cup-sized batter mounds onto pan, spreading with spatula. Cook for 2 minutes or until tops are covered with bubbles and edges look cooked.
- Carefully turn pancakes over and cook one minute more, or until bottoms are browned.
- Repeat procedure with remaining batter.
- Combine butter and honey in small bowl and serve with pancakes and syrup.
- Or make a drizzle icing to top.
- Maybe even a cream cheese icing.
- Yields approximately 12 pancakes. 3 pancakes each.

337. Vanilla Buttermilk Pancakes With Blood Orange Marsala Syrup Recipe

Serving: 4 | Prep: | Cook: 25mins | Ready in:

Ingredients

- 2 tablespoon butter
- 1 vanilla bean
- 2 eggs
- 1 egg yolk
- 30 g powder sugar
- 200 g buttermilk
- 1/2 teaspoon baking soda
- 2 teaspoon baking powder
- 150 g flour
- 4 blood oranges
- 1 lime
- 3 tablespoon sugar
- 1 pack vanilla sugar
- 1 tablespoon marsala

Direction

- For the syrup use the juice of 3 oranges and 1 lime.
- Out of the fourth orange make filets and add into the syrup when it is ready.
- Cook the juice of the citrus with sugar, vanilla sugar and Marsala until it is viscous.
- Melt butter and let it cool.
- Mix eggs and egg yolk with powder sugar and the pulp of the vanilla bean.
- Add buttermilk, baking soda, baking powder, cold melted butter, flour and mix well.
- Heat some butter and on low heat bake the pancakes really slow for about 7-8 minutes.

338. Vegan Cinnamon Pancakes Recipe

Serving: 2 | Prep: | Cook: 10mins | Ready in:

Ingredients

- 1 C flour (I like to use 1/2 white and 1/2 whole wheat flours)
- 1/2 tsp baking soda
- 1/2 tsp baking powder
- 1/2 tsp cinnamon
- 1 C vanilla Soy milk
- 1 T oil
- 1 tsp Vanilla*
- 1/4 C sugar

Direction

- Sift together flour, soda, baking powder, and cinnamon.
- Mix the rest of the ingredients together then add to dry ingredients and stir till just mixed.
- Toss in any extras if you'd like (Ex: Blueberries, etc.).
- Heat lightly greased skillet to medium heat.
- Drop a 1/4 cup of batter in skillet and cover.
- Turn when center starts to bubble and cover again.
- *If you don't have any vanilla on hand, using 1 tbsp. of maple syrup instead works nicely.

339. Vegan Pancakes Recipe

Serving: 2 | Prep: | Cook: 6mins | Ready in:

Ingredients

- 1 cup soy milk, vanilla flavor ideal
- 1 cup whole wheat/buckwheat flour
- 1/4 cup unbleached, raw cane sugar
- 1 T agave nectar (optional)
- 1 T olive oil
- 1 t vanilla
- 1/2 t baking soda
- 1/2 t baking powder
- 1/2 t cinnamon

Direction

- Sift together flour, soda, baking powder, and cinnamon
- Mix the rest of the ingredients together then add to dry ingredients and stir till just mixed.
- Toss in any extras. I've used chopped apples, frozen blueberries, and carob chips- very tasty additions!
- Grease pan with olive oil or butter, heat on medium.
- Drop a 1/3 to 1/2 cup of batter in pan.
- Turn when center starts to bubble and cover again.
- Serve with natural unsweetened maple syrup, organic butter and you're set!

340. Wheat Free Milk Free Corn Cakes Recipe

Serving: 4 | Prep: | Cook: 15mins | Ready in:

Ingredients

- 2 cups yellow cornmeal
- 1/2 teaspoon baking soda
- 1/2 teaspoon salt
- 2 cups soymilk
- 2 eggs
- 1 teaspoon vanilla
- 3 tablespoons melted butter

Direction

- Combine dry ingredients in a bowl. Stir liquid ingredients together in a separate bowl. Stir liquids into dry. Pour 1/4 cup of batter on hot greased griddle. Fry until brown on one side and then flip and brown second side. If your batter is too thick add a little more soymilk. If it is too thin, add a little cornmeal. Serve hot and top with butter, syrup, or whatever you like.

341. Wheat Germ Pancakes Recipe

Serving: 2 | Prep: | Cook: 10mins | Ready in:

Ingredients

- Your favorite pancake mix or recipe
- 1/4 cup Kretschmer's toasted wheat germ (jar with the red lid)
- 1/2 cup melted sweet butter
- 1 tsp. vanilla extract

Direction

- Make your pancake recipe as usual, adding the rest of the ingredients.
- Let batter rest for 3-5 minutes till lightly bubbly.
- Spoon batter on to a heated pan or griddle and bake as you usually do.

342. Wheat Germ Pancakes With Yogurt And Berry Sauce Recipe

Serving: 4 | Prep: | Cook: 15mins | Ready in:

Ingredients

- Pancakes:
- 1 c. Whole- Wheat pastry flour
- 1/2 c wheat germ
- 1/4 c. raw sugar
- 1 1/4 c. buttermilk
- 1/4 c. canola oil
- 2 large brown eggs, separated
- oil for the griddle or skillet
- 2 c. Sliced bananas, berries, or raisins
- Sauce:
- 1 pt. blueberries or other berries of choice, washed and dried
- 1/4 c. raw sugar
- 1 Tbsp. lemon juice
- 2 c. low or non fat vanilla yogurt

Direction

- Pre-heat oven to 200F.
- Pancakes:
- Combine dry ingredients in a large bowl.
- Mix buttermilk, oil and egg yolks in a cup.
- Beat egg whites until stiff peaks form.
- Mix the yolk mixture into the dry ingredients just until moistened and then fold in the egg whites.
- Heat a non-stick (cast iron) skillet or griddle over medium heat until hot.
- Lightly oil it and then drop 1/3 cup portions of the batter onto pan, spreading a bit if batter is thick.
- Drop in fruits and press them down with the edge of the spatula.
- Reduce heat to medium-low.
- Cook pancakes until bubbly.
- Flip them over and cook for a couple of minutes.
- Transfer to an oven safe platter and hold until all pancakes are done.
- Sauce:
- For the sauce, mix the fruit, sugar, and lemon juice in a saucepan.
- Heat over medium heat, stirring constantly, until it comes to a boil.
- Remove from heat and add yogurt.
- Sauce will thicken as it stands.
- Serve pancakes topped with yogurt and berry sauce.

343. Wheat Pancakes My Kids Will Eat Recipe

Serving: 4 | Prep: | Cook: 5mins | Ready in:

Ingredients

- 1/2 c. wheat flour
- 1/2 c. all purpose flour
- 1 tsp baking soda
- dash of sea salt
- 1 egg
- 3/4 c. skim milk
- 1 Tbl olive oil

Direction

- Mix dry ingredients together.
- Add egg, milk and oil and mix till blended.
- Heat pan over med. heat.
- Cook pancakes on each side until done (just about a minute or so).

344. Wheat Free PancakesWaffles Recipe

Serving: 4 | Prep: | Cook: 15mins | Ready in:

Ingredients

- 1 1/2 cups barley flour
- 1 1/2 cups oat flour
- 1 T baking powder
- 1/2 t salt
- 3 T honey
- 3 T safflower oil
- 3 eggs
- 1 1/2 cups rice milk
- 2 t vanilla

Direction

- Mix dry ingredients.
- Mix wet ingredients.
- Add wet to dry.
- Make them on the skillet.
- Yum!

345. Wheat N Ter Pancakes Recipe

Serving: 4 | Prep: | Cook: 15mins | Ready in:

Ingredients

- 2 eggs
- 2 cups whole wheat flour
- 2 1/2 cups plain yogurt
- 3 tablespoons applesauce
- 2 tablespoons brown sugar
- 4 teaspoons baking powder
- 1 teaspoon salt
- 1/2 teaspoon baking soda

Direction

- Mix ingredients. Griddle to perfection.
- I like to sprinkle cornmeal on the pancakes after I pour them on the griddle.

346. Whole Grain Pancakes Recipe

Serving: 8 | Prep: | Cook: 10mins | Ready in:

Ingredients

- 5 cups rolled oats
- 3/4 cup wheat germ
- 3/4 cup brown sugar
- 7-1/2 cups whole wheat flour
- 2-1/2 cups dry milk flour
- 7 teaspoons baking powder
- 2-1/2 teaspoons baking soda

Direction

- Insert metal blade in food processor.
- With motor running pour in oats, wheat germ and sugar.
- Add flour, milk powder, baking powder and soda.

- Process with an on/off action until just well blended.
- Pancakes:
- 2 eggs
- 2 tablespoons vegetable oil
- 1 cup milk
- 1/2 teaspoon vanilla extract
- 2 cups whole grain pancake mix
- In a large mixing bowl beat eggs, oil, milk and vanilla extract.
- Stir in pancake mix but do not over mix.
- Allow to stand 5 minutes then pour 1/4 batter onto hot griddle.
- Cook until brown on both sides.

347. Whole Wheat Applesauce Pancakes Recipe

Serving: 1 | Prep: | Cook: 2mins | Ready in:

Ingredients

- The Mix:
- 2 cups whole wheat flour
- 1 cup all purpose flour
- 3 tbsp sugar
- 2 tbsp baking powder
- 4-1/2 tsp ground cinnamon
- 1-1/4 tsp salt
- The pancakes:
- 1 cup mix
- 1 egg
- 4 tbsp apple sauce
- Approx 3/4 cup milk

Direction

- 1) Sift ingredients of pancake mix into a sealed plastic container. Keeps unrefrigerated for 3 months. Store until needed.
- 2) I Use a 2 cup measuring cup to make a breakfast for 1. Makes for less clean-up.
- 3) Break egg into measuring cup and beat with fork.
- 4) Add 4 tbsp. applesauce and beat again.
- 5) Add enough milk to measure 1 cup of liquid (approx. 3/4 cup). Beat again.
- 5) Slowly stir in 1 cup of mix with fork. Mix should be a bit stiff, do not over mix.
- 6) Pre heat non-stick electric griddle to 300F. Add a small amount of oil. More oil is required if griddle is not non-stick.
- 7) Use 2 heaping tbsp. of mixture per pancake. Cook 4 pancakes at a time. Swirl skillet immediately after dropping mixture in to slightly spread mixture.
- 8) Cook 3 minutes (until bubbles form on top) and flip. Cook for additional 3 minutes on other side.
- 9) Serve with favourite toppings.

348. Whole Wheat Buttermilk Blueberry Pancakes Recipe

Serving: 4 | Prep: | Cook: 30mins | Ready in:

Ingredients

- 1/2 cup all-purpose unbleached flour
- 1/4 cup whole wheat flour
- 2 tablespoons toasted oat bran
- 1 tablespoon brown sugar
- 1/2 teaspoon baking powder
- 1/2 teaspoon baking soda
- 1/2 teaspoon ground cinnamon
- 1/8 teaspoon kosher salt
- 1 cup bulgarian buttermilk
- 1 large organic egg
- 2 tablespoons olive oil
- 1 cup fresh blueberries
- unsalted butter, for greasing pan/griddle, about 1-2 tablespoons

Direction

- In a large bowl whisk together all the dry ingredients. Set aside.
- In a medium bowl whisk together the buttermilk, eggs and olive oil. Add the wet

ingredients to the dry, and mix until just combined. Do not over-mix the batter, which will have small lumps. Allow the batter to rest at room temperature for 15 minutes.
- Heat your griddle or non-stick skillet over medium heat and lightly grease with butter. Wipe the griddle with a thick wad of paper towel.
- Use 1/4 cup of batter for each pancake. Once the batter is on the griddle sprinkle blueberries on top and gently press them into the batter with your fingers. Cook about 2 minutes, or until bubbles begin to form on the surface and the underside of the pancake is golden (you can check with your spatula by gently lifting an edge). Flip and cook for about 1-2 minutes on the other side.
- Serve immediately, or if you are making pancakes for more than one person keep the pancakes warm by placing them on a baking sheet in an oven heated to 200 degrees F.
- Serve with warm maple syrup

349. Whole Wheat Nutty Pancakes Recipe

Serving: 6 | Prep: | Cook: 15mins | Ready in:

Ingredients

- ¾ cup Quaker Oats
- ¾ cup whole wheat flour
- 2 teaspoons baking soda
- 1½ teaspoon baking powder
- ½ teaspoon salt
- 1½ cups buttermilk
- ¼ cup vegetable oil
- 1 egg
- ¼ cup sugar
- 1/3 cup finely chopped pecans

Direction

- Grind the oats in a blender or food processor until fine, like flour.
- Combine ground oats, whole wheat flour, baking soda, baking powder and salt in a medium bowl.
- In another bowl combine buttermilk, oil, egg and sugar with an electric mixer until smooth.
- Using an electric mixer, add the wet ingredients to the dry ingredients.
- Add nuts and mix well with the mixer.
- Lightly oil a skillet or griddle; preheat it to medium heat.
- Ladle ⅓ cup of the batter onto the hot skillet and cook the pancakes for 2 to 4 minutes per side or until brown.
- Serve with syrup or topped with powdered sugar or fresh fruit - and a dollop of whipped cream is always a nice addition, if you've got it!
- Note - this batter will not keep in the refrigerator, so I prepare all the pancakes, then freeze them with a piece of waxed paper between layers. Pop them into the toaster, right from the freezer, and they will come out warm and crisped up just a bit - reheats great.
- Note - these are good with blueberries or mashed bananas added to the batter, also. I use about 1 cup and just fold it gently into the batter at the very end.

350. Whole Wheat Ricotta Pancakes With Citrus Buttered Honey Syrup Recipe

Serving: 0 | Prep: | Cook: 30mins | Ready in:

Ingredients

- 2 cups whole wheat flour
- 2t baking powder
- 1/2t salt
- 1/4t fresh nutmeg, grated
- 4 eggs
- 1 1/2 cups ricotta cheese, strained well, if not the 'dry' variety
- 1 1/2 cups buttermilk

- 2T honey
- 1t vanilla
- shortening, bacon grease, butter or oil for griddle, if desired
- For Citrus buttered honey Syrup
- 1 1/2 cups honey
- 2T fresh lemon or 3T fresh orange juice(I used orange, but lemon is great with ricotta, so your choice)
- 4T butter
- 2t lemon or orange zest

Direction

- In medium bowl, combine all dry ingredients and mix with fork.
- In another medium bowl, whisk eggs until slightly foaming and bubbly around the edges.
- Fold in cheese, vanilla and honey then add buttermilk and combine well.
- Slowly add liquid ingredients to dry ingredients and fold to mix until JUST combined.
- Cook on prepared, hot griddle(medium heat for no stick, but you can cook on a lower heat if using cast iron, like I do) until bubbling on the edges, about 3 minutes or so, then flip, and cook another 2-3, until done.
- For Syrup
- Heat honey, juice and butter over medium heat, in small, heavy saucepan, to boil. Immediately reduce heat to very low and simmer about 10 minutes, just to reduce slightly. (Do not over heat or over cook, or you will make candy ;)
- Add zest and stir. Let cool slightly before serving over pancakes.

351. Wholesome Cornmeal Pancakes Recipe

Serving: 12 | Prep: | Cook: 10mins | Ready in:

Ingredients

- 1 c whole wheat flour
- 1/2 tsp sea salt
- 1/2 tsp baking soda
- 2 tsp baking powder
- 2 tbsp wheat germ
- 1/4 c cornmeal, ground coarsely
- 1-1/2 c Soy milk
- 1 egg
- 1 tbsp ground flax
- 2 tbsp water

Direction

- Combine milk and cornmeal and let sit 7-10 minutes.
- Mix together ground flax and water and whisk for a few seconds till goopy.
- Add the flax and egg to the milk mixture.
- Combine dry ingredients and then add those to the wet mixture.
- Grill cakes until golden brown.

352. Wild Blackberry Pancakes Recipe

Serving: 4 | Prep: | Cook: 10mins | Ready in:

Ingredients

- 1 egg
- 1 cup buttermilk
- 1 tablespoons oil
- 1 tablespoons honey
- 1 cup whole wheat flour
- 2 teaspoons baking powder
- 1/2 teaspoon baking soda
- 1/2 cup wild blackberries

Direction

- Mix together egg, buttermilk, oil and honey.
- In separate bowl combine dry ingredients with blackberries.
- Add together and mix just until it forms a batter.

- Drop 1/3 cup batter onto 400 degree griddle and flip as soon as bubbles form.

353. Wildcat Cafe Blueberry Pancakes Recipe

Serving: 4 | Prep: | Cook: 20mins | Ready in:

Ingredients

- 1 1/2 cup all purpose flour
- 1 1/2 cup whole wheat flour
- 1 1/2 tsp salt
- 2 tsp baking powder
- 2 tsp baking soda
- 1/2 cup of sugar
- 3 eggs
- 1/2 cup melted butter
- 1 cup plain yogurt
- 1 cup milk
- 2 cups blueberries, fresh or frozen

Direction

- Electric frying pan set to 350 degrees.
- In a large bowl combine first 6 ingredients.
- In a separate bowl beat together the eggs and add melted butter, yogurt and milk.
- Pour over flour mixture and mix/stir until just blended but still lumpy.
- Spoon 1/3 cup batter onto greased grill and sprinkle with blueberries.
- When bubbles form on the top, flip and cook until bottom is browned. Approximately 4 minutes per side.
- Keep the pancakes warm in the oven at about 200 covered with a slightly dampened tea towel.

354. Wisconsin Buttermilk Pancakes With Strawberry Sauce Recipe

Serving: 8 | Prep: | Cook: 15mins | Ready in:

Ingredients

- 2 cups all-purpose flour
- 2 tablespoons granulated sugar
- 2 teaspoons baking powder
- 1 teaspoon baking soda
- 1 teaspoon salt
- 2 cups buttermilk
- 2 eggs beaten
- 2 tablespoons melted butter
- Strawberry Sauce:
- 3 tablespoons firmly packed brown sugar
- 1 teaspoon cornstarch
- 1/3 cup fresh orange juice
- 1 teaspoon finely grated orange zest
- 2 cups sliced fresh strawberries
- 1/2 cup fresh blueberries
- 2 tablespoons butter

Direction

- In a large bowl combine dry ingredients then add buttermilk, eggs and melted butter and stir until dry ingredients are just moistened.
- Preheat skillet over medium heat then rub skillet with additional butter.
- Spoon about 1/3 cup batter for each pancake into preheated skillet.
- Cook until top bubbles then turn and cook other side.
- Cook second side until lightly browned then serve with warm strawberry sauce.
- To make sauce in a 2-quart saucepan combine brown sugar and cornstarch then stir in orange juice and zest.
- Cook over medium heat stirring constantly until thickened.
- Add berries and butter then cook and stir until butter melts.
- Pour over warm pancakes.

355. Zucchini Pancakes Dated 1964 Recipe

Serving: 4 | Prep: | Cook: 10mins | Ready in:

Ingredients

- 1 pound small zucchini coarsely grated
- 1 tablespoon freshly chopped parsley
- 2 teaspoons chopped lemon zest
- 1/2 teaspoon chopped garlic
- 1 teaspoon salt
- 1 freshly ground black pepper
- 2 eggs
- 1/2 cup flour
- 1/2 cup olive oil
- 3 lemon wedges for garnish

Direction

- Combine grated zucchini, parsley, lemon zest and garlic then season with salt and pepper.
- Stir in eggs and flour then heat 1/4" oil in skillet until it ripples.
- Spoon batter by tablespoons into skillet and flatten each mound into a 3" pancake.
- Cook pancakes 1 minute on each side then remove with spatula to paper lined baking sheet.
- Keep warm in a 250 degree oven while you continue to prepare remaining batter.
- Arrange pancakes on platter then sprinkle with salt and garnish with lemon wedges.

356. Zucchini Pancakes Recipe

Serving: 0 | Prep: | Cook: 30mins | Ready in:

Ingredients

- about 4-5 small zucchinis (about 1 lbs or so)
- 2 eggs
- 4 tbsp of flour
- garlic powder
- salt & pepper
- cooking oil

Direction

- 1. Grate zucchini (skin on) and drain the liquid.
- 2. Mix in 2 eggs, garlic powder (amount is up to you), salt and pepper to taste.
- 3. Add flour; if the mixture appears to be too liquidy add more flour.
- 4. Heat oil in the skillet over medium heat; spoon the zucchini mass into small pancakes; cook on each side till golden-brown (each side literally takes only about 1 minute).

357. Zuider Zee Pancake Recipe

Serving: 6 | Prep: | Cook: 20mins | Ready in:

Ingredients

- 1 jar Kraft Marshmellow Creme (7 oz)
- 1/2 cup dairy sour cream
- 1/2 cup milk
- 2 eggs
- 1/2 cup flour
- 1/4 teaspoon salt
- 1 tablespoon butter
- 4 cups sliced strawberries or 2 (17 oz) cans peach slices, drained
- frozen strawberries can be used, thawed and drained.

Direction

- Combine marshmallow crème with sour cream, mixing until well blended; set aside
- Combine milk, eggs, flour and salt; beat until smooth and well blended.
- Heat a 9 inch oven proof skillet in 450 degree oven until very hot.

- Add butter to coat skillet; pour batter in immediately.
- Bake on lowest rack at 450 degrees, 10 minutes.
- Reduce heat to 350; continue baking 10 more minutes or until golden brown.
- Fill with fruit; top with marshmallow crème mixture.
- Serve immediately.
- 6 to 8 servings.

358. Banana Pancakes Recipe

Serving: 4 | Prep: | Cook: 20mins | Ready in:

Ingredients

- 2 cups flour
- 1/2 cup sugar
- 2 tblspn melted butter
- 1 egg
- +-1 cup milk
- sliced bananas
- peanut butter
- golden syrup
- pinch of salt
- 2 tspn baking powder
- oil

Direction

- Sift flour, sugar, salt and baking powder to butter add eggs and milk, whisk.
- Add to dry ingredients, mix.
- In a pan put a little oil, and spoon batter.
- Once bubbles start to form slightly press the bananas.
- Turn over.
- Once done, read peanut butter and pour syrup.
- Enjoy

359. Chocolate Chip Pancakes Recipe

Serving: 8 | Prep: | Cook: 10mins | Ready in:

Ingredients

- • 1 1/2 cups all-purpose flour
- • 3 1/2 teaspoons baking powder
- • 1 teaspoon salt
- • 1 tablespoon splenda
- • 1 1/4 cups milk
- • 1 egg
- • 3 tablespoons butter, melted
- • 2 bananas - ripened to your taste
- • chocolate chips.

Direction

- 1. In a large bowl, Wisk together the flour, baking powder, salt and sugar. In another bowl, mash the bananas well and add the milk, mix well, add the butter and eggs, mix well. Make a well in the center of the flour mixture and pour in the banana concoction; mix until well blended.
- 2. Heat a lightly oiled griddle or frying pan over medium high heat. Pour or scoop the batter onto the griddle, using approximately 1/4 cup for each pancake. Brown on both sides and serve hot.

360. Cornmeal Pancakes Recipe

Serving: 164 | Prep: | Cook: 10mins | Ready in:

Ingredients

- 1 1/2 cups yellow cornmeal
- 1/4 cup flour{Not self rising}.
- 1 tsp. soda
- 1 tsp. salt
- 1 Tsp. sugar
- 2 cups buttermilk

- 2 Tablespoons salad oil
- 1 egg yolk (Slightly beaten
- 1 stiffly beaten egg white

Direction

- Mix dry ingredients Add buttermilk oil egg yolk
- Fold in egg white. Let stand 10 minutes Bake on hot griddle
- Makes 16 4 inch pancakes. Butter pancake pour syrup over them or Molasses. Enjoy.

361. Fiber Full Bran Pancakes Recipe

Serving: 8 | Prep: | Cook: 12mins | Ready in:

Ingredients

- 3/4 cup whole wheat flour
- 1/2 cup bran flakes cereal, crushed
- 1/4 cup wheat germ
- 1 1/2 tsp baking powder
- 1/8 salt
- 1 cup milk
- 1 egg
- 1 egg white
- 1 tbsp vegetable oil

Direction

- In medium bowl, combine flour, bran flakes, wheat germ, baking powder and salt. Set aside.
- In small bowl, blend together milk, egg, egg white and oil; stir into bran mixture until combined.
- For each pancake, pour 1/4 cup batter onto non-stick griddle or frying pan. Cook, turning once, for about 1-2 min per side or until golden.

362. German Potatoe Pancake Lippischer Pickert Recipe

Serving: 4 | Prep: | Cook: 10mins | Ready in:

Ingredients

- 10 big potatoes
- 300 g flour
- 4 eggs
- 4 tbs sugar
- 1 tsp salt
- 1/4 ltr warm milk
- 1 sqare yeast
- raisins

Direction

- Peel and grate potatoes
- Add sugar
- Add eggs
- Add salt
- Add flour
- Dissolve yeast in milk
- Combine milk/yeast with grated potato mix
- Dust raisins with flour and add to mixture
- Cool dough about 45 min until it doubles in its size
- Heat oil in pan
- Create pancake size pickert in pan and bake until golden brown.
- This dish is being served with apple sauce, cinnamon sugar mix or also a type of syrup which is made from sugar beet (it's delicious). For all my Americans out there feel free to serve any other syrup with it. Enjoy!

363. Homemade Pancakes Recipe

Serving: 10 | Prep: | Cook: 20mins | Ready in:

Ingredients

- 1 1/2 cups all-purpose flour

- 3 1/2 teaspoons baking powder
- 1 teaspoon salt
- 1 tablespoon white sugar
- 1 1/4 cups milk
- 1 egg
- 3 tablespoons butter, melted

Direction

- Mix all ingredients together until thoroughly blended.
- Heat an electric skillet or frying pan to medium high. Pour 1/4 cup of batter onto the hot skillet and cook until cooking side is brown or bubbles cease to form in the batter. Flip and cook until brown (or desired state of cooking is reached).
- Remove from skillet and enjoy with your choice of condiments (butter, syrup, whip cream, strawberries, peanut butter, etc.)

364. Mixed Berry Pancakes Recipe

Serving: 4 | Prep: | Cook: 30mins | Ready in:

Ingredients

- 4 cups basic whole wheat pancake batter
- 2 cups mixed fresh berries[blueberries, red and black raspberries, blackberries] substitute I.Q.F. if no fresh on hand
- 1 cup maple syrup
- 1/2 tsp. dried hot pepper flakes
- 6 egg whites
- 1 tsp vanilla
- 1 tbsp superfine or powdered sugar
- pinch cream of tartar

Direction

- Mix pancake batter as per directions and cook.
- Mix pepper flakes into syrup and let set for a few minutes.
- Layer pancakes and berries into an 8 by11 pan covering each layer with syrup mix.
- Beat egg whites, sugar and tartar to stiff peaks and cover pancakes entirely, piling as high as needed.
- I bake in a 400 degree oven until meringue tips and edges are a dark brown, but this step can reflect your personal choice.
- After baking allow to set a few minutes before cutting.
- HINT, this is very sweet, so a little goes a long way. Bon Appetite

365. Peanut Butter Banana Pancakes Recipe

Serving: 3 | Prep: | Cook: 8mins | Ready in:

Ingredients

- 1/4 cup peanut butter
- 1 very ripe banana
- 2 eggs
- 1/2 tsp baking soda

Direction

- Mash banana well, add peanut butter, eggs and baking soda and mix very well.
- Drop by tablespoonful onto hot, ungreased griddle.
- DO NOT MAKE TOO BIG or you won't be able to flip them!
- Flip when bubbles appear on top (5 minutes?)
- Cook an additional 2 minutes until done.
- Makes about 15-18 3" pancakes.

Index

A

Almond 3,6,7,10,11,15,16,112,113,115,141

Anise 104

Apple 3,4,5,6,7,12,13,14,15,20,29,47,52,53,56,60,65,76,77,78,79,81,84,86,97,101,102,107,112,128,134,147,148,154

B

Bacon 3,4,18,19,49

Baking 7,133

Banana 3,4,5,6,7,8,19,23,24,25,26,27,28,49,68,69,100,111,118,144,159,161

Beer 3,30

Berry 3,4,5,6,7,8,25,26,44,97,112,152,161

Blackberry 3,6,7,18,32,33,34,121,156

Blueberry 3,4,5,6,7,10,12,23,24,32,36,37,38,39,40,41,43,100,130,135,146,154,157

Bran 3,6,7,36,126,131,160

Bread 3,4,24,42

Buckwheat 3,4,5,16,25,37,43,44,48,68,96

Butter 3,4,5,6,7,8,9,23,25,30,31,33,37,39,45,46,48,63,70,75,77,78,84,86,92,94,98,101,102,104,105,113,114,116,123,126,127,128,134,135,138,142,144,150,154,155,157,160,161

C

Cake 3,4,5,6,7,12,42,44,59,69,74,75,99,126,133,136,141,149,151

Caramel 4,6,25,47,111

Carrot 7,149

Caviar 132

Cheese 3,4,5,6,22,32,38,39,48,55,60,62,72,102,127

Cherry 4,6,45,112,113,129,131

Chestnut 4,7,49,144

Chips 6,64,116,125

Chocolate 4,6,7,49,50,51,52,64,101,102,113,125,126,159

Cider 6,107

Cinnamon 3,4,6,7,23,31,33,50,51,53,54,55,56,67,101,102,128,151

Coconut 3,4,6,7,28,29,58,68,116,148

Coffee 67

Coriander 3,19

Cranberry 4,45,60,61,62,123

Cream 4,5,7,49,50,51,55,58,62,81,101,135,136,146

D

Date 4,7,65,136,158

E

Egg 4,5,6,16,69,74,96,122

F

Fat 5,67,71

Flour 3,4,5,10,68,97,147

Fruit 4,5,6,7,42,58,75,76,94,120,137,140

G

Gelatine 75

Gin 3,5,6,20,29,79,80,81,115

Grain 3,4,5,7,9,59,94,139,153

H

Ham 7,147

Hazelnut 4,40

Heart 5,85

Herbs 89

Honey 3,6,7,22,92,124,128,155

I

Icing 78

J

Jam 42,134

Jus 30,84,121

K

Ketchup 95

L

Lemon 5,6,7,78,90,91,92,130,139,140

M

Mango 5,7,93,149

Maple syrup 86,138

Marmalade 3,21,29

Marshmallow 5,94

Milk 5,6,7,94,96,104,136,151

Molasses 160

Mozzarella 127

Muffins 6,113

N

Nut 3,4,5,6,7,17,26,27,28,42,53,56,59,75,76,101,102,111,155

O

Oatmeal 3,4,5,6,15,36,40,46,70,75,84,102,103,104

Oats 155

Oil 5,100

Onion 3,10

Orange 3,4,6,7,11,29,33,35,39,92,106,119,150

P

Pancakes 3,4,5,6,7,8,9,10,11,12,13,14,15,16,18,19,22,23,24,25,26,27,28,29,30,31,32,33,34,35,36,37,38,39,40,41,42,43,44,45,46,47,48,49,50,51,52,53,54,55,56,57,58,59,60,61,62,63,64,67,68,69,70,71,72,73,74,76,78,79,80,81,82,83,84,85,86,87,88,90,91,92,93,94,95,96,97,98,99,100,101,102,103,104,105,106,107,108,109,110,111,112,113,114,115,116,117,118,119,120,122,123,124,125,126,127,128,129,130,131,132,134,135,136,137,138,139,140,142,143,144,145,146,147,148,149,150,151,152,153,154,155,156,157,158,159,160,161

Peach 3,4,6,21,22,46,62,104,112,113

Pear 3,5,6,22,76,87,115

Pecan 3,4,5,6,7,22,43,73,111,115,123,124,138

Peel 52,61,65,75,85,86,88,107,128,149,160

Pie 3,14,122

Pineapple 6,116

Plain flour 130

Plum 6,117

Pomegranate 123

Port 5,18,19,74,75

Potato 3,4,5,6,7,10,48,56,85,88,89,118,144,160

Prune 7,147

Pumpkin 5,6,7,71,82,83,117,122,123,124,140

R

Raspberry 6,23,124

Rhubarb 5,98

Rice 6,126

Ricotta 4,5,6,7,41,92,100,106,126,127,128,129,130,155

S

Salsa 7,135

Salt 42

Sausage 3,18

Semolina 7,141

Squash 6,105

Stew 94,147

Strawberry 4,6,7,63,113,114,115,141,142,157

Sugar 3,5,6,36,64,71,78,129

Swede 108

Sweets 7,145

Syrup
3,4,5,6,7,11,22,28,29,32,42,44,45,51,61,62,78,104,114,115, 121,123,132,134,147,150,155,156

T

Tea 97,104,113,130

Thyme 3,10

V

Vegan 4,7,68,119,151

W

Waffles 6,7,123,124,153

White chocolate 109

Conclusion

Thank you again for downloading this book!

I hope you enjoyed reading about my book!

If you enjoyed this book, please take the time to share your thoughts and post a review on Amazon. It'd be greatly appreciated!

Write me an honest review about the book – I truly value your opinion and thoughts and I will incorporate them into my next book, which is already underway.

Thank you!

If you have any questions, **feel free to contact at:** *author@bisquerecipes.com*

Nancy Maye

bisquerecipes.com

Printed in Great Britain
by Amazon